D0554219

MUSSOLINI'S ISLAND

Also by John Follain

A Dishonoured Society

Jackal

Zoya's Story

City of Secrets

MUSSOLINI'S ISLAND

THE BATTLE FOR SICILY 1943
BY THE PEOPLE WHO WERE THERE

JOHN FOLLAIN

HODDER &
STOUGHTON

Copyright © 2005 by John Follain

First published in Great Britain in 2005 by Hodder and Stoughton
A division of Hodder Headline

The right of John Follain to be identified as the Author
of the Work has been asserted by him in accordance with the
Copyright, Designs and Patents Act 1988.

A Hodder and Stoughton book

1 3 5 7 9 10 8 6 4 2

A CIP catalogue record for this title is
available from the British Library

ISBN 0 340 83362 9

Typeset in Sabon MT by Palimpsest Book Production Limited,
Polmont, Stirlingshire

Printed and bound by Clays Ltd, St Ives plc

Hodder Headline's policy is to use papers that are natural,
renewable and recyclable products and made from wood grown
in sustainable forests. The logging and manufacturing processes
are expected to conform to the environmental regulations
of the country of origin.

Hodder and Stoughton Ltd
A division of Hodder Headline
338 Euston Road
London NW1 3BH

To all those who were there

You have seen grow before your eyes the state of military preparedness on land, sea and in the air which protects the island. Only the greatest folly could lead one to contemplate an invasion. No one will ever land here, not even a single soldier!

Benito Mussolini, speech in Palermo, Sicily
20 August 1937

CONTENTS

THE PROTAGONISTS

THE BRITISH

DAVID FENNER: age 21, Lieutenant, Officer Commanding Thirteen Platoon, C Company, 6th Battalion, Durham Light Infantry.

DAVID REPARD: age 22, Sub-Lieutenant, Gunnery Officer, HMS *Tartar*, Royal Navy.

TONY SNELL: age 21, Flying Officer, 242 Squadron, Royal Air Force, flying Spitfires, based Malta.

THE AMERICANS

ALFRED JOHNSON: age 20, Sergeant, Artillery Forward Observation Officer, 16th Regimental Combat Team, 1st Infantry Division.

JOSEPH ROSEVICH: age 28, Sergeant, private secretary to Lieut.-General George S. Patton.

THE ITALIANS

LIVIO MESSINA, age 21, Second Lieutenant, 1st Battalion, 33rd Infantry Regiment, Livorno Division.

RITA FRANCARDO: age 9, Refugee, living in Catania, Sicily.

THE GERMAN

WERNER HAHN: age 20, Lance-Corporal, 2nd Company, 504th Heavy Panzer Battalion, Hermann Goering Division.

Europe and the Mediterranean

0   500 km

EAST
PRUSSIA

POLAND

ECHOSLOVAKIA

TRIA

HUNGARY

RUMANIA

Black Sea

YUGOSLAVIA

BULGARIA

ples
alerno

ALBANIA

GREECE

Messina

Peloponnese

alta (Valetta)

M e d i t e r r a n e a n   S e a

Crete

Alexandria

El Alamein

Cairo

*Suez
Canal*

EGYPT

Gulf of
Akaba

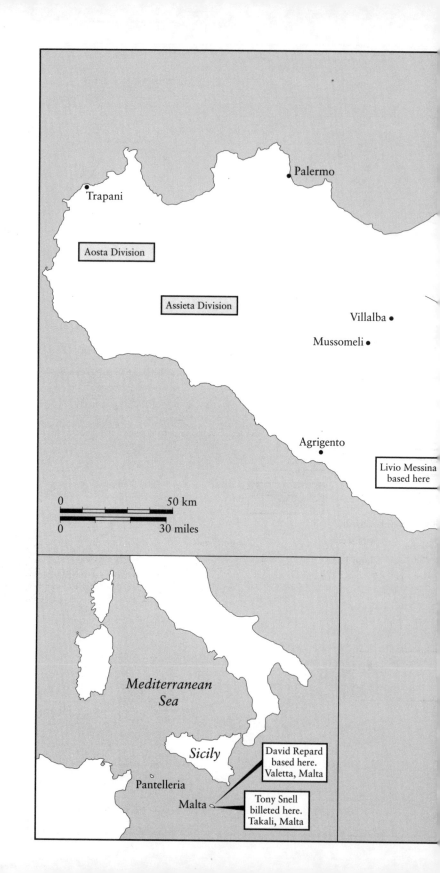

Trapani

Palermo

Aosta Division

Assieta Division

Villalba •

Mussomeli •

Agrigento

Livio Messina
based here

0   50 km

0   30 miles

Mediterranean
Sea

Sicily

Pantelleria

David Repard
based here.
Valetta, Malta

Malta

Tony Snell
billeted here.
Takali, Malta

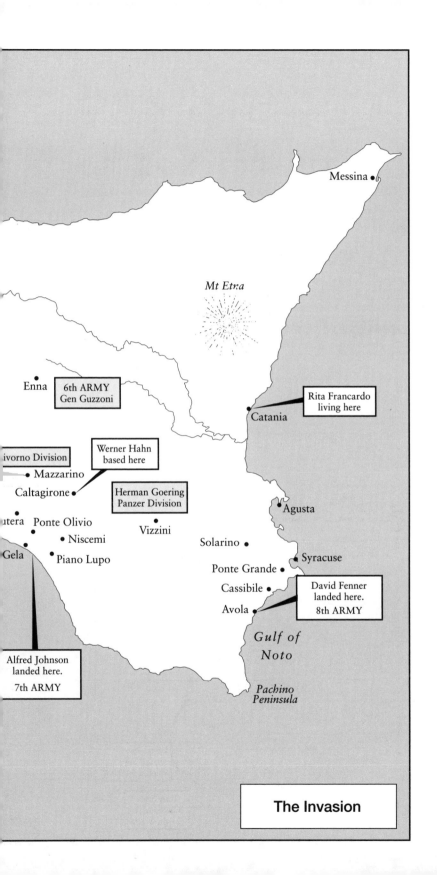

Messina •●

Mt Etna

Enna •

6th ARMY
Gen Guzzoni

Rita Francardo
living here

Catania •

Werner Hahn
based here

ivorno Division

• Mazzarino

Caltagirone •

Herman Goering
Panzer Division

• Agusta

utera

Ponte Olivio

Vizzini •

Solarino •

• Niscemi

Gela •

• Piano Lupo

• Syracuse

Ponte Grande •

Cassibile •

David Fenner
landed here.
8th ARMY

Avola •

Gulf of
Noto

Alfred Johnson
landed here.

7th ARMY

Pachino
Peninsula

The Invasion

PROLOGUE

On the last day of March 1943, Lieutenant Norman Jewell, commander of the submarine HMS *Seraph*, reported to Submarines Headquarters in a requisitioned block of flats in Swiss Cottage, north London. Jewell had been summoned to receive orders for a new mission which was to be one of the most ambitious deception stratagems of the entire war. In a little over three months' time, the lives of several thousand British and American soldiers would depend on its outcome.

At only twenty-nine, Jewell was already a veteran of special missions. He had taken part in the Dunkirk evacuation three years earlier, and had also put the American General Mark Clark ashore in north Africa before the Anglo-American landings there the previous year. His superiors knew they could trust both him and his crew to perform the most sensitive tasks.

At the red-brick Northways building which housed Submarines Headquarters (Operations and Administration), he met Lieutenant-Commander Ewen Montagu of the Naval Intelligence Division. Montagu handed Jewell his orders, which were typed up on a few sheets of paper. HMS *Seraph* was to ensure that a body, dressed in the uniform of a major of the Royal Marines, would drift ashore close to the town of Huelva on the south-west coast of Spain, where the Germans were known to have a highly active agent. The enemy must be fooled into believing that the 'major' died in an air crash at sea, while traveling from Britain to Allied Headquarters in north Africa.

The body would be carrying a briefcase. Montagu briefed Jewell on a 'need to know' basis, and did not tell him what would be inside the briefcase. If Jewell were to find himself forced to abort the mission, he must sink the body and its container in deep water, making sure the body did not escape. He should also burn the briefcase and its contents, without opening it. With a raw sense of humour, the mission was codenamed Operation Mincemeat.

After the briefing, Jewell spent an enjoyable few days helping to build up a background for the fictional Royal Marine, who was given the name of Major William Martin. Jewell and other officers impersonated Martin with outings to the theatre, restaurants and nightclubs, accompanied by young women from the Admiralty posing as Martin's girlfriends. After consultation with a distinguished pathologist, a suitable body was obtained by clandestine means – its true identity was kept secret – and dressed in a new uniform purchased from Gieves & Hawkes of Savile Row. Two ticket stubs for the Prince of Wales Theatre, a photograph of an attractive 'fiancée', two love letters from her, and a bill for a diamond engagement ring were placed in the pockets.

On 18 April, as HMS *Seraph* prepared to sail from Holy Loch at Greenock in Scotland, Montagu entrusted a tubular steel canister to Jewell. A little over six feet long and under two feet wide, it weighed some 400 pounds, and was marked 'Handle with Care – Optical Instruments'. The ratings who placed it in a forward chamber thought the canister odd, and asked what it was for. Jewell told them it contained a secret experimental device for reporting on the weather. The explanation didn't convince the crew, and because of the canister's shape and weight they joked about what they called 'John Brown's body' and 'our new shipmate, Charlie'.

Shortly after 0400 hours on 30 April, the conning tower of HMS *Seraph* broke the surface of the water off the coast of Andalucia in south-west Spain. Four junior officers, led by Jewell, climbed through the tower and took their first breath of fresh air since the previous afternoon.

The night was pitch black as the new moon had set and the

sky was overcast. The men could see lights shining in Fascist Spain, whose government had claimed neutrality but which in reality had sided with Germany. Just over a mile away were the mouths of the rivers Odiel and Tinto.

Jewell ordered the officers to help him haul the airtight steel container through the tower, and lay it gently to rest on the deck. Then, Jewell revealed the secret he had kept to himself since leaving Britain. Inside the container, he told the men, was a body. The body carried documents, and the enemy must believe that 'Major William Martin, Royal Marines', whose corpse this was supposed to be, had died in an air crash at sea.

'Isn't it pretty unlucky carrying dead bodies around?' one officer asked.

Two of the men served as look-outs as the engineering officer helped Jewell unscrew the sixteen bolts on the canister's cover with a spanner. It was no easy job, and took them ten minutes. At 0415 hours, Jewell and the engineering officer slowly extracted the body. The men stiffened as they saw the sodden corpse, packed in dry ice to slow down the rate of decomposition. Jewell sensed that the look-outs were not at all keen to handle the body. He suspected that they had never seen a corpse before. It was the first time Jewell had laid eyes on this one, and to him it looked very ordinary. His father a surgeon and his brother a doctor, Jewell wasn't squeamish about such things.

He knelt down and untied straps securing a blanket which had been wrapped around the body to prevent friction during the journey. Over the Royal Marines uniform, the corpse wore an old trench-coat, and on top of that a Mae West lifejacket blown up very hard. Jewell checked the condition of the uniform and its array of badges. He also checked that the hand was clenching the handle of the black briefcase, which bore the royal cipher, and that the chain clipped to the briefcase was securely fastened to the belt of the trench-coat. Jewell still had no idea what the documents in the briefcase were.

The officers stood over the body, their bare heads bowed, while

Jewell recited what he could remember of the Burial Service. A passage from Psalm 39 seemed particularly apt for the men he had sworn to secrecy: 'I will keep my mouth as it were with a bridle: while the ungodly is in my sight. I held my tongue, and spake nothing: I kept silence, yea, even from good words; but it was pain and grief to me.'

At 0430 the service ended. The officers bent down, picked up the body and slid it over *Seraph*'s side. It began to drift towards the shore, the inflated Mae West helping to catch the wind, which was alternating between south-westerly and south-easterly. Jewell ordered the submarine's engines full speed astern, so that the wash from the screws would help the body on its way. Half a mile further south, a damaged RAF aircrew dinghy was also slipped into the water, upside down to help persuade the enemy that Major Martin had drowned.

Seraph plunged to the seabed, to surface again at daybreak for the last part of the mission. The crew had not seen daylight since leaving Britain almost two weeks earlier, as until then the submarine had only surfaced under cover of darkness. The empty canister was thrown into the water, and an officer attempted to sink it by firing some 200 bullets from a Vickers gun and a .455 revolver. The canister continued to bob on the water and *Seraph* had to go alongside to allow the men to haul it out. This time, they put plastic explosive inside it and attached more to the outside before slipping it back into the water. The submarine withdrew, the canister blew up, and Major Martin's bizarre coffin finally disappeared.

Jewell and the men of the *Seraph* had played their part. He sent off the agreed signal: 'Mincemeat completed'. In London, Naval Intelligence waited to discover whether Major Martin, better known as 'The Man Who Never Was', would dupe Adolf Hitler and Benito Mussolini. The Allies were planning an invasion of Sicily, but their aim was to trick the Axis dictators into believing that the attack would be launched against two other locations – Sardinia and Greece.

PART 1
THE WAIT

January – 5 July 1943

CHAPTER ONE
5 JULY 1943

The stirring notes of 'Land of Hope and Glory' blared from the loudspeakers of the *Winchester Castle*, penetrating every corner of the big passenger liner and floating across the calm waters to other ships in the convoy as they sailed out of Port Said, their decks crowded with troops. Some of the men went on cleaning their guns or sharpening their bayonets, but most stopped what they were doing to listen. A few sang along quietly.

Like almost all the troops sailing out into the Mediterranean, Lieutenant David Fenner of the Durham Light Infantry had no idea where or when the planned assault on what Hitler called Fortress Europe would take place. For him and the Thirteen Platoon he commanded, the long guessing game had continued on the journey all the way up the Suez Canal.

Once, as they passed by, an American had shouted from the bank of the Canal: 'Where you going?'

'Home!' the men on board replied, although they knew this could hardly be true.

'Looks damned likely, with those canoes strung alongside,' the American retorted. The *Winchester Castle* had been stripped of its lifeboats to make room for Landing Craft Assault, or LCAs for short, which hung from the davits for everyone to see.

As the ship left the Egyptian coast, the twenty-five men of Thirteen Platoon bet on Burma, Crete, Greece and the South of France. A tall, quiet-spoken man with a steely pale-blue gaze which commanded respect, Fenner didn't take part in the betting. He couldn't see the point. He was something of a fatalist and the only thing that mattered to him was getting his job done – wherever the landing took place.

A relative newcomer to the Durham Light Infantry, having only joined nine months earlier, Fenner had quickly realised that getting the job done was the best way to win acceptance. Several veterans in the Durhams had been on the march since the war began in 1939. They had fought in France and were among both the last to leave Dunkirk and the first to return overseas afterwards for the assault on north Africa. Theirs was one of the most experienced battle units in the British Army.

In the short time he had served with the Durhams, Fenner had never shirked his duty – the only time he missed a battle was when he had suffered from jaundice – and the platoon looked up to him as a result. He liked its North Country character – many of the men he led were former miners, physically strong, quick-witted with a caustic sense of humour, and who did not suffer fools gladly. They were a tight-knit unit; whenever they bumped into other troops in the dark, they would yell out: 'Durhams! We're Durhams!'

A few days before sailing, when Fenner was having a drink at the Suez camp in the officers' mess, which was just a big marquee with a bar at one end, he had met a friend who was a member of the SAS. The friend said to Fenner: 'You must come and join the SAS after this operation because there will be plenty of room.'

'There'll soon be plenty of room in the Durhams too,' Fenner replied grimly. He'd never felt so loyal to his unit before.

Further to the west along the north African coast, another convoy set out eastwards from Algiers, carrying the men of the American 1st Division. More famous as the Big Red One, it was the most prestigious unit in the US Army.

Shortly after the USS *Samuel Chase* had weighed anchor, a GI on deck started day-dreaming aloud. 'How about it,' the infantryman said. 'Put Hitler, Mussolini, Churchill and Stalin in a football stadium. We can all watch. Give them all baseball bats, and let them beat each other's brains out. The last one still standing is the winner. War over.'

'If they don't like baseball bats, they can have a gun and a bullet,' echoed another.

'Razors.'

'Swords.'

'Spears.'

Sergeant Alfred Johnson ignored them. If someone had asked him, the restless twenty-year-old Johnson would have said that he was sick of the Army and of the war, that he didn't give a damn for anything or anybody. He was as disenchanted as the rest of them with Uncle Sam's Army, and with Uncle Sam's war. And yet, part of him felt that war was beautiful, clean and justifiable. Sometimes it was even romantic. Part of him was proud of the Big Red One, which had been the first to fight in the First World War, and deeply believed in its motto: 'No Mission Too Difficult, No Sacrifice Too Great; Duty First'.

Loyalty to the cocky 1st Division meant a lot to Johnson. It was his new family. Of Scottish-Irish descent, Johnson was six-foot-two, and had a heavily-built frame, an infectious grin and big powerful hands which were always useful in brawls. Thanks both to his size and to his cheek, he'd got away with forging his parents' signatures on the Army recruitment papers and joined up in Atlanta at the age of sixteen.

He'd wanted nothing more than to get away from his parents' violent rows. His mother suffered from some kind of paranoia, and she couldn't bear living somewhere for longer than a year so he and his older brother kept moving – across the American South, from Georgia to Alabama, from South Carolina to Florida, then back to Georgia. The constant moving played havoc with Johnson's education. Over eight years he went to fourteen different schools, most of them one-room schoolhouses. His mother beat him with a switch to make him learn to read, and when he became so passionate about reading that he would use a torch under the bedcovers at night, she beat him again.

When Johnson had signed up and got his first crew cut, he didn't stop to think that he might get wounded or even killed in combat, he thought he would live for ever. The world was a great big choice plum and war would be an adventure, just like in the movies. He knew it would be, because he'd seen all the fun everybody had in war movies. The heroes always got the girl in the end. There was one movie, however, *All Quiet on the Western Front*, about German trench soldiers in the First World War, which he didn't like because the hero got killed. Johnson figured the Navy would be safer and planned to join that. But at the Atlanta post office where the armed forces had their recruitment centre, an Army sergeant got to him first.

Johnson didn't tell his parents that he'd joined the Army. But after a few weeks of training and sleeping in a vast dormitory, he wrote asking them to get him out. If he'd had enough brains to walk and chew gum at the same time, he told himself, he would never have signed up.

Several days later, he saw his father drive up. 'He's come to fetch me,' Johnson thought, and rushed towards him.

His father got out of the car, looked at him for a moment and said: 'Son, you made your bed, now you lay in it.' Then he shook hands – the first time that father and son had ever shaken hands – got back into the car and drove off.

If there was a lesson his father had taught Johnson, it was that as a man you had only one thing – your word. If his father shook hands with someone on a deal, Johnson knew his father would stick to it, even if it cost him every nickel he had on the face of the earth. So Johnson stuck with the Army.

As he fell asleep in his bunk on the *Samuel Chase*, Johnson started to feel more optimistic. He had learnt to fight in north Africa, and he felt confident that he would hold his own. His Division had pulled through the slaughter on the Kasserine Pass in February, when the forces of the German Field Marshal Erwin Rommel had claimed some 6,000 American casualties, held down the equivalent of two Panzer Divisions and then kicked the Germans into the Mediterranean. 'The damn, old, cumbersome Americans who weren't supposed to know shit from apple butter whipped their arses bad,' he told himself. Three months later when the Allies conquered north Africa, they had taken some 250,000 German and Italian prisoners.

Johnson hoped that the battle for Sicily would end the war. He hoped that the Germans would quit and go home. And he hoped that then, he would go home too. He kept these thoughts to himself – he would have been ashamed to voice them to anyone else.

On the island of Malta that same day, Royal Navy Sub-Lieutenant David Repard made his last preparations ahead of the imminent departure of his ship HMS *Tartar*, a 2,500-ton destroyer. As the officer in charge of firing *Tartar*'s guns, he had learnt much from other people's deaths at sea and he devised a personal survival kit for himself.

Repard had seen enough men thrown unconscious into the water and then pulled out dead later, to make him devote some effort to scrounging a bright yellow lifejacket, which floated much better than the Navy's regulation Mae West, from a merchant navy ship. He resolved to wear it at action stations, and a lifebelt too whenever possible, even though he knew he'd look a little odd.

He'd also seen men pulled out of the sea virtually dead from exhaustion, so he obtained small packs of Horlicks tablets which he thought would help him to keep going. And he'd seen how flashes of fire from explosive shells burned the skin, making it peel off in ugly strips, so he made sure he had plenty of long trousers and long-sleeved shirts, which he determined to wear despite the summer heat.

The unorthodox uniform gave Repard a jaunty air, in keeping with his chatty and inquisitive nature. Blessed with good looks, he had a high forehead, a dimpled chin and long, sensitive hands. He had long ago lost the illusion which had prompted him to join the Navy in the first place – that war would be as thrilling as the most exciting rugby match he'd ever played. His mother was an Australian-born actress, his father a property developer who exploited the craze for penny-flicks and retired a wealthy man in his early forties. Repard had enjoyed a privileged childhood in a world of chauffeured cars and skiing holidays at the chic Swiss resort of St Moritz. Then when he was only eight, his father died of pneumonia, just at the time of the Great Crash of 1929, and suddenly the family fortune disappeared.

At first he wanted to follow in his mother's footsteps and become an actor, but by the time he was sixteen he had changed his mind and decided to join the Navy. Before his interview, in the ballroom of a hotel off Piccadilly in the summer of 1939, his mother coached him in her best theatrical style. 'Don't sit down before they tell you to. Whatever you do, look them in the eyes and answer them directly,' she advised. 'Try to avoid saying "um" and "er" all the time.' On the day of the interview, she insisted that he read the leader in *The Times*. War had not yet broken out, and no one asked him if he was ready to fight.

The Navy recruited him. During his training he and other cadets were taken to see from close-to the damage which an enemy shell could cause. The recruits silently inspected a wrecked turret on HMS *Exeter* in Devonport. The shell had exploded inside, setting cordite alight and sparking a huge flash of flame which had rubbed out all the men in the turret. It dawned on Repard that something similar could happen to him too, and he wrote a one-page letter to his mother, to be given to her if he died at sea. In it, he told her how wonderful she had been and how much he appreciated everything she had done for him. For safe-keeping, he gave it to his godfather who put it in a safe deposit box at his bank.

Today, three years later, Repard wanted to believe that his survival kit would see him through.

As the band played a fast martial tune, Second Lieutenant Livio Messina ran down the parade ground outside the medieval town of Mazzarino in central Sicily, struggling to hold his rifle at the proper angle in front of him and keep up with the music. Why, he asked himself for the hundredth time as his shorts and shirt dripped with sweat, should he learn the bizarre 'running march', typical of a unit he didn't even belong to, the Bersaglieri?

The reason was simply that Colonel Mario Mona, the new commander of Messina's infantry regiment, the Livorno Division, had previously served with the Bersaglieri and believed his new charges were too soft. He made them learn the speed-march and do gymnastics from 0445 until 0545 in the July heat, even on Sundays. Messina, his fellow-officers and the soldiers all complained. The commander, they said, was turning their Livorno Division into a circus and they bitterly referred to their unit as 'the Mona Circus'. This wasn't what Messina had signed up for.

Messina's move from the Italian mainland to Sicily was somewhat of a homecoming for him. Born in the Sicilian capital, Palermo, he had grown up near Naples and his extrovert, playful character was more Neapolitan than Sicilian. He was stocky, with a wide chubby face, a ready grin, and dark hair which he parted and sleeked fashionably with brilliantine. On 10 June 1940, he had stood in a drizzle in the Piazza Plebiscito in Naples as loudspeakers relayed Benito Mussolini's declaration of war from Rome. Messina applauded at the dictator's '*Vinceremo!*' (We will win!) An old woman was standing next to him at the time and Messina suddenly realised she was in tears. She lifted a hand to his face and stroked his cheek. 'My son, you don't realise what is going to become of us,' she told him.

The old woman's words meant nothing to Messina. He wanted war – not because he hated the enemy, but because he dreamt of Italy demonstrating its greatness. Mussolini, a great statesman who embodied the nation, would do just that by conquering a new empire to rival that of ancient Rome with what he called an army of 'eight million bayonets'. That was what Messina had learnt at school: in the Young Fascist movement he had no choice but to join and then at university where he took a course in Colonial Studies; he saw no reason to challenge what he had been taught.

His faith in Mussolini was only a little shaken when, after conquests in Africa, Italy began to suffer defeats. The death of his uncle, a soldier, in Albania affected him personally. But when he was called up at the age of nineteen, he responded with enthusiasm because he respected the Italian royal family and the tricolour, and hoped to repeat the valour of Italian First World War heroes he had been taught about at school. Seeing him off at the railway station, his father had given him a razor, complete with brush and soap, but to Messina's dismay for months afterwards his face remained so smooth that he had no need for the gift.

A year and two days later, his right hand raised over his pistol which he had been told to lay on the desk in front of him, he had stood before the commander of his regiment, and proudly taken his oath as an officer to observe the laws of the Italian state 'with the only objective the good of the state, the King and the mother-country'. Since November he had been stationed in Sicily and he was now in charge of a signals platoon. Messina was so naïve and so used to the Army sending him from one city or camp to another, that it never crossed his mind that this latest move had brought him closer to the enemy. He had pushed the old woman's warning to the back of his mind.

CHAPTER TWO

JANUARY–APRIL

When Churchill secretly met Roosevelt in Casablanca in January 1943, the question the two leaders had to answer was where to strike next. As Allied troops looked set to sweep German and Italian forces from north Africa, the time had come for Churchill to fulfil his private promise to Stalin that the Allies would open a 'second front' in Europe in 1943.

But the British and the Americans did not see eye-to-eye on just where their first assault on Hitler's Fortress Europe should take place. Churchill was convinced the best target was Sicily, which he called 'the soft under-belly' of the Axis. Victory on the island, he believed, would not only provide the Allies with a stepping stone for landings on the Italian mainland, where they would seek to overthrow Mussolini, but also help the Allies control shipping routes in the Mediterranean. He saw a further advantage: by prompting Hitler to send reinforcements southwards, it would weaken German troop deployments in Russia and France.

The Americans, however, wanted to mass troops in Britain to prepare for the earliest possible invasion of France. They worried that Churchill had imperialistic ambitions in the Mediterranean. In Casablanca, the Americans argued that a Mediterranean operation, including Operation Husky as the Sicilian invasion was codenamed, could not defeat Germany. 'Is Husky a means to an end or an end in itself?' they asked pointedly.

The British delegation – so numerous that one American compared it to a swarm of locusts – retorted that once Italy had surrendered, the Allies would at last be able to launch the invasion of France. The attack on Sicily was not only a rehearsal for the landings in France, it was also a prerequisite for them. The willingness of both sides to compromise ensured that the British won the argument and Husky was set for June or July – two months when the moon would be favourable. At the same time, everything would be done to launch the French landings as soon as possible.

As the planners drew up the blueprint for the invasion of Sicily, Churchill and many others could not forget the outcome of the last major Allied assault against an enemy-held nation: the tragic Gallipoli campaign which twenty-eight years earlier had claimed more than a quarter of a million casualties. Churchill, then First Lord of the Admiralty, had himself ordered the assault through the Dardanelles.

Wary of repeating any such tragedy, the Royal Navy and the Royal Air Force insisted that the most important Sicilian airfields and ports be seized immediately. As a result, the original plan provided for small forces to land on all three sides of the triangular-shaped island – its eastern, southern and northern coasts. Some of the attacks might fail but others would be bound to succeed and these would be swiftly reinforced, or so the planners thought.

For Lieutenant-General Bernard Montgomery, a favourite of Churchill, the invasion plan which he first studied in mid-March amounted to military suicide. The commander of the Eighth Army and victor of El Alamein was not shy of making his views heard. 'In my opinion the operation breaks every common-sense rule of practical battle fighting and is completely theoretical. It has no hope of success and should be completely recast,' Montgomery wrote.

The key was what he called the 'break-in', the initial assault. Speed and violence were vital. Instead of landing at various points, the Allies should concentrate their effort on the south-east of the island. The British troops, he decided, must stage not five landings, as the planners argued, but just two – at Avola and on the Pachino peninsula. The invaders should then race towards the vital eastern seaports – Syracuse, Augusta, Catania and finally Messina. But he predicted that the mountains of Sicily would play into the hands of its defenders, forcing 'a prolonged dogfight battle'.

Montgomery had no intention of allowing planners to force their harebrained ideas on him, when his reputation and the lives of his men were at stake. He unleashed a blizzard of signals and letters, making many personal visits to planners and other commanders. He soon became unpopular with both British and American staff officers. Admiral Sir Andrew Cunningham, Commander-in-Chief Mediterranean, complained in the deceptively mild but cutting tone of the well-bred British officer: 'Montgomery is a bit of a nuisance; he seems to think that all he has to do is to say what is to be done and everyone will dance to the tune of his piping.'

Montgomery himself found it all exasperating. In one letter home, he confided: 'The battles I am having now with the planning staffs are far more exhausting than my battles against the Germans.' Montgomery had every confidence in his own judgment and very little in other people's, including that of General Dwight D. Eisenhower, Supreme Commander in the Mediterranean theatre. In a letter to his friend General Sir Frank 'Simbo' Simpson in April, marked 'Most Secret', Montgomery wrote after spending an evening with Eisenhower that the latter was 'a nice chap and probably quite good in the political line', adding a typically outspoken and damning assessment: 'But his knowledge of how to make war, or to fight battles, is definitely NIL. He must be kept right away from that sort of thing . . . otherwise we shall lose the war.'

Montgomery was just as damning of Americans in less elevated positions: 'The real trouble with the Americans is that the soldiers won't fight; they have not got the light of battle in their eyes. And the reason they won't fight is that they have no confidence in their Generals. If they had confidence that their Generals would put them into battle properly, then they would fight.' Montgomery advised Eisenhower to focus on training his generals. Later, he even suggested that American land forces should be placed under his command. None of this endeared him to the American commanders, in particular to the man who was to be the other major commander in the invasion of Sicily – Lieutenant-General George S. Patton.

Relations between the best Allied combat generals of their time had hardly got off to a good start. In mid-February, Patton had attended a conference at which Montgomery lectured military chiefs on the art of war. Perhaps in part irritated by Montgomery's ban on smoking, the chain-smoking Patton commented audibly as the Eighth Army commander finished one lecture: 'I may be old, I may be slow, I may be stupid, and I know I'm deaf, but it just don't mean a thing to me.' In his diary, Patton wrote that Montgomery was 'very alert, wonderfully conceited, and the best soldier – or so it seems – I have met in this war.' Patton's opinion was confirmed by Air Chief Marshal Sir Arthur Tedder, who told him during the period when Montgomery was busy overhauling the Sicily plans that the Eighth Army commander 'thinks of himself as Napoleon'.

For the time being at least, Patton was willing to play second fiddle to Montgomery. Patton knew little about the planning for Sicily, and cared even less. 'George is spectacular,' General Omar Bradley commented. 'Does not like drudgery. And that is drudging work. No glamour in that.' All that mattered to Patton was throwing himself into battle and ensuring his troops were ready to follow him into it. Watching one practice landing at Arzew, in Eisenhower's presence, Patton strode up to a group of soldiers, his face red, and yelled at them: 'And just where in hell are your goddamned bayonets?' He then let loose a volley of oaths.

In the end, it was thanks to an American that Montgomery finally imposed his plan for the invasion. In early May, in the unlikely setting of a lavatory at Allied Forces Headquarters in Algiers, he cornered Major-General Bedell Smith, Eisenhower's

Chief of Staff. There and then, Montgomery persuaded him to cancel plans for American landings at Palermo, and instead send Patton's Seventh Army ashore on the south coast in the Gulf of Gela. To the east of this, Montgomery's own Eighth Army, with Canadian troops also under his command, would land on either side of the Pachino peninsula, in the Gulf of Noto and at Cassibile.

But no master plan was ever drawn up detailing how Sicily would actually be won, once the landings had taken place – an oversight which set the stage for damaging tension between Montgomery and Patton later on.

A weary Montgomery wrote in his diary that some people would take the line of least resistance and always agree with everything. But that was not in his nature: 'Personally I will always fight for what I know is right, and which means men's lives if you don't get it.'

On the evening of 16 April, nine-year-old Rita Francardo clung to her grandfather by a window in the main room of her home, staring out as what looked like fireworks of a thousand different colours rained down on her home town of Catania at the foot of Mount Etna.

'*Madonna mia*, what beautiful colours!' her grandfather exclaimed, before wondering aloud after a bomb exploded: 'Who knows where that one fell?'

Rita's mother, six months pregnant and sitting in a corner of the room with Rita's brother Pippo and her three sisters, shouted to her to keep away from the window. The tiny Rita, a pretty, blue-eyed girl with a mop of black hair her mother tied in ribbons in an effort to keep it tidy, ignored her. She knew perfectly well that a bombing raid was under way, targeting the industrial port of Catania, Sicily's second city, but the display was so much more impressive than celebrations she used to watch on the feast day of the city's patron, Saint Agatha, before the war.

Rita had no bad memories of her early years under Fascism. She was the favourite of her father, a taxi-driver who often took her to see Laurel and Hardy at the cinema. He took Rita because he loved the sound of her laughter and the way she would jump up and down the aisle during the film, laughing uproariously. She was by far the liveliest of his children. Once, when he took all the family out for a ride in a horse-drawn carriage down Catania's main street, the Via Etnea, she found it hard to keep still because she was so excited by the sound of the horse's hooves on the lava paving stones, the red feathers swinging on the horse's head, and the unfamiliar sense of pride she felt at being high up above all the people on the pavement.

When Mussolini visited Catania shortly after her fourth birthday in the summer of 1937, he stopped to pick her up, and kissed her. Rita, whom her parents had dressed in the blue skirt and white shirt of a Young Fascist girl for the occasion, remembered the Duce as a big gentle fellow. To her he was the leader of the world and she was proud to discover that she was born (albeit fifty years later) on the same day as the Duce, 29 July. At her school near the fishmarket she jumped up eagerly with the rest of her class whenever the teacher came in, throwing her right arm upwards in the Fascist salute, and shouting: '*Viva il Duce!*' Rita shouted as loudly as she could.

But Fascism took away her father. Sent to Africa to help Mussolini conquer a new Roman empire, he sent her postcards which she treasured. 'When I see the sun I say "Rita",' he wrote. 'When I see the stars I think "Rita".' One night shortly after he had returned home, the whole family were woken by police bursting into their house and the sound of chains as they arrested him. He had told fellow taxi-drivers that he wanted the war to end soon so that he could afford to buy petrol for his car, and feed his five children. He was released a month later.

The schools closed, and bombing raids on Catania, and on the harbour near Rita's home, became increasingly frequent. The port was a key link in the German chain, and much of the Afrika Korps had sailed from there bound for north Africa, only to return defeated. Many local people sought refuge in the ruins of the Roman amphitheatre in the centre of the city, once home to gladiators and animals.

Early in 1943, Fascism again stole Rita's father away. He had got into a discussion with a police officer, and the argument became so heated that he was jailed for offending the policeman. Their chief breadwinner gone, the family relied on the small earnings of Rita's grandfather, who occasionally worked as a waiter in a restaurant. To raise money, the family sold what little furniture they had in the few rooms they rented on the ground floor of a small house. There was no electricity, and the only source of light was a rudimentary oil lamp – a wick fixed to three corks which floated on top of a glass filled with water and oil.

One morning Rita's mother shepherded them all outside, everyone carrying as much luggage as they could, and they all headed for the bus station. The plan was for them to travel to a relative's home in the country west of Catania, far from any bombing raids. But the buses had stopped running, and the family had to go back home.

As the bombs continued to fall from the evening sky, Rita heard her mother pray as she worked the beads of the rosary. 'Hail Mary, protect our children, protect all my family,' her mother recited. 'Saint Rita, look after this family, look after these children.' Rita tried to make her already tiny frame as small as possible.

The morning after the firework-raid, Rita found out that a bomb had destroyed a house four doors away down her street, killing the neighbour and all his children. Later that day, an aunt called on Rita's family and offered them hospitality in her home on the city's northern outskirts which was higher up the slopes of Etna, away from the harbour. 'Come to my house, that way you'll be far from the centre and out of danger,' the aunt said.

Rita's mother accepted. All that Rita carried in her bundle, which was just two pieces of material her grandmother had sewn together to make a bag, were the only two dresses she owned – one for the week, which was washed every evening, and one for Sundays. They had to walk two miles uphill and Rita found it hard to keep up. She had never been so far up the slopes of Etna before. 'Hurry, hurry, we don't want to be caught out by another raid,' her mother urged her. Rita didn't like raids any more, and the first sight of German soldiers carrying awful-looking weapons she had never seen before made her afraid. She rushed to catch up.

Just a hundred yards short of the aunt's house, her mother tripped and fell over. A one-litre bottle of precious olive oil in her bag broke as it hit the ground and the family stopped to stare at the green puddle. 'Spilt oil brings bad luck,' her mother said as she picked herself up.

CHAPTER THREE

MAY–13 JUNE

One night in late May, more asleep than awake, Repard rose from his bed and left his cabin in the stern of the destroyer HMS *Tartar*, which was docked at Algiers. As usual, the Royal Navy officer had gone to bed fully clothed, with his lifejacket on. He dreamt he could hear the alarm bells, and the call to action stations which always sent men running, even the ones who were in the heads at the time and who fastened their trousers as they ran.

It was only some way from his cabin that he woke up and realised he had been sleep-walking. He was in such a confused state that he just kept on going, making his way forwards and then starting the climb up towards the round platform above the bridge, similar to an eagle's nest, from which he would direct fire on the enemy.

'Right, I'll take her,' Repard said as he reached the entrance to the platform.

A shout from the officer in charge snapped him fully awake. 'David, what are you doing here? You're not due for a couple of hours!' the officer cried out.

Repard was embarrassed. He had imagined it all – both the alarm bells and the call to action stations. 'Bother,' he said. The other men looked at him in silence as he turned and left to return to his cabin. In the Navy, it simply wasn't done to show sympathy for someone suffering from frayed nerves.

Repard's sleep-walking was the legacy of the horrors he had witnessed at sea. Aboard his first ship, HMS *Sheffield*, he sailed in the Atlantic and was on watch duty when its gunners shot up a German supply ship and took the wounded on board. Repard walked into an unlit compartment, fell over something, and found that the hatch above him was closed. Stumbling around, he touched things that were sticky and messy, and realised they were bodies. When he got to the light, he found that he was covered in blood. The corpses were of Germans wounded in the attack who had died after the *Sheffield* picked them up. A shaken Repard went to an officers' bathroom to clean himself up, only to find a leg in the bath – the cabin was sometimes used as an operating theatre. For quite a few weeks afterwards, he had a recurring nightmare in which he was shut up in a dark space with something nasty.

On HMS *Tartar*, his home for the past year, Repard had witnessed more horror. The ship was a member of the Tribal class, the fastest and most heavily-armed destroyers in the Navy, which meant it was thrown into action time and again. In an encounter off the north African coast with German E-boats – a dreaded enemy as they were even faster than *Tartar* and were equipped with torpedoes – Repard couldn't get a precise bearing so he decided to experiment. He set the fuses on his shells to explode just above the ships, a method usually reserved for firing at aircraft. Shortly afterwards, he heard on his headphones the sound of a man dying on one of the E-boats, apparently the officer who had been commanding the ship. *Tartar* had tuned in to the enemy's communications. The 'headache operators', as the eavesdroppers were called because of the headaches they suffered after long shifts on the job, were delighted with the death rattle but Repard, sickened, tore the phones off his head.

Repard saw enemy soldiers die aboard his own ship. When half a dozen German prisoners were brought up to the deck for some fresh air on a bright sunny day, some Dutchmen whom *Tartar* used to intercept and translate German signals ordered them to stand close to the side of the ship. The Dutchmen pointed, and the prisoners did as they were told. One of the Dutchmen then opened fire with a pom-pom gun at point-blank range with the explosive shells designed for hitting aircraft. The crew had to pick the ship clean of prisoners' remains. No action was taken against the Dutchmen, and Repard vowed he would keep as close an eye as possible on what people on his ship got up to.

The cute little Algerian girl stood out among the rabble of children who fought over the US Army food which GIs threw down a twelve-foot-high bank on the edge of their camp as they cleaned out their mess kits. Sergeant Johnson saw her hold back, unwilling or perhaps too weak to compete for the filthy scraps which the others picked out of the dirt and crammed into their mouths.

Johnson, who figured the girl must be about ten years old, beckoned to her. After a little coaxing, she approached and he bent down to give her his mess kit. She finished what was in it with her hands. The following meal, Johnson ate first, then went back for seconds and gave that to the girl. He did that every day for several days at the camp near Algiers where his 1st Division was holed up for most of the month of May.

One morning before daylight, Johnson was sleeping in his tent when he was woken up by someone grabbing his toe. He saw the little girl standing in front of him, and she held out an egg to him. She insisted that he take it, and then she vanished. He had no idea how she had got into the camp, let alone found his tent.

Johnson went on feeding the girl for several days, until one day she failed to turn up. There was still no sign of her the next day, so Johnson asked one of the other children, and found out that she was sick. Johnson knew the Arab quarter was off-limits to American soldiers, but he decided to seek her out anyway.

With a boy guiding him, Johnson walked through the dirty streets. He felt safe – he figured that everyone knew he had been feeding the girl. He found the shack where she lived. The girl was lying on some rags, feverish, soaked in her own sweat, and delirious.

'Why don't you get a doctor?' Johnson asked the boy, who could speak a little English.

'Doctors no come,' the boy replied.

'By God, yes they will,' Johnson said.

He rushed off and found a doctor, a French civilian. The doctor refused to go to the Arab quarter, saying he would be killed because of widespread anti-French feeling. Johnson pulled out his pistol and pointed it at the doctor. 'You come with me or I'll kill you,' Johnson said.

The drawn gun, and Johnson's powerful frame – the muscles on his legs were so big that he had trouble finding trousers to fit him – quickly made the doctor change his mind. '*D'accord, d'accord* (All right, all right) I'm coming,' the doctor said.

They followed the boy back to the shack where the doctor examined the girl and prescribed some medicine which Johnson bought.

Four days later, Johnson was walking outside the camp when he saw the little girl coming towards him. A man accompanied her, carrying a bundle of what looked like clothes.

'You have saved her life so she belongs to you. Here she is,' the man said.

'You crazy? What the hell can I do with her?' Johnson protested. The man took some persuading before he agreed to take her back home.

Not for the first time, Johnson asked himself what he was fighting for in north Africa – for people who gave away a little girl just because you brought her a doctor?

In early June, some two weeks after he had sleep-walked to his action stations on HMS *Tartar*, Repard was summoned by a superior officer as the destroyer still lay docked at Malta.

'You're going ashore for two days. Rest camp,' the officer told him.

Repard didn't ask why, he knew the reason. 'Good oh,' was all he said.

It was obvious that his nervousness had been noticed and reported to the Captain, Reginald St John Tyrwhitt, even though

Repard hadn't confided in anyone. Mindful that his condition risked deteriorating and could prompt him to do something he might be ashamed of afterwards, Repard was grateful for the break. It wasn't for nothing that, among themselves, the officers jokingly referred to 'action stations' as 'panic stations'.

Repard knew he could count on the Captain's sympathy. Even the most senior man on board, who was widely admired and who had pledged to make *Tartar* the hardest-working, hardest-fighting destroyer in the Navy, wasn't immune from 'the twitch'. On a couple of occasions when he was on the bridge before a battle, Repard had noticed that the Captain gripped the rail in front of him with both hands, and guessed it was to mask their trembling. For Repard and the other officers this was more than understandable, given that the Captain's last ship, HMS *Juno*, had turned over and sunk two years earlier when it was bombed off Crete. The Captain had managed to swim off the bridge to safety, but most of the company drowned. He was sent back to Britain to rest, but kept pestering the Admiralty until he got another commission.

The Captain was far from alone in suffering from the after-effects of trauma. On a ship Repard had served on as a midshipman, a baronet's son who served as a look-out had taken off his headphones and run from his post during an attack. Repard punched him in the stomach as he raced by. The man crumpled to Repard's feet and said: 'Terribly sorry, sir.' Repard, who carried a revolver for just such emergencies, could have shot him there and then for cowardice in the face of the enemy, but he didn't even charge him.

Repard had heard that a friend of his on another ship, a fellow-officer, had shot dead a crew-member who had panicked during combat. Repard thought about it at length, and became convinced he would have drawn his gun and done the same thing, if it was essential to do so. But he had the greatest difficulty in deciding precisely what would make such a gesture essential.

Only a few days earlier on 10 June, after no less than 6,400 tons of bombs had beaten to a pulp the island of Pantelleria south-west of Sicily, *Tartar* had been jumped from the stern by a Focke-Wulf 190 diving out of the evening sun. Repard had shouted for one of his guns to open fire but nothing happened and the German dropped his bombs, which barely missed the ship and gave Repard a wet shirt. He discovered that the gunner had abandoned the gun and run away. The man was found crying in a corner. He got off with a reprimand.

Alcohol was often the only refuge for desperate men. At one stop in north Africa, a drunken sailor whom Repard had reprimanded threw himself on top of him. The sailor apparently couldn't make up his mind whether to gouge Repard's eyes out with his thumbs, or to strangle him. So the sailor tried both, until Repard, lying flat on his back and crushed by his attacker's weight, found a fairly large stone and hit the sailor over the head with it, splitting his scalp. The sailor recovered.

Repard had heard another drunken sailor shout: 'Look at me, I'm a seagull!' as he jumped down some fifteen feet onto the steel deck, injuring himself severely. Repard blamed himself for that accident, as he had not realised how drunk the sailor was, and should never have allowed him to climb up to the higher deck.

Drinking was not confined to the lower decks. When *Tartar* was docked at Algiers, a senior officer had got very drunk. Brandishing a couple of revolvers, he decided to find out whether he could shoot through the wardroom portholes. Bullets started to ricochet around the wardroom, so Repard draped a tablecloth over the officer and, wielding a golf club, knocked him unconscious with a single blow to the head. When the officer recovered shortly before dawn, he tottered up to the Captain, claimed there had been a mutiny on board and accused Repard of attacking him. The incident was hushed up.

The more Repard saw others go to pieces during combat, the more determined he became never to do so himself. He slept as much as he could at the rest camp in Malta, which was actually a hospital. No one ordered him to action stations, no alarm bells sounded. He needed the rest. During the German and Italian evacuation from north Africa, he had set a new record for time spent in the gunnery director, the platform above the bridge from which he oversaw the firing of *Tartar*'s guns: a total of sixty-two hours, with only one four-hour break.

He relaxed, swam in the sea, roasted in the sun, and picked big juicy figs which grew everywhere. He thought of home. He wrote to his girlfriend back in England, Jane, a pretty admiral's daughter and the sister of one of his best friends. The two had become close when Jane, working as a physiotherapist at the hospital in Portsmouth, had massaged his legs which he had injured playing hockey. When they parted, she gave him a silver pencil.

In her last letter, she had written to say that she was on board a ship leaving Liverpool and headed for north Africa, but he had received no news from her since. Repard felt very much in love with her, but he'd refused to become engaged because he thought there was too high a chance of his getting killed and he didn't want to tie her down.

Repard was at the young man's stage in which he falls in love with great enthusiasm as often as possible, and at the Maltese hospital he became attracted to a beautiful nurse. She agreed to go for a couple of long walks with him at dusk on a pathway along the coast. Repard thought she would be lovely to kiss. On the last of these walks, when they knew he would be leaving the following morning, they kissed near some prickly pears.

Lieutenant Fenner stood to attention in front of his Thirteen Platoon, as stiffly as he could after the long wait in the desert heat. Some 700 men of the Durham Light Infantry were on parade on the afternoon of 13 June, strung out along a track in the desert near the Gulf of Aqaba. Out of the corner of his eye he saw the slim, wiry figure of Montgomery stride closer. Montgomery, wearing his trademark black beret, came to within a few feet of Fenner, who got a good look at him. Fenner was struck by Montgomery's piercing blue-grey eyes and his angular, hawk-like profile.

Later that day, at a specially erected building the size of a cinema, Fenner listened to Montgomery give a lecture. The subject, as far as Fenner could tell, was how he, Montgomery, fought battles. Montgomery, speaking in his clipped, slightly high-pitched voice, took them through the north African battles, making no effort to conceal his respect for the opponent he called 'Wommel', rather than Rommel, apparently because of a speech impediment.

At one point, Montgomery paused. Then he said: 'Ah, the Mareth battle. That was very interesting, you know.'

Fenner did know, and the comment shocked him. His battalion had lost many officers and men in that one battle, and he wouldn't have described such a scenario as 'interesting'. But Montgomery was a good speaker, and he captivated his audience. He was generous in his praise of the 50th Division, saying that he used it to attack the enemy's front door, while sending other troops round the back. The problem was, Fenner thought, that banging on the front door was sure to get us a bloody nose.

As the audience dispersed after Montgomery had left, Fenner realised that Montgomery had made no mention of the task ahead, nor of where they were all bound. But for the past two days, he had taken part in Exercise Bromyard, which consisted of manoeuvres involving thousands of troops in the Gulf of Aqaba. Fenner had tried to find out from a superior officer where the real target was, but the officer had just smiled at him and said: 'Lucky old you, you're going in first.'

Thirteen Platoon had taken part in the exercise using bizarre boats which Fenner had seen for the first time only a short while earlier: the assault crafts, or LCAs, looked like floating boxes. From the way Fenner and his twenty-five men were made to storm off his boat when the front was lowered onto the beach, it was obvious that what lay ahead was an assault landing, and that they would be the first ashore.

Wherever they were going, Fenner felt he and his men were as ready as they ever would be. Apart from Exercise Bromyard, they had been put through long route marches – the men called them 'stick and dog walks' – up desert hills every morning at five o'clock for days on end. At the start of the route marches, the officers told the men: 'If you need any water, it's six miles that way.' By the time the men got there, the water carts had been standing in the sun for so long the liquid was almost hot enough to brew up with. One morning, Fenner had to endure all this with a hangover made worse by an anti-typhus inoculation – the previous evening, officers had managed to get hold of some gin and, given the few opportunities at the squalid, sandy camp, Fenner had joined the party, despite his injection.

The guessing-game in his platoon over their destination turned gloomy when medics distributed mepacrine anti-malaria tablets, handing them out to the soldiers lined up on parade with water-bottles ready. The men were convinced that the sour-tasting tablets meant they were bound for Burma. They knew there was plenty of malaria there, and the latrine gossip focused on that destination. But many soldiers spat the tablets out instead of swallowing them. The troops thought they were so tough that mosquito bites could not possibly hurt them. Besides, rumour had it that the tablets were not against malaria, but were aimed at controlling their sexual drive.

Fenner took the tablets. He had been brought up by his aunt, a devout Catholic, to respect discipline and would never have dreamt of disobeying the medics' orders. Born in India, Fenner had been entrusted to his aunt in Kent after his mother died when he was only three years old. His father, an officer in the Royal Indian Navy, could see his son only once every four years when his tours of duty ended.

As a teenager, Fenner wanted to follow in his father's footsteps and joined the merchant navy. He sailed to Australia and back, but a year after war was declared, he decided the merchant navy was too passive for him. Although at eighteen years old he was under call-up age, he enlisted in the Army, because at the time a Nazi invasion seemed imminent and he wanted to be there on the ground to stop the enemy. He knew he had been exceptionally lucky so far.

CHAPTER FOUR
14 JUNE–4 JULY

Captain John Henderson, Montgomery's twenty-three-year-old aide-de-camp, had to hand it to his superior. Eager to see and be seen by as many of his men as possible, Montgomery, five feet seven inches tall, would stand in his jeep to deliver speech after speech as he toured the north African camps. It was the same speech, with the same jokes, again and again, and yet even to Henderson it sounded fresh every time. Even when Montgomery was particularly worried about some aspect or other of planning for the coming invasion, he gave the impression that he had not a care in the world. And he managed to enthuse the men, to give them the most amazing sense of confidence, that they were going to win that next battle, together.

After the speech ended, Henderson reached in the back of the command car and handed packets of Victory cigarettes to the teetotal, non-smoking Montgomery, who distributed them to the troops with the remark: 'Do you use these things? I find them no good.'

Montgomery had let it be known that gifts of cigarettes would be very welcome, and people in Britain sent him a huge number of packets. At any time, there were fifty parcels of cigarettes in the car, ready for distribution. It was a typical touch of Montgomery, who often asked Henderson to take down the names and home addresses of soldiers he met, so that he could send handwritten letters to their parents with a few kind words about their sons. The letters, sent by air mail and uncensored, in turn prompted warm letters of thanks from the front line.

A member of the 12th Lancers, a former cavalry regiment, Henderson had not taken to his new boss at first. Montgomery had questioned him closely – what school had he gone to, why had he joined the 12th Lancers? Henderson wasn't used to being probed so relentlessly, and didn't like it. 'Things are quite easy here really,' Captain John Poston, Montgomery's other aide-de-camp, reassured him. 'Try it for a fortnight. If he doesn't like you, you'll be off, and if you don't like it, you can leave.' Poston had two bits of advice for him: be yourself, and never tell Montgomery a lie.

After a few days in Montgomery's service, a bizarre incident broke the ice. During a visit to Cairo, Montgomery asked Henderson to be part of his guard of honour early the following morning before a thanksgiving service for the El Alamein victory. With a free afternoon on his hands, Henderson and a friend toured the local zoo. They went to see the elephants, who showed no interest in visitors offering them bread. The friend grabbed Henderson's hat, a smart thing with a peak, and offered it to an elephant. The elephant grabbed the hat. Henderson tried to go and save it, but a zoo-keeper restrained him. The elephant ate the hat except for a small part which it spat out, perhaps because of the badge on it. By that time it was early evening and all the shops were shut. Henderson failed to find a new hat for himself and stayed away from the guard of honour the next day.

'Why weren't you at the guard of honour?' Montgomery asked him after the service.

'I'm very sorry. I didn't have a hat. It was eaten by an elephant yesterday afternoon,' Henderson said, mindful that he should never tell Montgomery a lie.

'Well if you feel as bad as that, you had better go and lie down,' Montgomery said.

Later, Henderson drove him back to headquarters, more than an hour's drive from Cairo. As usual during such journeys, Montgomery said nothing. Henderson would drive Montgomery for miles and miles through the desert, and he just sat there, thinking. But over dinner that evening – Montgomery always relaxed for an hour over his supper, when talk of military matters was banned – he turned to Henderson and asked: 'What was that extraordinary story?'

Henderson's account, and Montgomery's amusement – it appealed to his schoolboy sense of humour – broke down a barrier. Henderson decided to stay. Henderson would never have dreamt of describing himself as a friend of Montgomery, but the two men respected each other and got on well together. For the first two weeks, Henderson had called Montgomery 'sir', but after that he dropped even that title. Montgomery called Henderson simply 'Johnny' and never asked him to salute.

Montgomery's routine was the same every single day. Awoken at 0630, he emerged fully dressed from the special caravan he used as his living quarters precisely an hour later, and began his breakfast at 0750. You could set your watch by it all. Then, he would start work in his second caravan which he used as his office. Inside, he had hung photographs of enemy commanders, including Rommel, which he liked to study, imagining how the opponent would react to his moves. In the evening, he always went to bed at 2100, even when the King or Churchill was visiting him.

Henderson soon understood that Montgomery needed to feel permanently in command with whoever he had dealings with, and that was the reason Montgomery picked young staff members. He could exercise more control over them than over older servicemen. Answering back was forbidden. On one occasion, Montgomery gave Henderson a training manual for captains, and later asked him: 'Well, what do you think of the manual?'

'Well, I'm afraid I haven't read it,' Henderson replied.

'Oh, you will never make a soldier,' Montgomery said.

Montgomery had to be always right. After the battle of Mareth in the north African desert, Montgomery no longer wrote up his diary every evening, but instead started to do so every three days. This, Henderson thought, enabled him to be wise after the event, and portray himself as infallible. But then again, his superior had pretty much proved himself infallible – at least so far.

For the Palermo-born Messina, life in the Italian Army was fun, an adventure in which an officer's uniform would inevitably open the door to female conquests. Like everyone else, he didn't much care for the daily six-mile marches with the infantry down winding Sicilian roads, and the weekly ones four times as long, with forty pounds of signals and other equipment on his back. Girls interested him more than anything else.

Before the Livorno Division sent him back to the island where he was born, Messina's knowledge of the female sex was non-existent. Two years earlier, after praying in church with his cousin Livia, his first love, he had found out that they had both asked for the same thing: to marry each other. He then kissed her for the first time, barely brushing her lips. They wrote to each other, until he was swept up in the Army and didn't bother to write any more.

His apprenticeship in Sicily had been slow. He took part in village dances held to celebrate the novena, prayers which lasted for nine successive days. Before each dance, held in someone's home, the young women and their mothers would line some chairs up opposite an image of the Virgin Mary and recite prayers in chorus. After the litany, a cloth would be hung over the Virgin so that she would not see the dancing couples. The mothers watched over them instead, reprimanding any soldier who held his companion too closely.

No matter how perfectly he pressed his uniform, or how neatly he slicked his hair back, Messina failed to make any headway with the girls he met at the dances. Some chaperone or other – a brother or a cousin – was always present, watching his every move. Apart from the dances, there was no other opportunity to meet young women; they rarely ventured out into the street, and never alone. The luckiest of Messina's fellow-officers, those who had been billeted in the homes of families whose menfolk were all away at war, boasted of their exploits with Sicilian girls whom they described as thirsting for men – males in smart uniforms, and from the mainland, were seen as an exotic catch. 'A massacre, my friend, a massacre,' one friend said of his multiple conquests in just one household.

Messina resorted to women he could pay to spend a night with him. Although rules on sexual diseases were strictly enforced – a soldier faced arrest if he caught one – prostitutes were tolerated in the camp, as long as they were discreet. The men were expected to treat the women properly; after a prostitute complained that a soldier refused to pay her, and threatened her with a bayonet, the company commander called all the men out on parade, and had the woman point out the culprit.

One prostitute, a Calabrian woman, came to Messina several evenings a week without asking for payment. She also went to other officers in the camp, but made them all pay. Messina could not hide the fact that such loss of sleep made him tired, and one morning he was stopped by his battalion commander, Lieutenant-Colonel Osvaldo Alessi, a dry, methodical leader who always wore a black glove over his left hand because of a First World War injury.

'What do you do at night?' Alessi asked.

'I sleep, sir,' Messina replied.

'That's not true. Make sure you get some proper sleep,' Alessi said.

Soon afterwards Alessi, who was also one of the Calabrian woman's – paying – customers, asked her which officers she preferred.

'The officers of your battalion,' she replied.

As the woman reported to Messina later, Alessi started to preen himself then asked: 'And which officer do you prefer?'

'Messina,' she said.

Messina felt great pride at being preferred over his commander.

Sergeant Joseph Rosevich stared, mesmerised, as the man he knew simply as 'The General' launched into a speech before the

45th Division, massed outside their camp in the north African desert on 27 June. Rosevich had never seen Lieutenant-General Patton, whom he served as personal secretary, so fired up.

The son of a modest Polish tailor who had emigrated to the East Coast, Rosevich was a handsome twenty-eight-year-old with smooth cheeks and thick wavy hair. His arched eyebrows gave him a permanently quizzical look. He noticed how swell the white-haired Patton looked. Rosevich thought Patton's uniform must have been made on Fifth Avenue, it was so fine and fitted him so beautifully. The two ivory-handled Colt Frontier revolvers at Patton's hips were as much part of his uniform as the row of bullets in his belt, and the three stars on his helmet and shirt collar.

'Clearly all of you must know that combat is imminent,' Patton began, his high-pitched voice sounding more strident than ever. 'You are competing with veterans, but don't let that worry you. All of them, too, fought their first battle, and all of them won their first battle just as you will win yours. Battle is far less frightening than those who have never been in it are apt to think.'

As he listened, Rosevich marvelled at the transformation in Patton. Over the past year and a half he had spent with the General, he had become used to him dictating his orders, letters and diary in a soft-spoken, aristocratic manner. This was a man who read the Bible, Shakespeare and poetry. And yet here was Patton delivering a speech which at times rose to fever pitch. Rosevich, who loved the theatre and had directed a couple of plays at high school, figured that Patton was putting on an act.

'All men are afraid in battle. The coward is the one who lets his fear overcome his sense of duty . . . Pride is the greatest thing a man can have,' Patton continued with an expression so fierce that Rosevich guessed he must have practised it in front of a mirror.

Patton made liberal use of obscene language with phrases like: 'We'll kick Hitler in the arse,' 'We'll kick Mussolini in the balls,' and worse – language which Rosevich had never heard him use in front of his staff.

Rosevich looked around him, at the crowd of faces which were all turned towards Patton. He felt much older, and much more experienced than most of these men, who had sailed straight from America via Oran. Although Patton didn't reveal to them their next destination, Rosevich already knew that they would receive their baptism of fire in Sicily. How in the heck, he wondered, did you get a young American boy to charge up a hill in the face of enemy machine-guns? Nice American boys knew all about working in drugstores and making milkshakes, but you didn't win wars with nice green guys. Rosevich had seen German prisoners; they were so military-minded they drilled and goose-stepped every day just to keep occupied, using bits and pieces as props.

You couldn't argue with Patton's military background. A descendant of Confederacy soldiers, he'd fought against Pancho Villa on the Mexican border in 1916, and had led a charge on a machine-gun nest in France during the First World War and been wounded. He'd become an authority on tank warfare. If Patton felt that a Jekyll and Hyde transformation, and coarse language, got through to the troops and helped to lick them into shape, then so be it.

To applause, Patton concluded his speech: 'We Americans are a competitive race. We bet on anything. We love to win. In this next fight, you are entering the greatest sporting competition of all times . . . for the greatest prize of all – victory.'

Rosevich applauded too. He felt as American as the rest of them. His father was a Pole, but his Jewish mother was, as she often proclaimed, 'American-born', and when the war started Rosevich, who was teaching shorthand, typing and book-keeping to high-school students, wanted to volunteer and join the Army. He hated Hitler, and was worried about his Jewish relatives in the Warsaw Ghetto. But his mother stopped him, and he wasn't in the business of going against her wishes.

He was glad to be drafted, and soon thankful that he was not in a combat unit. But as Patton's secretary, Rosevich had quickly found out that the General, at fifty-seven almost thirty years his senior, drove his staff hard. Everything had to be just right, and that kept Rosevich's nerves on edge. Luckily, he was bright and hard-working enough to satisfy Patton, but he lost sleep doing so.

Before Operation Torch, the November 1942 invasion of Morocco and Algeria, Patton had discovered that propaganda leaflets from the Office of War Information, destined to be dropped on French Vichy forces in Casablanca and written in French, were missing accents. 'Whoever did these leaflets has forgotten all the accents!' Patton had exploded. 'The French think we Americans are barbarians, and now here we are looking just like barbarians!' It took Rosevich and a dozen other GIs several hours to write the accents in. There were many thousands of the damn leaflets, and he thought he'd go blind.

But Rosevich liked his job, and above all he was proud of serving 'the General' – Patton was so unique that it was as if the other generals didn't exist. Rosevich would never have dreamt of calling him 'Old Blood and Guts' – the name he knew was popular among the soldiers. Patton's enthusiasm and confidence were so great they were catching, and Rosevich found himself looking forward to the battle ahead. He thought it would be easy.

Montgomery handed his aide-de-camp Henderson the Order of the Day which he had just finished writing at the hotel in Malta where they had arrived on 3 July. It was Henderson's job to ensure it got printed in time to be read to the troops on the eve of the invasion.

Henderson glanced through the text, which Montgomery had written long-hand as was his habit, printing all the names in capital letters, and drawing circles around the full stops. The Italian Overseas Empire had been exterminated, it said, and now the time had come to carry the war into Italy, and into the Continent of Europe. It continued:

I want all of you, my soldiers, to know that I have complete confidence in the successful outcome of the operation.

Therefore, with faith in God and with enthusiasm for our cause and for the day of battle, let us all enter into this contest with stout hearts and with determination to conquer.

The eyes of our families, and in fact of the whole Empire, will be on us once the battle starts; we will see that they get good news and plenty of it. To each of you, whatever may be your rank or employment, I would say: 'Good luck and good hunting in the home country of Italy.'

There was of course no hint of Montgomery's dismissive view of the American military, or of the feeling of apprehension which Henderson had seen weighing over Montgomery in the past few weeks. As far as Henderson could guess, Montgomery felt he hadn't been involved in the planning for the invasion as much as he would have liked, and he wasn't sure the plans were as perfect as they should be.

On the eve of the invasion, much of which he spent in an Operations Room that had been set up in caves, Montgomery wrote in his diary: 'It will be a hard and very bloody fight, and we must expect heavy losses.' It would take all the Allies' resources to capture Sicily. As for events after the battle for Sicily, Montgomery confided: 'The further exploitation on to the mainland – with a view to knocking Italy out of the war – is definitely unlikely to be possible.'

Johnson spent his last night in north Africa, 4 July, getting drunk and getting into fights with GIs of other divisions. His whole outfit was under orders to sail in the morning, but no one knew where. They were at Patton's beck and call – 'Old Blood and Guts' had himself insisted that Johnson's 1st Division go into battle under him in a few days' time, telling Eisenhower: 'I want those sons of bitches! I won't go on without them!'

Johnson was as lonely as hell in the middle of so many

hundreds of men. He hadn't heard from his quarrelsome folks in Georgia for what felt like years, and he had as few friends today as he'd had when he'd been forced to keep changing school as a child. Getting into trouble was one of the ways he could attract attention to himself. So he drank, and used his fists to give other soldiers a good licking. Any time Johnson saw a 1st Division man in a fight with someone from another unit, he would hop in there and help him out. He and his friends had once locked up the colonel in charge of the MPs (Military Police) in his own jail. Johnson hated the sight of rear-echelon troops who wore ribbons on their cotton uniforms, so he picked fights with them. The 1st Division didn't wear ribbons, but they were on the front line.

Besides, neither the maverick Major-General Terry 'Terrible' Allen, the Division's commander, nor his eccentric deputy, Brigadier-General Theodore Roosevelt, the eldest son of the American President, did anything to impose tight discipline. Johnson heard that Allen had tried to stop a brawl in a bar in Oran, when the Division had celebrated the end of the Tunisian campaign in typically rowdy fashion, but had given up when he'd been thrown out onto the street. Local officials in Oran were so exasperated by the Big Red One's rioting, including fighting rear-echelon soldiers and looting wine shops, that they banned the Division from ever returning to their city.

Apart from drinking and brawling, the only relaxation north Africa offered was the sea. For the last few days the troops spent on the continent, the long sandy beaches were as crowded as Blackpool or Coney Island. Except that there were no girls and no bathing suits, only thousands and thousands of men relaxing as they tried to forget what lay ahead.

PART 2

THE INVASION

6–17 July

CHAPTER FIVE
6–7 JULY

The island which the Allies chose as their stepping stone into Europe, with the ultimate goal Berlin, was no stranger to invasion. Shaped like a jagged arrowhead with its point broken to the north-west, Sicily is the biggest island in the Mediterranean. It has been a land of conquest ever since the eighth century BC when Greeks settled there. Waves of invaders from the great empires which held sway over Europe or the Mediterranean landed on its shores – among them Carthaginians, Phoenicians, Romans, Vandals, the British and the Spanish.

Although only two miles from the Italian mainland across the Strait of Messina, on either side of which lay Scylla and Charybdis, monsters which dwelt on dangerous rocks in Greek mythology, Sicily never had much in common with the rest of Italy. In Sicily time stood still. The long history of foreign rule left a legacy of fortified hilltop towns and villages, and made the people of Sicily strong-minded, and mistrustful. The failure of foreign rulers to ensure efficient government and law and order spawned the Mafia which from the nineteenth century onwards grew into a sinister brotherhood loosely based on traditional popular values such as honour and loyalty. Sicilians took the law into their own hands and settled their disputes through personal vendettas.

The Mafia's stranglehold, together with the barren mountains and infertile plateaux in much of the island, condemned most Sicilians to live in poverty. The most fertile terrain was limited to a narrow green belt of vines, olive groves and fragrant lemon and orange trees which stretched along most of the coast and circled the foot of the snow-capped Mount Etna, Europe's highest

41

volcano. Otherwise, the countryside was mainly desolate and suffocatingly hot for much of the year.

In his novel *Il Gattopardo* (*The Leopard*), Giuseppe Tomasi di Lampedusa captures the essence of 'this landscape which knows no mean between sensuous sag and hellish drought; which is never petty, never ordinary, never relaxed, as should be a country made for rational beings to live in . . . this climate which inflicts us with six feverish months at a temperature of 104°.'

In the late nineteenth century, Tuscan sociologist Leopoldo Franchetti journeyed across Sicily to study the peasantry. At first he was stunned by the savage beauty of the Sicilian landscape. But as he heard story after story of Mafia violence, he 'felt everything change around him little by little. The colours change, the appearance of things is transformed . . . After a number of such stories, all that scent of orange and lemon blossom begins to smell of corpses.'

Mussolini did nothing to dispel the Sicilians' diffidence towards the State. He made grand promises to the island, which he proclaimed 'the geographical centre of the Empire' in the early days of the Fascist regime, but failed to keep any of them – among the most extravagant were claims that he would turn Sicily and its impoverished estates into 'one of the most fertile regions on Earth', overhaul the water supply, and throw a patchwork of new roads across the island. With much pomp, he laid the foundation stone for a new town which he named 'Mussolinia'. Although it was supposed to become 'a garden town for peasants' and an idyllic home to at least 10,000 people, Mussolinia never made it onto the map.

His biggest initiative in Sicily was a relentless offensive he called 'Fascist surgery' against the Mafia, which he regarded as a challenge to his totalitarian vision of the State. The Fascist regime tortured, jailed or sent into exile thousands of Sicilians, many of them innocent. Although the sharp edge of Mussolini's scalpel spared the most senior Mafia bosses because of their powerful political allies within the Fascist regime, it was the furthest any government had gone in tackling organised crime in Sicily.

In July 1943, Sicily's defences had been severely weakened by Operation Mincemeat, the Allied deception stratagem launched ten weeks earlier. Five hours after the corpse of the supposed Major William Martin was slipped into the water off the Spanish coast, a fisherman spotted it. He reported his find to the authorities.

Despite their country's claim of neutrality in the war, Spanish officials, before handing over the body to the British vice-consul, surreptitiously copied the contents of the briefcase attached to the corpse and passed their findings to a local German agent – which was precisely what the creators of Operation Mincemeat had hoped would happen.

The Germans discovered that one of the two letters inside the briefcase was addressed to General Sir Harold Alexander, who at the time commanded an army in Tunisia under Eisenhower. The other was addressed to Admiral Cunningham, Commander-in-Chief Mediterranean, and – an insiders' joke – described Major Martin as 'quiet and shy at first, but he really knows his stuff'. Taken together, the letters summed up the Allies' intentions – or so the enemy was led to believe. They said the Allies would launch two attacks against Europe at the same time. One would target southern Greece, and the other Sardinia. Beforehand, an offensive would be launched against Sicily, but this would be only a feint.

The Major Martin ploy was a double-bluff, born of Allied concern that attacking Sicily after north Africa was simply too obvious. As Churchill put it: 'Anybody but a bloody fool would *know* it is Sicily.'

Berlin took the bait. After studying the letters as closely as it could, the German Intelligence Service pronounced: 'The authenticity of the captured documents is above suspicion.' Until this new piece of intelligence, the German High Command had believed that Sicily was the most probable next Allied target, ahead of Crete, with Sardinia and Corsica third. But by mid-May, Major Martin and his letters had convinced Hitler himself that the planned attack would be directed not at Sicily but mainly against Sardinia and the Peloponnese.

In a message to all commands on defences in the Mediterranean, the High Command of the German Armed Forces decreed: 'Measures for Sardinia and the Peloponnese to have priority over everything else.' Defences in Sardinia, Corsica and Greece were reinforced at Sicily's expense. Hitler dispatched the 1st Panzer Division from France to Tripolis, a town in the Peloponnese, and another strong Panzer force to Corsica. Navy commanders ordered the laying or completion of three new minefields off Greece. A fleet of motor torpedo boats, known as R-boats, were sent from Sicily to the Aegean Sea.

Operation Mincemeat, combined with Hitler's distrust of Mussolini's commitment to the war, and his doubts over Italy's military efficiency, led the Führer to station only two German divisions in Sicily in the early summer of 1943. Both divisions had suffered severe losses before withdrawing from north Africa.

The German presence on the island was estimated to number between 40,000 and 60,000 men. The Hermann Goering Armoured Division had only three battalions of infantry, was poorly trained and had no battle experience. The 15th Panzer Grenadier Division, made up of three regiments, was stronger, mobile and had supplies which would see it through twenty days of combat. Together, the Germans could however deploy only 160 tanks and 140 field artillery guns.

In death, Major Martin had accomplished his mission, and even duped Hitler. It was one of the most successful deception operations of the war. As the Chiefs of Staff put it in a message to Churchill: 'Mincemeat swallowed whole.'

Unlike Hitler, Mussolini had long held firm to the conviction that the Allies would invade Sicily. But the Italian Army presence in the island, although more numerous, with four mobile divisions amounting to about 200,000 troops, was a far from perfect fighting force. Two of the divisions, the Aosta and the Napoli, were to a great extent made up of Sicilians who had as low an opinion of Mussolini and the war as the island's civilian population. Morale in the Assieta Division was stronger, but it was short of men, vehicles and field artillery. Only the Livorno Division was a powerful force, but it was short of ammunition.

The defences along the 600 miles of coastline were manned by poorly equipped and poorly trained troops – one report noted that soldiers were afraid of injuring themselves with their own bayonets. Many of them were Sicilians, too old or too unfit for active service, who insisted on going home to spend Sundays and feast days with their families, war or no war. Pillboxes had been sloppily built, and much of the artillery dated from before the First World War.

To all appearances, the German and Italian forces deployed in Sicily would be no match for the force which the Allies were about to unleash.

To Johnson, the sand-table with its model of the combat zone looked just like the real thing. There it stood in the briefing room on the USS *Samuel Chase* – the beaches, roads, houses and pillboxes, everything tiny, clean and neat. On 6 July, two days into his journey, he had finally found out where he and his men, as a forward observation unit, would start calling in artillery fire on the enemy.

'You will land right here on Red Two beach, east of the town of Gela on Sicily's southern coast,' an officer was saying, tapping the model with a pointer, 'and you will proceed towards Piano Lupo and beyond.' Another tap. 'The airborne troops will fly over the ships, and land here.' Tap.

Piano Lupo – is that the name of an instrument or of a town? Johnson asked himself. He wondered who was going to sing first, the Americans or the enemy. In fact, Piano Lupo was a fortified position at a road junction which controlled all inland access to Gela, and was made up of sixteen blockhouses and pillboxes.

'The German Panzer Division is away near Messina,' the officer continued, 'so it'll be two or three days before it can get down to where we are.'

'Great,' Johnson said. 'That gives us a chance to get off, get set up, and get puckered up for them.'

Usually, the officers didn't even tell the men the time of day, they just pointed you in a direction and told you to 'go at them'. But this time the planners, previously so tight-lipped, told Johnson everything. For hours on end, they deluged him with briefings and told him exactly where on the south coast he was headed. They made him memorise roads and slopes and enemy gun emplacements on the superb scale models and in photos of the beach and the coastal plain which was dotted with vineyards, orchards and olive groves in small fields separated by dry-stone walls. The information had been gathered over the previous months by reconnaissance flights and Naval and Army intelligence teams which sneaked up to beaches at night.

Johnson noticed that the planners avoided anything complicated. The officers, he had learnt, always made it all look as simple as they possibly could, because they worried that giving it to you straight would scare you.

It never dawned on him that the plan outlined in the briefing might fail. The absence of the Panzers meant that Johnson's unit would face mainly Italians on the beach. In north Africa he'd seen that the Italians didn't, or rather couldn't, put up a good fight. Mussolini could spew and spout and carry on about everything he had, but his troops were under-equipped, under-fed, under-motivated, under-everything. They knew they were up the creek.

Johnson felt a little pity for them because the Kasserine Pass disaster had taught him what it meant to be the underdog, and that's what the Italians were. He'd watched through his binoculars as the Germans placed the Italians between themselves and the Americans. If the Italians fought, the Americans shot them. If they tried to surrender, or to rush back, the Germans shot them. But Johnson still hated the Eyeties as well as the Krauts. The sons of bitches were trying to kill him and his people, and Johnson hated them and wanted to kill them. He was fighting for his country, and anywhere his unit went was America. If his unit won ten feet of sand on a foreign beach, that was America. Johnson fought for his outfit, for his men, and for his buddies. It was that simple.

He learnt that the moon would be in its second quarter on the night of the invasion. Until midnight, it would ease the path of airborne forces who would be the first to attack. After the moon had set, Johnson and the seaborne troops would launch their assault, taking advantage of the darkness.

H-Hour was set for 0245 hours on 10 July, two hours before first light.

The news that Sicily was the target didn't mean much to Fenner as his British troop-ship sailed westwards through the Mediterranean. Sicily was better than Burma because he'd be closer to home, although it didn't feel very close, given the hell of a lot of Italians and Germans who stood in the way. Sicily was just another bloody battle. The idea of the war ending one day was so remote that all he could think about was the job at hand, the next meal, and the next night's sleep. What was the point of looking any further ahead?

'I'm going to land at a holiday resort,' Fenner thought when on 7 July he was shown the scale model and air photos of Marina D'Avola, a small fishing harbour, and its Lido, a waterfront where a pier and a concrete circular dance floor jutted out into the sea. The place reminded him of Bournemouth, except that its defences included not only twenty-foot-high cliffs but also barbed wire, anti-personnel mines and guns protected by pillboxes.

Fenner's company was scheduled to land between the fishing harbour and the Lido at 0300 on 10 July, when he would race to a point south-west of the main town of Avola further inland, clear up the Italian troops he would find there, and seize a road leading into it to stop any enemy approach.

Fenner concentrated particularly on photographs of the skyline for the stretch of coast he was due to aim for. He would be landing in darkness, and the skyline would be one of the few clues as to whether he was in the right place. One other clue was a pair of white columns, part of an archway above the path which led to the dance floor built out in the sea.

The intelligence people seemed to know all there was to know. A week earlier, a Navy team had got so close to the shore that they had watched a group of Italian soldiers come down to the water-line, take off their boots, and wash their feet in the water. According to the intelligence people, the troops defending the coast were all Italians. Fenner felt less apprehensive than if they had been Germans, because the Italians weren't expected to put up as much of a fight. They didn't have the efficiency, discipline or strength of the Germans.

But further inland a more serious threat awaited the invaders. Two German divisions were expected to launch a counter-attack pretty soon after the landings. It could hardly have been a co-incidence that, for a service on the mess deck the previous Sunday, 4 July, a colonel had chosen an extract from the Book of Deuteronomy, which began: 'Hear, O Israel: Thou art to pass over Jordan this day, to go in to possess nations greater and mightier than thyself, cities great and fenced up to heaven.'

The British troops were also expected to be pitted against the Sicilian population. *The Sicily Zone Handbook*, prepared by the Foreign Office and handed to all officers, described the history of Sicily as 2,500 years of 'exploitation of the island by foreigners', and warned: 'It would be rash to suppose that the population would welcome a British invasion. The islanders would probably oppose any invader, whoever he might be.'

Should he bump into any unidentified forces, the planners told Fenner, the password for the landings was 'Desert Rats'. The answer to the challenge was 'Kill Italians'. Fenner thought it was a bloody silly password, and wondered who had invented it. Why only Italians? he asked himself.

At the Livorno Division's camp near Mazzarino in central Sicily, neither Messina nor any of his fellow-officers believed in the

alarm that sounded, inconveniently, in the middle of the swelter-
ing afternoon of 7 July. Messina had witnessed so many false
alarms over the past couple of weeks, as well as manoeuvres and
exercises, that he assumed this was yet another drill. For two
days the troops had been put on alert because of the full moon
at the end of the previous month, and then again a week later.

Messina got his signals platoon ready all the same. His Division
prided itself on its sense of discipline – so much so that on the
train journey to Sicily nine months ago, a soldier who stole an
orange from a tree during a stop in open country had been threatened with the firing squad. The Division, Messina believed, was
the elite of the infantry, and Mussolini himself had proved as
much by marching at its head for a whole morning just outside
Rome. But the men had little recent experience of combat. The
Division had seen only skirmishes in the Alps with the French in
June 1940, and since then plans for it to fight in Russia, invade
Malta, and land in Tunisia, had all come to nothing. Inactivity
earned the unit an unflattering nickname – the 'Ghost Division'.

Messina gathered his men and checked their equipment,
making sure they were ready to move to the front, wherever it
might be, and meet the enemy supposedly invading Sicily.
Messina supervised the loading onto the trucks of the field telephones and the spools of wire that his men would unwind on
the battlefield.

The heightened state of readiness was irritating and unnecessary, Messina thought. For the next few hours, or however long
the alarm lasted, he would have to keep his uniform on, and his
rifle near him, all the time. Under Army regulations, he wasn't
even allowed to take off his uniform to get washed at the camp's
rudimentary showers – a line of fuel tanks that had been drilled
with holes and fitted with taps, usable only in the early hours
of the morning before the water got too hot.

It was all for nothing. If the enemy really was about to land in
Sicily, Messina would surely know by now. Someone would have
spotted the Allied fleet long before it ever came close to the island.

CHAPTER SIX
8–9 JULY, 2100 HOURS

Nine-year-old Rita Francardo crouched close to her mother in the dark cave. The air stank with the acrid smell of acetylene lamps, and rivulets of water ran down the jagged black lava rocks jutting out of the walls. From outside came the sound of explosions. Over and over again, her mother, almost nine months pregnant, recited prayers.

The bombs had followed Rita's family up Mount Etna since their move to their aunt's home in a northern neighbourhood of Catania, which soon revealed itself no safer than their own house near the city's harbour. Shortly after their arrival, they discovered that the Germans had turned a nearby school into a barracks, making the area a target for Allied bombers. Then, in early July, warships had begun to shell Catania.

On the afternoon of 8 July, as she squatted with her brother Pippo and her three sisters on slabs of lava slippery with damp, Rita listened to the sound of prayers recited by her family and dozens of other people crouching nearby. The prayers in the cave reminded Rita of the crypt of a local sanctuary she had visited with her parents before the war.

Rita's mother had brought with her to the shelter various things she would need if she went into labour there. Proclaiming that she didn't want to suffer 'the fate of a rat' and be buried alive deep in the shelter, she had found a space close to the entrance. Rita liked feeling her mother's hand stroking her head, but hated not being able to jump around as she usually did – the only time she stayed still at home was at mealtimes.

A chorus of subdued voices echoed through the grotto: 'Our

Father, who art in heaven, hallowed be thy name. Thy kingdom come. Thy will be done . . .'

From his gunnery director, the cramped platform which dominated virtually all of HMS *Tartar* and which he called his 'draughty nest', Repard scanned the horizon with his binoculars as dusk sucked the light out of the sea off the coast of Libya. He sat on a small metal seat, which reminded him of those on tractors back home, one of three men on a cramped platform with a diameter of only eight feet and ringed by thick steel. He wore his lifejacket over a blue shirt, a waistcoat from Gieves & Hawkes and an old uniform jacket. Two sweaters round his shoulders acted as a cushion for his back. He knew his outfit was odd, but he wanted to be comfortable, and safe.

Slowly detaching itself from the horizon came an extraordinary sight which lifted Repard's spirits. An enormous convoy of ships, large and small, was steaming towards him from the east, the sky over them speckled silver with barrage balloons. As *Tartar* rushed over at 25 knots to the new charges it would escort from now on, he could make out destroyers and minesweepers, trawlers and tankers, cargo-vessels and converted cross-channel ferries. Everyone on deck stared at the great troop-ships in the convoy, pointing out to each other the most famous, and arguing violently about the rest. Those who had a copy of *Jane's Merchant Ships* leafed through it to settle arguments.

The oldest of the liners, with their high, nearly vertical, smoking funnels, reminded Repard of the posters advertising exotic cruises which he had seen at railway stations back home, and made him think of his mother seeing him off when he left for boarding school, he not knowing quite where to look when the time came to say goodbye. Together with the rest of the battle-fleet, *Tartar* formed up around the convoy. The destroyer quickly took up its appointed station on the bows of the convoy, and turned to head towards the setting sun, and Sicily.

Since *Tartar* had sailed from Malta just before dawn, Repard's mood had kept swinging from elation to depression and back again. One moment he was eagerly looking forward to the landings ahead, and the next he was worrying about just how close they would have to get to the Sicilian coast and the enemy guns which would be awaiting them. *Tartar*'s mission was to lead the troop-ships to a point south of Syracuse where the soldiers would embark in the landing craft.

The three days' rest he had enjoyed at the Maltese hospital were long forgotten and Repard had gone back to living in fear. Over the past weeks he had heard more reports of fellow-destroyers of *Tartar*'s Tribal class being sunk by the Germans, especially in the Mediterranean. The casualties included several men he knew from his Navy training days. Repard found out that of the eighteen Tribal-class destroyers with which the Navy had entered the war, only four had so far survived. He was careful to show none of his fear when, in Malta before sailing, he briefed his gunnery crew. He was much younger than they were, but as an officer it was up to him to put them in the picture.

A short distance from Malta, *Tartar* had met up with its battle-fleet for the Sicily landings which included HMS *Rodney*, part of the force that sank the battleship *Bismarck* in the Atlantic two years earlier, and the flagship HMS *Nelson*. It was the first time a battle-fleet had managed to reach Malta for more than a year, and he felt a sentimental lump in his throat at the sight of the 'old boots', as he called the warships ploughing along under a grey sky.

In all, sailing through the Mediterranean towards Sicily at that time was a huge force – 2,500 ships and landing craft carrying a total of eight divisions, with 250,000 British and 228,000 American troops, 400 tanks, 14,000 vehicles, and 1,800 guns. The assault on Sicily would be the biggest amphibious invasion the world had yet seen.

As the Squadron Leader outlined the plan for the invasion of Sicily in the airfield's briefing room at Takali, Malta, on the morning of 9 July, Flying Officer Tony Snell exchanged glances with his fellow-pilots. This was why he had joined the Royal Air Force: to get up there and do something. He had known for some days that something was up – he could tell from the ships which filled the harbours and creeks of Malta – and it would have been terrible to be left out.

Tall and dashing, Snell wore a handlebar moustache that he had grown to make himself look older than his twenty-one years. He had always been in a hurry to get involved. The very first day that war was declared, Snell was still attending Cheltenham College, one of the best public schools. He and his father, a solicitor who served as a captain in the First World War, reported to the police station in Tunbridge Wells to join the Local Defence Volunteers. Snell, equipped with a 2.2 pistol and a pitchfork, spent many happy nights with his father in the bell-tower of the local church, watching for invaders.

The invaders never came, but Snell found another way of contributing to the war effort A guitar-player, he joined a band which gave concerts for soldiers, and organised several get-togethers to raise money for the Spitfire Fund – the RAF said it cost £5,000 to make a Spitfire, and many people were keen to make a contribution. The band's signature tune was 'We'll meet again', and Snell would join in: 'We'll meet again, don't know where, don't know when, / But I know we'll meet again, some sunny day. / Keep smiling through, just like you always do, / 'Til the blue skies drive the dark clouds far away.'

After he turned eighteen, Snell joined the RAF – he thought he'd be allowed to do his own thing in the Air Force, not like the Army where some vicious sergeant-major would order him around. With other young cadets, he sailed to America where he was taught to fly by US Air Force instructors. But he was so airsick that he forced himself to spend hours on a roller-coaster at a fairground near the base in Albany, Georgia, loathing every trip but determined to get his stomach together. The hours of torture didn't stop him throwing up at any aerobatics during training, but apart from that he suffered much less than before.

He found much of the discipline in the American Air Force pretty ridiculous – he was expected to salute his superiors even if he was in a swimming-pool and an officer chanced to walk by. He used up all his leave hitch-hiking, and once got as far as the Mexican border after travelling 1,400 miles in three days.

Back home, Snell felt very much the new boy when he joined 242 Squadron in North Weald, Essex. The Squadron struck him as very formal at times – he soon learnt to pass the port down the left during formal dinners. On missions over France, Gibraltar, north Africa and, in the last month, Sicily where he often used Mount Etna at 11,000 feet and its wisp of white smoke as a convenient bearing, he took a respectable toll of enemy trucks and tanks, including a few Tiger tanks which he was particularly satisfied with.

Snell also flew many missions escorting American bomber boys, whom he felt sorry for because they had a much worse time than he did, spending all those ghastly hours in the air from African bases to Sicily and back. When the flak started, the Spitfires could dart about but the bombers ploughed on steadily in tight formation. And a lot of them didn't come back.

But he was more and more frustrated with his failure to bag a 'confirmed kill' on an enemy aircraft, especially as several other pilots could boast as many as a dozen such kills. The last few days in particular had been too quiet for his liking, as the enemy hadn't put in much of an appearance. He prayed that the invasion would bring him face-to-face at last with his first chance for a really good show – a nice sitting duck, he hoped, a German bomber flying straight and steady.

That morning, Messina picked his way through piles of rubble in the deserted streets of the town of Mazzarino. The false alarm imposed on his Livorno Division had been lifted the previous evening after twenty-four hours, but this morning's gymnastics had been halted by bombers. Such raids had become frequent over the past few weeks, and neither Messina nor his companions gave the latest one any significance. It simply meant he had work to do, as the raid had spared the camp but struck Mazzarino less than a mile away, and he volunteered to follow a company of sappers armed with shovels, pickaxes and stretchers.

Messina noticed a house with parts of its front wall smashed by a bomb. He walked into the house, pushed open a door, and stared, aghast. Lying on a bed was the body of a beautiful, dark-haired girl who looked to be about eighteen years old. She was naked, her skin pale, with an ugly gash under her chest. She had apparently been killed by a piece of shrapnel which had entered through the nearby window.

The girl must have been sleeping naked because of the heat. Messina hurriedly drew a sheet over her, careful not to touch her. She was the first corpse he had seen, and the one thing he could still do for her was protect her decency. Then he ordered some of his men to take care of the body, and continued his search for survivors.

As dusk fell that day, the eve of the invasion, Repard took out the notebook and pencil he had brought on board his destroyer, and started to write. 'Operation Husky, or the Assault on Sicily,' he wrote on top of the first page, the notebook resting on his thigh as he sat at action stations in the gunnery director. Then, underneath, he began: 'For 2 days we've been at sea . . .' Repard hoped that putting his thoughts down on paper would help steady his nerves. He planned to confide only to his diary the fears that plagued him. He would never have dreamt of mentioning them to his fellow-officers, or to his family back home.

Over the past day, his convoy had frequently met so many other ship formations that he knew the sea was for thirty miles a seething mass of floating steel, and would be all night. At one stage, *Tartar* had overtaken ships carrying troops and tanks, steaming five deep in a plunging carpet that stretched from one horizon to the other.

Despite the Spitfires and Bristol Beaufighters which occasionally circled overhead, Repard couldn't stop himself feeling that with so much to tempt the enemy, he was sitting on top of a dirty great target which could be hit at any moment. Questions raced through his mind. Is our attack still a surprise? Where is the enemy? Will the landing craft make it to the beaches? Repard did his best to keep his mind focused on the job at hand, but right now this involved little more than keeping his eyes peeled. Nothing was happening, and the inactivity and the wait were sapping his morale.

That afternoon, the Mediterranean had changed colour from a lovely blue to a very dirty grey. The gale which no one had predicted had increased to Force 7, with gusts of up to 40 mph, and the waves grown higher, so much so that Repard felt seasick and worried how much worse things would become. Siroccos of this kind usually lasted at least forty-eight hours, and he couldn't imagine airborne troops being dropped in such weather. In the convoy, he glimpsed a boat loaded with soldiers which plunged so heavily into the water it looked like a submarine alternately submerging and surfacing. The gale may have one advantage, he thought wryly – it might make the soldiers keener to storm ashore.

Trapped in the stuffy hold of the USS *Samuel Chase*, Johnson was heavily ill. From his bunk, he could tell easily that everyone else in the great 1st Infantry Division was sick too – no fresh air got through, so the place smelt disgusting. The ship's crew refused to unlock the doors of the holds. They said the sea was so rough that the waves would sweep overboard anyone out on deck. Off the beaches of Sicily, the surf would be so big that surely it would be impossible for the landing craft to force its way through.

'Thank God we didn't get that damned steak,' someone groaned.

Earlier, Johnson had complained when the mess-crew failed to serve up the lavish steak supper he was expecting. Now he was glad all he'd had to eat was a boloney sandwich. He tried to distract himself from thinking about his stomach and the stench. What if I'd stayed at home? he thought. What if I hadn't signed up when I was sixteen? They couldn't have put me in a draft for another two years. I was too young. What if I had joined another division? His mind went round and round, asking a series of 'What if's?' to which there was no answer. But he tried anyway, because he felt he just had to discover whether he could have done something to avoid being here now.

Although he was surrounded by soldiers, and his ship was flanked by several thousand other ships, Johnson felt alone. He had learnt on the battlefield that all a soldier cares about is what he can see and hear – it's a very small patch most of the time, but as far as he is concerned, all the rest is hearsay. Johnson knew that he was taking part in an invasion, and that somebody would try to stop him. His heart beat so damn loud that he worried someone else would hear it. He would have been so ashamed if they had. He was a sergeant, he was in charge, he couldn't let them see his fear.

But he wasn't a hero, he was just a plain GI. He was there because he had no choice. He figured they were all there for the same reason.

CHAPTER SEVEN

9 JULY: 2100–2400 HOURS

Lance-Corporal Werner Hahn joined in the early evening sing-song as his friend, tank commander Alfred Günther, strummed his guitar, playing 'Lili Marlene' and their favourite Italian tunes. A few yards away the company's seventeen Panzer Tigers lay buried under camouflage among the olive and eucalyptus trees, but the music and a few sips of the heady local Marsala wine made Hahn forget the tanks, and the war.

His Protestant mother, a painter, played the guitar but not as well as Günther. She had encouraged Hahn to learn to play the violin. A slight figure with a boyish, finely chiselled face, he had inherited her artistic sensibility – his best subjects at school were painting, drawing and music – and he became adept enough to take part in Hitler Youth concerts in his home city of Dresden, performing Mozart and Beethoven in a symphony orchestra. He enjoyed the Hitler Youth, apart from the boring political slogans like 'One Führer, One People, One Fatherland' which went in one ear and out the other. He liked its militaristic character, the discipline and the twice-monthly marches which he had done ever since he was fifteen, covering thirteen miles in four hours, a brick in his rucksack.

Inspired by the Hitler Youth, and by reading about commanders like Frederick the Great and Bismarck, Hahn decided he was going to be an Army officer. Perhaps he would become a hero. But his father, a pharmacist, vetoed the idea – 'In our family, you have to study,' he said, explaining that the Army didn't pay well. His father had himself served with the infantry as a lieutenant in the First World War, but never talked about it, and all Hahn knew was that he had fought near Verdun and earned the Iron Cross, First Class. His father's word was final – children were expected to obey at all times, and at mealtimes only his parents were allowed to talk – so Hahn gave up on the idea of an Army career. He decided instead to follow the family tradition and promised he would be a doctor.

The outbreak of war suddenly gave Hahn, then seventeen, a chance to cut his studies short, and join the Army. With his father's reluctant agreement, Hahn volunteered because this would automatically earn him his end-of-school diploma, without having to sit the examinations. He applied for the Panzer Regiment, convinced that only front-line combat would allow him to shine. He was impressed by the speed with which the tanks had powered through France and all the way to Dunkirk. Speed and daring, he believed, made the tank regiment superior to any other.

He was impressed by the aristocratic character of the regiment – because of its roots in the cavalry, it boasted many officers whose names began with the noble 'von'. He also took great pride in his black uniform, which stood out among the sea of grey in the street when he came home on leave – he was especially proud of the death's-head on his collar and on his cap. The infantry, Hahn believed, was for lesser mortals, and he disliked having to learn to march around the parade-ground, his leg and waist muscles aching from so much goose-stepping.

His company proved its worth in Russia. In December 1942, in Rzev to the west of Moscow, it became the most successful one in the entire German Army, destroying more than 200 enemy tanks. Russia, where Hahn served as the loader for the main gun of his tank, a Panzer III, was his first experience of combat. His worst fear was of being taken prisoner by the Red Army, because they tortured you or starved you to death. During the siege of Stalingrad, he had heard the loudspeakers of the Red Army taunting: 'Stalingrad, *massengrav*' (mass grave). One Panzer which failed to receive an order to pull back was found the next day, its crew slaughtered and their eyes gouged out.

Two months later, in February, 94,000 Axis troops surrendered at Stalingrad.

At one time, when Hahn's battalion was surrounded, he decided that the last bullet in his pistol would be for himself. But a German division managed to break through and free the battalion. Hahn's own company didn't take prisoners. The Russians, he heard, played dead when they lay in the foxholes they had dug for themselves, and as soon as a Panzer had passed by they jumped up and fired on it from behind. So the Panzers made a habit of rolling over the foxholes, crushing men inside. Hahn knew this was a horrible death for the men, but it was necessary.

Sicily, in contrast, was a country at peace. Apart from the odd Allied plane flying overhead, nothing had disturbed the three months he had spent there so far. Hahn found Sicily beautiful, but couldn't bear the heat. In Germany everything was green, but here the landscape was hot and dusty, and everything was either yellow or brown. The men seized any chance to shower and wash off their sweat. During one train journey across Sicily, they had spotted a water tank for locomotives, and had stripped naked to wash. All the windows of the nearby houses were soon full of locals, mostly women, staring at the Germans.

Thankfully the German Army adapted itself to the Sicilian heat. Training was restricted to early morning before the sun started beating down. But German standards were respected – when the training meant a run up a hill towards a cluster of grey-stone houses and red-tiled roofs huddled around a big church, the officer in charge would stop the men just outside the village and order them to adjust their ties before marching in.

Every afternoon, they had a three-hour siesta. In the evening they were free to chat, sing and get drunk on Marsala wine – but not too drunk. On one visit to a brothel with Hahn and some friends, Günther played his guitar and the girls danced for them while they knocked back wine, cracked jokes and roared with laughter. On Sundays, Hahn relaxed, cooling off in the sea, or visiting the ruins of ancient Greek and Roman temples.

He expected an invasion to take place soon – he reasoned quite simply that Sicily was the logical next step for the Allies after the loss of north Africa – but he was too young and self-confident to worry too much about it. Field Marshal Albert Kesselring, Commander-in-Chief South, had inspected Hahn's regiment two months earlier, and ordered it to be based near Caltagirone some twenty miles inland from Gela on the south coast. Kesselring placed many of his forces further west, to ensure they could get anywhere in Sicily pretty quickly.

'When they come, throw them straight back into the brook,' Kesselring had quipped.

Hahn's company was the best; its Tigers were the German Army's most feared weapon, and it would do just that.

The two Maltese sisters – one blonde, the other dark – were rather pretty, and fun to go out with, but dating them carried a price. At 242 Squadron, they were known as 'the Jinx sisters' because so many of the Spitfire pilots who spent an evening with them got shot down sooner or later. So far, the girls had given thirteen pilots what the men called only half-jokingly the kiss of death. That didn't stop Snell from asking the blonde sister out on the last evening before the invasion. He wasn't superstitious.

Besides, Snell was convinced he and his squadron had a lucky streak. He never thought he might get killed, although everyone knew some men might not come back. Even the loss of fellow-pilots had failed to dent his faith. In north Africa, Snell had stayed up late one night listening to a Canadian boy who wanted to tell him his life story. The next day, the boy couldn't get his wheels down, and he was told to bale out because it was feared that his plane would break up on the base's airstrip which had been laid with pierced steel planking. Snell and several other pilots searched for the boy but they couldn't find him or his parachute. Then they saw a greenish stain in a bog filled with water. They guessed the stain was the dye packet from the boy's

Mae West, and that his parachute must have failed to open. The boy had been twice unlucky, a senseless casualty.

That kind of loss was one of the reasons why, in the evenings, Snell was desperate to have as much fun as he could. That was the great thing about being a fighter-pilot, you were free to live it up after sunset. That meant alcohol, and women. In north Africa, Snell discovered that even dusty Algerian towns had bottles of champagne for sale. He had a brief fling with a French Tunisian girl who sang German songs for him – she'd learnt them from a previous, enemy boyfriend.

In Malta, after nearly three years of bombings as the Axis forces laid siege to the island, locals were so thirsty for revenge that whenever new RAF squadrons arrived, they would climb onto the wings while the planes were still taxiing and tell the pilots to go straight off and start shooting. The Maltese were also bursting with the desire to make up for the wasted years of hardship and death, and military personnel were fêted every-where. Snell went to as many parties and dances as he could. Nightly 'passion wagons' carried servicemen to bars, cafés, dance halls and cinemas in the island capital, Valletta, and to brothels in a neighbourhood known as 'The Gut'. One party however had proved a disappointment as servicemen were allowed just two beers each. Snell drank his allocation through a straw, in the hope that this would make the alcohol stronger. It didn't.

Snell, his handlebar moustache carefully groomed, took the blonde 'Jinx sister' to a café near the airfield, and they danced for most of the evening. In America, Snell had learnt some nifty moves for dancing to ragtime music, but there was no jukebox at the bar, and he did his best to adapt his steps to the fiddles and accordion of the Maltese band. During a break in the danc-ing, Jack Lowther, an Australian fellow-pilot, came up to Snell.

'You've had it now, Tony,' he said in his Australian drawl.

Snell answered with an obscene gesture. 'Boloney, old boy. I'm seeing her tomorrow night,' he said. Snell hadn't got any further than dancing with the blonde girl, but the main thing was that she had agreed to go out with him again.

In the fading red glow of the sunset, Repard caught sight of Sicily from his vantage-point, his platform high above the destroyer HMS *Tartar*. He could make out the outlines of a mountain range, black against the sky. The island didn't look at all welcoming.

The sun had barely set when the wind suddenly veered eight points to the north-west. It continued to blow with gale force, making the sea much too choppy for the assault craft which were supposed to bring the troops to the beaches. Depression took hold of Repard. It was all hopeless, he thought.

But a little more than an hour later the wind died away, the white horses vanished and the fleet was left tossing in a vacuum of heat. Darkness made the swell look larger than it was, but the half-moon gave it a fascinating glitter which seemed to deny its menace. Repard's spirits began to lift.

From the south he heard the sound of aircraft engines, and out of the moon roared dozens of tow aircraft, all pulling silent shadows across the starry sky, gliders of the British 1st Airborne Division bound for eastern Sicily. The transports switched on some lights as they passed overhead, but their exhaust flames already made them visible. As the planes approached the black mass of the Sicilian coast, random red lines of tracers flecked the darkness, and shells sparkled overhead. The beams of four searchlights swept wildly across the sky, chasing the clusters of aircraft flares but, as far as Repard could tell, they failed to find the planes.

A few minutes later, the ship's radio broadcast a terse message: 'Landing craft reported glider dropped short of coast, sunk.' Later, Repard found out that many other gliders had suffered the same fate – instead of landing behind the enemy defences, they had hit the stretch of water between the defences and the landing craft. This was bad news not only for the poor devils ditched in the sea, he thought, but also for the troops closing in on Sicily. They would have to land without anyone paving the way for them.

The men of the Durham Light Infantry on the troop-ship *Winchester Castle* cheered when they saw the outlines of British tugs and gliders sweeping towards Sicily in the moonlight, just beneath the clouds.

'Good, someone else is going in ahead of us. We won't be alone,' Lieutenant Fenner thought.

Earlier, against the setting sun, he had seen the summit of Mount Etna, lit up by the ever-active contents of its crater, glowing through a break in a bank of low cloud, as if detached from the earth. Low on the horizon was Sicily. Europe lay within reach.

Fenner went down to have supper in the first-class lounge, where he found some twenty battalion officers already sitting around a long table. He was struck by how gentlemanly it all was – the bright lights, the stewards in white jackets, the white tablecloth, and the fine china embossed with the liner's crest. The food was good and plentiful – so different from desert rations, and what's more it didn't have any sand in it. If he had to go to war, this was the way to do so. The only drawback was that, on General Eisenhower's orders, the ship was 'dry'. Fenner didn't feel like drinking much, but he would have welcomed a beer.

'Oh, this is the Last Supper,' someone said. The quip got only a couple of laughs.

Hardly anyone spoke, and everybody looked grim. Fenner looked around the table at the faces of the men. Some of them would be lucky, and some wouldn't. He thought this was the last time they would all be together, because once he got into his assault craft he would have no news from them for days until he would bump into another company and someone would say: 'Have you heard? So-and-so's got the chop.' He pushed the thought to the back of his mind. He needed to

think about the task ahead – he must not make a cock-up, or
let down his men.

Some fifty miles to the west, from the deck of his troop-ship,
Johnson watched in horror as Allied ships fired on Allied planes.
Moments after the first of the aircraft carrying paratroopers
approached the coast of Sicily, flying at just a couple of hundred
feet, engines roaring like hell, someone on one of the ships had
opened fire. Within seconds red tracer bullets were slicing
upwards through the darkness. The firing spread with the speed
and deadliness of a virus, and enemy anti-aircraft batteries also
opened up from the coast.

A patch of flames lit up the night sky as the shells hit a target.
Then the flames hurtled downwards, to be briefly reflected on
the surface of the sea before the plane vanished underwater.
Johnson had seen planes shot down before, but he figured an
Allied ship had shot the plane down, and it was the first time
he'd ever seen that happen. He looked out for men who had
managed to save themselves by jumping out with their para-
chutes, but didn't see any.

'They ought to shoot the son-of-a-bitch who started it,'
Johnson said to nobody in particular. He had never been known
to keep his mouth shut, especially when speaking his mind could
get him into trouble. 'There goes the surprise – the enemy will
be ready and waiting,' he said.

Also waiting for the invaders, some ten miles to the south-east
of Johnson, was HMS *Seraph*, the submarine at the heart of
Operation Mincemeat. It had been ordered to act as a beacon
to guide the American 45th Division to the coast. Lieutenant
Jewell, *Seraph*'s commanding officer, had sat through a briefing
from Patton a few days earlier, and had been unfavourably
impressed by the General's arrogance, and the fact that he spent
very little time outlining what he expected of the British officers
– Patton clearly didn't think much of his ally.

As the fleet approached, Jewell was so stunned by its size that he later wrote: 'The English language needs a new descriptive noun to replace the hackneyed word *armada*.'

Both British and American airborne troops flew into Sicily ahead of their seaborne comrades in a two-pronged attack. First off from Tunisia, at dusk, were the gliders carrying 2,075 Red Devils of the 1st Airlanding Brigade. The mission of the British, who had earned their nickname from the Germans because of their valour and red berets, was to seize the Ponte Grande bridge near Syracuse, which had to be taken in order to allow the Eighth Army to push up the east coast with its guns and tanks.

But lack of training in night navigation and in judging distance across the water off the coastline, combined with winds that were still blowing strongly when the aircraft approached Sicily, had disastrous results. Living up to the 'flying coffins' label given them by soldiers, gliders released from their tugs much too soon dived into the sea, where the men drowned without even reaching the island. The men who managed to hack their way out of their aircraft and cling to the wreckage in the water were often fired on by coastal batteries. Of 147 gliders, sixty-nine crashed into the sea where 252 men drowned. Those that landed in Sicily very often crashed into orchards, boulders, or stone walls. Only twelve landed near enough to the target to be of any use, but a force of seventy-three Red Devils did however manage to take Ponte Grande bridge.

Little went to plan for the American airborne assault either. Leaving north Africa two hours after their British counterparts, 3,045 paratroopers of the 82nd American Airborne Division were under orders to form a buffer-zone to the north-east of the port of Gela where the 1st Infantry Division and other American units would land. The paratroopers' key mission was to seize the Piano Lupo strongpoint controlling access to Gela.

As with the British, inexperience and strong winds threw the aircraft off-course, and the men dropped down to earth up to sixty-five miles away from their targets. Eight aircraft were shot down – luckily after their men had jumped. The only battalion which reached Sicily intact found itself twenty-five miles away from its planned landing zone. Many men hid wherever they could; others wandered in small groups across the countryside, searching both for their units and for the enemy. Their commander, Colonel James Gavin, had been expecting to meet Italian troops only, and was shocked to see a destroyed German scout car – his superiors, afraid that a security leak might reveal that the Allies had cracked the cipher on the German Enigma machine, had deliberately withheld the knowledge that the Hermann Goering Division was in the area.

In Malta late that night, Admiral Cunningham, without bothering to change out of his uniform, tried to grab some sleep before H-Hour. He summed up the frustration of the Allied commanders at that moment, writing: 'The die was cast. We were committed to the assault. There was nothing more we could do for the time being.'

CHAPTER EIGHT

10 JULY: 0000-0300 HOURS

Although it was just after midnight, the stateroom on board USS *Monrovia* was packed. The flagship had left Algiers two days previously just after General Patton was piped aboard. At first – before the storm hit – Rosevich had enjoyed the opportunity to relax. He had brought his typewriter with him, but Patton had little need for his secretary because in the hours before the invasion, the Navy was in charge.

There wasn't much to do for either Patton or Rosevich apart from read. Rosevich knew what Patton had been reading, because of the General's diary entry a few days earlier: 'Last night I sat up till 0100 reading a detective story, hundreds of pages about the death of one fool. I am sending possibly thousands to death and glory and don't or won't think about it. The human mind is very queer – only God could have devised such a complex machine.'

A few moments before Patton's staff and the Navy's top brass assembled in the stateroom, the radar of *Monrovia* had latched onto the Sicilian coast. Rosevich could feel the tension in the air as, the invasion just under three hours away, Patton prepared to lead a ceremony that would mark the formal creation of the first fully-fledged American Army in Fortress Europe.

No one spoke as the First Armoured Corps flag was taken down from its stand and the Seventh Army standard put in its place. Then, standing to attention, his pale blue eyes flashing with pride, Patton spoke briefly: 'Gentlemen, it's now one minute past midnight 9–10 July 1943, and I have the honour and the privilege to activate the Seventh United States Army. This is the first army in history to be activated after midnight and baptised in blood before daylight.'

Rosevich was shocked to see that Patton had tears in his eyes. The only other time Rosevich had seen his boss so moved was four months earlier, after the funeral of his aide, Captain Dick Jenson, who had died in the bombing of a forward command post. In the diary entry he dictated to Rosevich at the time, Patton had described how, at the funeral, he had got on his knees to say a prayer in front of Jenson's body which was wrapped in a white mattress cover – there was no wood for a coffin. Patton had said that he couldn't see any reason why such fine young men should get killed.

As he returned to his cabin, Rosevich heard the voice of Admiral Cunningham on the ship's loudspeakers. 'We are about to embark on the most momentous enterprise of the war,' the Admiral said in a recorded message, 'striking for the first time at the enemy in his own land.'

'Move to your waiting area. Take up position by your assault craft,' a voice on the *Winchester Castle*'s speakers said shortly after midnight.

Fenner, who had been trying to read George Bernard Shaw's *Major Barbara* as the ship tossed, rolled and squeaked, left his cabin and made his way through the ship, which was in virtually complete darkness. Pinpoint lights guided him along to the boat deck. The only sounds were those of boots on the deck, and high above him, the wind whistling in the rigging.

He had got into his battledress straight after dinner. The chaplains had given communion that evening, and later the medical officer came round handing out condoms. The men burst into laughter. 'What are these for? Are we going to an orgy?' one of them asked. Fenner thought for a moment, then dropped his watch into his condom, to keep it dry.

When the order to embark came, the steel assault craft, which hung virtually level with the boat deck, was swinging heavily – something all the rehearsals over the past few weeks had failed to prepare the men for. Several in his platoon swore as they lost their balance, or as bits and pieces of their heavy equipment got caught on the sides of the ship. The men who swore loudest were the ones carrying the PIAT, a bloody awful anti-tank gun which no one liked because the first one they ever fired had killed a chap in the company.

Fenner got into the small assault craft, and made his way to the front. He sat on a bench which ran along the boat's side, under a steel ledge which stuck out horizontally over him. All he could see was a small patch of overcast, moonless sky. With him was his platoon of twenty-five men, plus three sappers carrying anti-tank mines in sandbags, which they needed to blow gaps in barbed-wire fences.

As Fenner's craft hung far above the sea for almost an hour as if suspended from some giant barrage balloon, he hoped he would have time if the boat was hit. Time to get rid of his equipment, and hopefully his boots too, if they hit the water. The pack on his back and all the other things he carried – Bren gun magazines, hand-grenades, World War One entrenching tool, groundsheet, gas mask, rations for two days and for emergencies, plus full water-bottle and everything else – were more than enough to sink a man.

Shortly after 0100, the engines of the *Winchester Castle* stopped. The first assault crafts were lowered into the heaving sea and the hooks that held them to the liner's davits unshackled. Fenner's craft began pitching and rolling like a little cockle-shell as soon as it touched the water. Breakers washed over the craft and in no time he and his men were soaked to the skin, dripping from head to foot. The swell, Fenner thought, was heavy enough to get the assault craft stranded on a sandbank long before they got to the designated beach.

The Royal Navy coxswain came up to him. 'Sir, my compass light is not working,' the coxswain said.

'Now you bloody tell me,' Fenner said.

He found a torch, and told the coxswain to use that instead, and to stick with the rest of the battalion's assault crafts. There was no point in going back now, they would manage quite well with the torch.

As Johnson's assault craft neared Red Two beach, east of Gela, he felt as if he was packed tight in the middle of a herd of cattle in his native Georgia. The boat was so cramped that again he worried furiously that someone would hear his heartbeat and unmask him as unfit to lead his men into combat. It was still dark. It wasn't the best of times to talk, so no one did. Squatting in the front part of the craft, Johnson concentrated on keeping his Thompson submachine-gun dry. He preferred it to the standard issue M1 Garand semi-automatic because he liked to shoot and the tommy gun could spit out 800 rounds a minute.

Johnson could handle war. He wasn't in the same state of terror as he'd been during his baptism of fire on the north African coast, when he kept asking himself what he'd done to upset the guy shooting at him. Johnson had got madder and madder about it until he'd started shooting back, which made him feel better. That was the best way of overcoming fear: start shooting, knock them down. But right now there was no one for him to shoot at. This was the worst time, when all he could do was wait for the coastal batteries to open up, or for his landing craft to reach the beach – whichever came first. Johnson wondered how close it would get to dry land. When he'd invaded north Africa, the boat had hit a sandbar and he'd had to wade in for what felt like miles.

He heard machine-gun fire. Some of it sounded pretty close. He prayed silently. He wasn't superstitious – he was the only GI he knew who accepted Army supplies with the number 13 on them – and he wasn't a religious type, but he figured that although praying might not do him any good, it surely didn't do him any harm. The rush of adrenalin made him feel thirsty, so he drank from his water-bottle.

The ramp dropped. Someone shouted: 'Come on, let's go!' Johnson jumped out and ran for the beach, the water reaching only up to his knees. His men following, he made straight for a pillbox.

The position was empty. The Italians had apparently run down a belt of ammo and then fled, leaving the gun sitting there. They'd also left hand-grenades lying all over the place. The hand-grenades, shaped like small tins, looked cute. But what really got the men talking was an empty bottle of American Schenley whiskey standing in a corner. 'Well I'll be damned. Here they are drinking our whiskey, and we can't get any,' Johnson said.

He understood why the Italians had fled. They didn't want to fight for that bastard Mussolini, so the best thing was to give them a chance to surrender. 'Don't just run in kicking arse,' Johnson told his men, 'give them a chance to give up and they will.' Taking a prisoner was always better than killing.

Some time later, Johnson lay under what he guessed was a peach tree. This invasion's easy, he told himself. The rush of adrenalin during the landing had left his throat parched, and he'd already drunk all his water. That was one of the problems with war: no matter how much water you carried, it was never enough to beat the thirst which adrenalin caused. He missed the milk he used to drink back home. The tree had little green peaches on it, a bit bigger than cherries. Johnson figured that chewing on one would give him a little saliva, so he reached up, grabbed one, and bit hard. It tasted so bitter, it was the worst thing he had ever put in his mouth. He'd bitten into an almond.

The sound of a motorcycle engine at about 0100 startled Messina out of his doze as he sat in a tent at the entrance to the Livorno Division's camp, where he was on twenty-four-hour sentry duty.

During the night, enemy planes had passed repeatedly over-head, and were fired at by Italian anti-aircraft guns. Expecting another bombing raid, most of the soldiers in the camp had abandoned their tents to spend the night in trenches. Several officers billeted in the nearby town had abandoned it, and also sought refuge in the trenches.

A dispatch rider, wearing a helmet and goggles, strode into the tent. He told Messina he had come from Army Headquarters in Enna, handed Messina an envelope, and left. Messina opened the envelope. The single sheet of paper inside, styled in typical military bureaucratese, was just two sentences long: 'This Battalion to place itself immediately on alert for possible util-isation. Further instructions will follow.'

Yet another pointless drill, Messina thought.

The land was an ill-defined blur, blacker than the sea, and quite unlike the photographs of the stretch of coast south of Syracuse which Repard had been shown at pre-invasion briefings. The moon had set and the night was darker and colder than ever. Away to the north, a great cluster of some fifty flares, looking like huge Chinese lanterns, hung over Syracuse as bombers attacked the ancient Phoenician port. From time to time whirling clouds of red tracer rushed up at the flares.

Repard couldn't recognise any landmarks and there was no sign of the midget submarines which he'd been told would guide ships to their designated beaches, their blue lights shining seawards. *Tartar* was supposed to be leading its own column of ships to beaches south of Syracuse, but judging by the exchanges which he could hear on his headphones, the destroyer was lost.

Tartar stopped and waited as, despite the confusion, the other ships lowered their assault crafts. As one came up astern, the destroyer switched on its shaded stern light and steamed ahead, bound for the coast. Repard put on his tin hat and scanned the coast with his binoculars, his frustration mounting. As the assault craft's engine hummed in the blackness, he thought nerv-ously of the next few hours. What would be the cost of an opposed landing? he wondered. Are we 'expendable'? Will some-one make a mistake? He hated it when there was so damn little for him to do. Every so often, he lowered his binoculars to look into the night sky, wondering if an enemy aircraft would appear.

On a beach four miles to the south, a searchlight switched on.

It swept towards *Tartar*, and lit up the destroyer. It seemed to pause, moved on and then returned as if to confirm its suspicions. Another searchlight came on, and lit up a beach. Before Repard had a chance to open fire both turned off, and the coast was again just a black blur.

Ten miles to the south, Fenner's assault craft pitched and rolled so much that the men soon threw away the small, cup-shaped cardboard containers they had been provided with and simply vomited into the foot or so of water swilling about at the bottom of the boat.

Everyone was soon soaked to the skin by the spray that splashed over the bow every time the boat plunged through the crest of a wave before crashing with a loud thud in the trough. The unlucky ones in the platoon had to sit on the floor of the flat-bottomed boat, the vomit swilling around their bottoms and their feet. Quite a lot of 'last suppers' coming back, Fenner thought as he managed not to be sick. But he couldn't avoid breathing in the air which smelt of vomit, engine fuel and fear.

The original plan had been for assault crafts lowered from both sides of the *Winchester Castle* to go round the cruise-liner three times, rather like a brood of chicks round a hen, before setting off together on what should have been a seven-mile trip to the coast. But the coast was some twelve miles away, and the rough seas made it impossible for them to stick together. It was so dark when Fenner stood up to look that he couldn't even see the coast. But he guessed they were heading towards Syracuse, which was under heavy air attack and too far north.

As he was trying to work out the best course, another assault craft loomed out of the darkness.

'Who are you?' Fenner shouted.

'King's Own Yorkshire Light Infantry,' came the reply.

'We're Durham Light Infantry,' Fenner called back.

A brief discussion established that the other craft was in the wrong place. Fenner managed to get his coxswain heading in the right direction, but moments later the craft gave a sharp jolt. They had rammed another craft. Fenner cursed the coxswain under his breath. How would they ever find the right beach with a coxswain whose compass had failed, and who couldn't even avoid ramming another craft?

The chaotic journey unnerved Fenner. He remembered the small bottle of Egyptian-made rum he carried in his web pouch and offered it around. Eisenhower or no Eisenhower, the craft was not a dry ship, but Fenner found few takers. Only the oldest veterans wanted some. He took a swig and found it eased his misery a little.

CHAPTER NINE

10 JULY: 0300–0600 HOURS

Snell strapped himself into the cockpit of the unfamiliar aircraft shortly after 0300 and sat there worrying as he waited for the engine to warm up. He'd managed to grab only a few hours sleep after his evening with the 'Jinx sister', and ahead of him lay his first night combat mission in a Spitfire. To make things worse, he wasn't going to fly his usual aircraft, a Spitfire Mark V model, but a brand-new Mark IX which needed to be tested. This was tricky because the new plane had a much bigger engine, the propeller went round the other way, and you had to allow for that on take-off. Snell would worry about landing later.

The orders at the pre-flight briefing had been short and to the point. The pilots were to prevent Allied troops being attacked by enemy aircraft. But over the sea they should fly no lower than 8,000 feet, because below that height they would be at risk from 'friendly' fire from the Allied fleet.

From his cockpit – it was virtually identical to the one he was used to, and it too felt cramped because of his lanky frame and long legs – he saw the navigation light on the wingtip of the Spitfire next to his as the pair prepared to take off. No one said anything on the R/T. Radio silence should be broken only when strictly necessary – not like the American blabbermouths, who over enemy territory would shout at each other things like: 'Hey, look at that big rock down there, looks like a cathedral.'

As Snell and his partner raced down the airfield at full throttle, he did his best to steer as straight a course as he could. As with all Spitfires, it was impossible to see straight ahead over the nose on take-off, which meant Snell had to look through the Perspex on the side of the canopy as he powered on with the navigation light on the other Spitfire his only guide. He used the left rudder to counter the pull of the propeller, and found the controls stiffer than on his usual plane. He was concentrating so hard on the controls, and it was so dark out there, that he lost his partner. He still managed to take off safely and for a brief moment felt relieved and quite lucky to have got off the ground without hitting anything.

Snell managed to rejoin his section and, as he flew over the seventy-mile stretch of sea which separated Malta from Sicily, he tried to relax a little but without success. The exhaust flames which the engine spat out obscured much of his forward vision. At least the sun wasn't beating down on the Perspex canopy above his head, he told himself. That almost always gave him a headache on long missions. And most satisfying of all, he could feel the extra power which the bigger engine gave him. He knew it was a match in speed for the Focke-Wulf 190s, and hoped to meet a few before very long.

Far below, just off the faint white ring of surf which marked the Sicilian coast, he spotted what looked like thin smudges on the surface of the sea. The invasion fleet. Snell was glad not to be part of that. As he gazed, he saw that something was pumping tracer bullets towards one of the smudges. Some enemy plane must be attacking a ship. Suddenly, the ship under attack started firing back. Snell still couldn't see the plane, but he was certain it was down there. It must have flown over the ship. Perhaps it had dropped some bombs and would repeat the manoeuvre.

The pre-flight briefing – *Fly no lower than 8,000 feet* – ran through his mind as he threw his Spitfire into a steep dive. He knew he was doing the wrong thing but he wanted to get the bugger down there. What mattered was scoring his first kill. For Snell, the sky was like a giant rugger field, the backdrop to a sporting competition between his team and the enemy. He knew what he had to do and was going to do it as best he damn well could. Even if his idea of what he had to do meant disobeying orders.

He was down to some 2,000 feet when all hell came up at

him. He could see the flak curling up towards him in long continuous streams. At the last moment it curved past the canopy without touching it, like the ribbon of a Morris dancer. He leapt upwards, thankful for the extra 250 horse-power on the new Spitfire. 'Serve me right for not obeying the rules,' he thought. But his luck had held.

Less than an hour before dawn, Messina stood by his truck, waiting for the order to start moving. Soon after receiving the order to sound the alarm, he had managed to alert all the company commanders of the Livorno Division with the help of a trumpeter and some soldiers he drafted in as messengers. Now all the companies were ready but, as so often in the military, for the time being the men had nothing to do.

Confident that he would soon be returning to the camp, he had left all his personal belongings behind – his camera, photographs of girlfriends, letters from his family, books. All he had with him, apart from his equipment, were small images of Saint Antonio and the Madonna of Pompeii, which his mother had given him as good luck charms.

The company medic joined him and held out an open pack of cigarettes. Messina took one, and both men lit up.

'So, another exercise, hey?' Messina said.

'What do you mean, exercise? They've landed,' the medic replied.

Messina felt as if a hand of cold steel had suddenly grabbed at his intestines and crushed them. The medic must have seen the panic on Messina's face, because he reached out and patted him quietly on the shoulder.

From the shore at 0410, a powerful beam of light flicked on, probing the sky. On his platform aboard *Tartar*'s bridge, Repard hurried to prepare his men and work out a range for the enemy searchlight. The enemy must have been alerted by the noise of aircraft, because the beam of light continued to swing across the sky. At any time it could descend and begin to sweep over the sea.

Repard was virtually ready to fire when he realised that several landing craft, their shapes silhouetted against the searchlight's beam, were in his path of fire. To take it out, he would have to fire just over the heads of the Allied troops. His guns were capable of firing as many as eight miles into the air, but the coast was at such a close range that his shells would hurtle along horizontally, only a few feet above the water.

Repard agonized over his dilemma. Should he give the order to fire, which risked not only killing Allied troops but would also alert the enemy – assuming they did not know already – that the landings were about to begin? A month earlier during the bombing of the island of Pantelleria, the gateway to Sicily, *Tartar* had steamed close to shore. He had been able to see at first hand the destructive effect of his guns. One house, hit by a single shell, had raised its roof politely and then fallen apart. The sight had given Repard a tremendous feeling of power.

Should he play safe this time and hold fire? But if he did, the searchlight might soon light up the landing craft and the rest of the Naval force. That was sure to draw enemy fire. Repard picked up the telephone which linked him to the operators in the transmission station below decks. It was their job to relay his orders to *Tartar*'s four turrets.

'Follow director,' he said, instructing his men to train the guns according to the aiming device that he operated on his platform, high above the bridge.

As he waited for the range-finder to make his calculations, he kept his binoculars trained on the landing craft, careful not to get too close to the searchlight. Its beam was bright enough to rob him of his night vision. The measurement came swiftly. Still Repard did not give the order to fire as he furiously debated whether he should become the first on his patch to open fire on Sicily. He was itching to have a go – he was fighting the Axis and was determined that if anyone looked like trying to kill him, he would get them first.

The enemy solved the problem for him: the beam of light

dived down from the sky and began to sweep across the sea, picking up one of the landing crafts. Within seconds, tracer bullets spat from a machine-gun on the shore. The poor devils were going to get hit even before they reached the beach.

Repard heard Captain St John Tyrwhitt's voice on his headphones. 'Sub, do you think you can take out that searchlight?' the Captain asked, his voice as calm as ever.

'I'll have a go, sir,' Repard answered.

Repard got back onto the transmission station. 'Load, load, load,' he ordered.

He pictured the crews at all four turrets lifting the heavy shells, and pushing them up into the breeches of the two guns in each turret with their clenched fists. The men were pretty competitive about how fast they could load the guns. Many of them regularly dipped their knuckles in methylated spirits to make them as hard as possible and be faster than the next chap.

Moments later, as soon as Repard received word from the transmission station that the guns were ready, he gave the final, one-word order: 'Shoot.'

Tartar jerked as the eight-gun broadside, its roar muffled by Repard's headphones, spat great orange flashes which briefly lit up the entire destroyer, turning the waters the colours of fire.

The searchlight went out, plunging the sea back into darkness. Repard's sense of relief at his stroke of luck was quickly crushed by the realisation that this was only the beginning. The alarm had been given now and along the whole coastline green Very signal lights showed the extent of the assault.

Shortly after 0400, Fenner saw tracer bullets coming for assault crafts to his right which were closer to the shore than his own. He was more than an hour behind schedule – he could tell from the watch he had stuck into his condom – and he was certain that he was in the wrong place, as he couldn't recognise any of the coast's features. Now the assault had to be made as the day was dawning, and not under cover of darkness, as planned.

In the early morning light he could see enemy guns at either end of the beach he was heading for. And the enemy could of course see him. Explosions hit the water between his craft and the one nearest to him. He assumed they were mortar bombs, because he couldn't hear the whine of artillery shells. Machine-gun fire cracked past. A searchlight came on, but fire from one of the boats switched it off instantly.

Worried that they would end up trapped inside their craft, the men had all got onto their feet. They were quiet and alert, their seasickness forgotten although the boat still stank of vomit. Most of them obeyed the rule that they should have as many as possible of the buttons on their clothes undone and all their equipment ready to dump quickly if they were in danger of drowning.

Fenner stuffed his binoculars under his shirt; if the enemy saw those they would easily identify him as an officer. He was standing by the bow of the craft, ready to jump as soon as the ramp was lowered, when the coxswain approached him.

Now what? Fenner thought to himself.

'Sir, I've dropped the anchor too soon and it's parted. I can't beach,' the coxswain said.

Several of the men heard him. 'Oh, bloody hell,' they moaned.

Fenner felt like shooting the coxswain – what a clown this man was! 'Stop the engine when the other assault crafts to port and starboard stop theirs,' Fenner ordered.

Moments later the boat came to a stop, and the ramp went down. Fenner stuck his pistol, a .38-calibre Smith & Wesson, into the air and, shouting 'Come on, chaps!', he jumped into the water and into the continuous enemy fire.

The water was only knee-high, and as he splashed through the shallows towards the sandy beach which mercifully wasn't too far away the Mae West flopped up and down on his chest even though he'd tied the tapes carefully around his waist. He was barely aware of the machine-guns which kept firing from either end of the beach; all his mind would allow him to think about as he ran faster than he had ever run was the need to cover as quickly as possible the exposed stretch of beach between the water's edge and the great big strands of barbed wire ahead.

That barbed-wire fence shouldn't be there, he thought. It wasn't on the models he had studied on board the liner. He barely had time to start thinking about how to get through it when the sappers came up from behind him and, with no need for a word of command from him, hung the two anti-tank mines on the fence and pulled the igniters. As he rolled back down the beach to get far enough away from the coming explosion, he saw that practically his entire platoon were lying on the waterline. 'Good God, what's happened?' he wondered before realising that they weren't dead, they were simply and quite sensibly waiting for the mines to go off.

The enemy was still firing, not very accurately. Fenner came to a stop and saw lying near him the body of a corporal from his platoon. Fenner couldn't see his wound, but the corporal was lying face down in the sand, immobile. Fenner simply registered the fact that the man was dead, and immediately began to worry that the platoon must be on the wrong beach. The plan had been for two companies to land ahead of him, but there was no sign of them on this beach.

The mines blew a big clean gap in the barbed wire. Fenner got up and ran, straight through the gap, thinking only that he must get off the beach and seize the road leading to the town of Avola as he'd been ordered to do – providing he could find the damn road in the first place. He'd been running for what felt like five minutes or so, vaguely wondering if he was going through a minefield, when he came up against a steep bank across his path.

One of his soldiers caught up with him, panting: 'Slow down! We can't keep up with you!'

Everything had gone quiet. Fenner was puzzled. He climbed the embankment, which was about a dozen feet high, and found himself on a railway line. The trouble was, it shouldn't have been there. Fenner and his platoon had definitely landed on the wrong beach. As he waited for his men to catch up with him, he had a drink from his water-bottle, lit a cigarette, and pulled out his map. He soon worked out that he was some three to four miles south of where he was supposed to be.

He'd been told to stick to the plan if he was dropped in the wrong place. He had no idea where his commanding officer or company HQ were. There was nothing for it but to start marching towards the planned objective, even though he would approach it from the south and not from the north as expected. He hoped to reach it soon; the last thing he wanted after all this was a ticking-off from the commanding officer.

As the dawn glimmered, it silhouetted the landing craft to enemy gunners. Repard saw one coastal battery open up and then another until the tops of the cliffs, fields and woods were covered in bright gun flashes. The craft had to move nearly a mile along the coast to reach the beaches and during that journey they were only a few hundred yards away from the enemy guns.

The landing craft put up a fight with machine-guns, but when they reached the beach the fire from what have must have been a howitzer battery, somewhere on the other side of the escarpment running parallel to the coast, was very accurate. Repard saw two direct hits and one of the crafts caught fire. Each round, Repard thought, must have sent splinters through the tightly packed boats.

The sun came up behind Repard and every detail of the coast and hills stood out. He saw shells drop onto the beach itself, in the middle of a crowd of troops who were just moving off the sand. The explosion threw the men up into the air. It looked murderous and he couldn't do anything to help them; the enemy battery was well-hidden, and he couldn't work out where it was.

CHAPTER TEN
10 JULY: 0600-0930 HOURS

Few men in Italy dared to take responsibility for disturbing the sleep of Benito Mussolini – invasion or no invasion – and it wasn't until 0600 that an Army colonel called at the aristocratic Villa Torlonia, the Duce's private residence in Rome, and insisted he be woken up immediately.

Minutes later, the dictator burst into his wife's bedroom: 'Rachele, the Anglo-Americans have landed in Sicily.'

His wife, a light sleeper, was instantly wide awake.

'I'm convinced our men will resist, and besides the Germans are sending reinforcements. We must be confident,' Mussolini reassured her, before leaving as abruptly as he had come.

Less than half an hour later, Mussolini telephoned General Guzzoni, whom he had pulled out of retirement in late May at the age of sixty-six to become commander of the Army in Sicily, at its Enna Headquarters in the centre of the island. At the Interior Ministry in Rome, a stenographer prepared to transcribe the conversation. On the orders of Mussolini himself, a small army of stenographers constantly recorded not only Mussolini's telephone calls but also those of leading Fascists.

Apart from helping him monitor any dissent, and verify that his orders were carried out, the transcripts fed Mussolini's maniacal appetite for petty detail and spicy gossip. This was a dictator who decided on what day open-air concerts could begin on the Venice Lido, and which announcers should be selected for the radio. He had even decreed which side of the road Romans should walk on, and then kept looking out through his office window in the Palazzo Venezia to check that his rules were being followed. Asked once by a Fascist party official why he dealt with such trivia as the price of bread, Mussolini had replied: 'Napoleon stated that there were no such things as details.'

From the General, Mussolini learnt that the enemy was constantly bombing major roads to stop reinforcements reaching the coast. The General explained: 'We will do all that is humanly possible, but we have to take account of the fact that, while we are finding it more and more difficult to get reinforcements, the enemy is drawing more and more strength.'

'Do all you can to throw them back into the sea or, at least, nail them to the shore!' Mussolini exclaimed.

'We will do our duty to the last!' the General replied.

Later that morning Mussolini set off to inspect the M Division at Lake Bracciano, north of Rome, as scheduled. He admired the performance under fire of the elite unit which Himmler had given him as a personal present. Trained by the SS, the unit was equipped with thirty-six Tiger tanks. Changing his schedule for the day, Mussolini believed, would be interpreted as a sign of weakness.

Fifty-nine years old, and worn down by a stomach complaint made worse by a string of defeats and humiliations, Mussolini was a shadow of the charismatic leader who had been an inspiration for millions when in 1922 he bulldozed his way to power with the Fascist movement's March on Rome, at the head of his squads of blackshirt thugs who claimed the lives of up to 2,000 victims.

The violence spawned a reign of terror based on a personality cult which had now endured for two decades. The new Fascist calendar began not with the birth of Christ, but with Mussolini's coming to power. The former schoolteacher's picture was carried in procession through villages and towns with the ecstatic devotion which traditionally accompanied the relics of a patron saint. Fascist leaders revered him as greater than Washington, Napoleon, or Michelangelo. One writer noted: 'Mussolini's smile is like a flash of the Sun god, long-awaited and craved for because it brings health and life.' His name was even used in hospitals as an anaesthetic.

When he bludgeoned Ethiopia into submission with the use of poison gas and wholesale destruction of villages in 1936, Fascist propaganda had trumpeted his victory in what he called 'the greatest colonial war in all history'. But no amount of lies could hide the catastrophes which had followed his entry into the world war at Hitler's side four years later.

His army of 'eight million bayonets' – in fact it numbered less than a million – failed hopelessly to live up to his triumphalist rhetoric and did little to help him realise his dreams of founding an empire. He had tried to unleash a Blitzkrieg on Greece that autumn, only to see his troops pushed back ignominiously into Albania, their uniforms falling to bits in the rain. In the summer of 1942, he travelled secretly to Libya, ready for his victorious entry into Alexandria and Cairo, which he was sure would take place as soon as the Axis troops had crushed the last British resistance at El Alamein. Events did not turn out the way he had hoped, and after kicking his heels a safe 500 miles or so from the front line for three weeks, he returned to Rome.

By the beginning of 1943, several of his most senior associates could see no reason to continue fighting, but Mussolini publicly insisted that 'war is the most important thing in any man's life'. In private, he toyed with the idea of pulling Italy out of the war, with or without German approval, but gave up on the idea when he discovered that the Allies would only be prepared to discuss peace terms with his eventual successor.

The Allies were not alone in counting on Mussolini being ousted. In Rome, speculation that he might be suffering from a terminal illness had fuelled the intrigue against him. Ever since the humiliating trip to Libya an ailment, diagnosed as acute gastritis due to nervous tension, had tormented Mussolini. Stomach cramps made him double up in pain and he would often vomit as soon as he tried to eat. He lost weight and his blood pressure fell. During one stay at his country residence, he suffered such severe stomach pains that he was reduced to rolling on the floor in a hopeless attempt to alleviate them.

Giuseppe Bottai, one of the Fascist chiefs, drew up a list of the signs of the Duce's suffering: 'his face ash-grey, his cheeks shrunken, a tired stare, his mouth turned down in an expression of bitterness'. Mussolini was not just tired, disheartened and saddened, he was also showing his age, Bottai remarked, blaming the Duce himself for the deterioration: 'He has killed in himself the man he once was.' The illness was all the more shocking in a man who liked to stage public displays of his skills in horse-riding, swimming, tennis and fencing.

Publicly, Mussolini refused to acknowledge any weakening of his hold on power and stifled any fears he had for Italy's military fate. In late June, he gave Fascist party leaders his prescription for the Army's response to an invasion of Sicily. 'If by chance the enemy troops get through,' he told them, 'the reserve forces must throw themselves on those who have landed, annihilating them to the last man. So that even if it has to be admitted that they occupied a strip of our land, it can be said that they occupied it remaining in a horizontal position for ever, and not a vertical one.'

At about 0630, the column of Italian trucks sped down the road from the camp in Mazzarino towards Gela and the coast, kicking up clouds of dust which covered the vehicles. The road wound its way through fields of wheat, a slight wind bending the stalks this way and that into attractive patterns.

Messina was struck by the sight of tranquil peasants reaping in the fields. The steel blades of their scythes shone in the sun as they inched their way forward, their typical Sicilian caps protecting them from the glare. Catching sight of the trucks, the peasants waved their caps at the men, and Messina waved back. They have no idea, Messina thought. This is just an ordinary working day for them. He tried not to think of what might lie ahead. But whatever it was, he was confident that, with the help of the coastal defences, the Livorno Division would come out victorious.

They had covered only a few miles when Messina heard a

knocking sound on the roof of the driver's cabin where he was sitting. 'Lieutenant, sir! Planes, planes, planes!' a soldier shouted.

Messina looked out of the window. He saw a dozen or so planes, close enough for him to make out the colours of the roundels on their sides. 'Don't worry, they're Italian!' he shouted back.

Seconds later he heard the planes' machine-guns opening up. Inexperience, and lack of sleep, had made him confuse the British roundels for Italian ones and he had failed to spot the distinctive silhouettes of P-38 Lightnings, known to friend and foe as the 'Fork-tailed Devils'.

Messina and all the other men tumbled out of the trucks. Finding himself on a bare hillside with no cover anywhere, he slithered down the side of the embankment and lay there, his head level with the road's surface, his body rigid. Perhaps the clouds of dust had given away the column's whereabouts.

A Lightning swooped down the length of the convoy, and Messina saw the lines of explosions in the dust as the bullets hit the ground rapidly coming closer and closer to him, the last spurt only a few yards from where he lay. As the plane's underbelly flashed past in a roar of engines and machine-guns, he felt something hot strike him on the shoulder and thought he had been hit, only to realise it was an empty cartridge from one of the Lightnings.

Again and again the Lightnings raked the convoy. Messina had never been under this kind of attack before and was overwhelmed by its power and his own helplessness. When the aircraft left at last, Messina was relieved to find all the men on his truck unharmed. Only a few of the rest were injured, he was told. The only victim he could see was a dead, straw-coloured horse lying on its back by the roadside, hooves raised skywards as if in prayer.

That morning, Johnson's unit ran into the first real resistance. It was on the right flank of the American force and came from machine-gun nests next to a big concrete pillbox at a fork in the road on the way to Piano Lupo. He raced his men up a hill to set up an observation post, and immediately started calling in artillery.

Before the firing could start, an American half-track, a dozen soldiers in the back, came down the road, heading towards the enemy a quarter of a mile away. The half-track only had quarter-inch armour, you could shoot through it with an armour-piercing bullet from a rifle if you were close.

'How in heck can we stop them?' one man asked.

Johnson had no idea. He didn't say anything. His mouth was still sore from the almond and talking made it worse, and in any case he had no idea what to do. He saw the tops on the half-track were open, which meant the men were so vulnerable they might as well be naked. He was still struggling to think of a way to stop the half-track when it turned off the road, away from him, and made for the far side of the pillbox. Two or three machine-guns started firing right down into the half-track. Grenades landed inside.

'The dirty son-of-a-bitches, they're gonna kill them all,' Johnson said.

He was furious that the enemy weren't giving the Americans the slightest chance to surrender. This was slaughter. None of them managed to get out. That kind of brutality made Johnson want to kill as many Krauts as he could. Every time he saw a dead American, he felt sick. And the sickest he'd felt was when he put his hand deep into the guts of a dead American, on Hill 609 in Tunisia. It wasn't just any American, it was Walker, his closest buddy.

Johnson and Walker had been holding out their mess kits for a helping of stew in the dark one night. An 88mm shell, recognisable by the *prrrr-crack* sound the cannon made when it fired, came in and hit so far off that nobody even ducked. Then Johnson saw Walker lying on the ground, and realised he'd knocked over the container of stew. He was so angry he kicked Walker in the butt. 'You sorry son-of-a-bitch, I gotta eat that,' Johnson said.

When Walker didn't move, Johnson reached down and started to pick him up. Horrified, he realised his hand had gone into his friend's side, right into a hole which the shrapnel must have carved out. Walker's dying like that left Johnson feeling guilty. He wouldn't have stuck his hand into Walker's side for a thousand dollars, he kept telling himself. He didn't have anywhere to wash it, to begin with. And who'd want to do a thing like that anyway?

Fenner's platoon marched along the road that followed the coast, the morning sun streaming down through olive trees and citrus groves, already hot enough to start drying the sodden clothes of the Durham infantrymen. Only the sound of their footsteps broke the quiet of the countryside. He could smell the wild garlic. There was no wind, and the stillness of his surroundings unsettled him.

'A lovely summer's day, and you're on your own in Nazi Europe,' he thought to himself. He had the odd feeling that his platoon were taking Sicily by themselves and couldn't stop wondering what lay ahead.

An old Sicilian man on a bicycle, a shotgun slung over his shoulder, suddenly emerged from a bend in the road. Before Fenner could give a command, several men in the platoon rushed up to the rider. They hauled him off his bicycle, grabbed his gun, and smashed both, leaving him shocked but unharmed.

Fenner felt sorry for the old Sicilian who stared after them as they marched on. He had probably gone out for a morning's shooting, and instead there he was with his gun in bits and his bike a wreck. Fenner knew that tension, and the mere sight of a weapon, had made the platoon act so drastically. Besides, there was always the danger that the old man could ride off somewhere to raise the alarm.

As the platoon entered a village a mile or so further on, locals – mostly old women dressed in black from head to toe, with some old men and children – emerged from the houses and started towards them. Fenner saw the fear in their faces and the hands clasped in prayer, and felt embarrassed that they should think the platoon meant to hurt them. He wondered what Mussolini's propaganda had told them. His men must have felt the same thing, because without any prompting they started pulling out cigarettes to give the old men, and chocolate and boiled sweets for the old women and children. His men were decent chaps, he thought, they had families at home and they didn't want to be thought of as the kind of people who would hurt women and children.

A soldier came up to Fenner. 'Sir, there's a cave full of bint up here,' he said. 'Bint', which meant 'women', was loosely based on the Arabic which the platoon had picked up in the desert.

The soldier's announcement started a general movement towards the cave, and soon the platoon was on friendly terms with the young women of the village who came out of their hideaway. Mussolini's propaganda had drummed into their brains that the Allies would rape them, and they were surprised to see how amicable these British men were. They're all getting on so well together, Fenner thought, that the men will be asking for photographs next. Time to move on. The joke in the British Army was that you were allowed a ten-minute halt every quarter of an hour, and the ten minutes were definitely up.

In towns and villages along several hundred miles of Sicilian coastline, civilians sick of Mussolini and Fascism gave the invaders a friendly welcome. Many of them had lived and worked in America, and in rusty English they asked the soldiers for news of Chicago or New York. Among the American invaders were intelligence officers come to seek out members of the Mafia who they knew would be able to give them information about the Axis forces on the island.

Already, in the run-up to the invasion, American military authorities had recruited the jailed, Sicilian-born gangster Charles 'Lucky' Luciano to help them establish contact with his underworld cousins in Sicily. From his prison, Luciano obliged, and four intelligence officers who landed with American troops on the first day of the campaign carried lists of contacts which included convicted Mafiosi deported from the United States to Sicily. One of the intelligence officers described these men as 'extremely cooperative and helpful, because they spoke both the dialect of the region and also some English'.

The extent of the Mafia's help is uncertain, but the Rome parliament's anti-Mafia commission reported on it after the war, and a couple of episodes have since come to light. In the town of Villalba in central Sicily, three American tanks arrived to fetch Calogero Vizzini, the Mafia's '*capo di tutti i capi*' (boss of all bosses), a man with thirty-nine murders and six attempted murders to his name. One of the tanks flew a yellow flag bearing the initial 'L' for Luciano in black. In Mussomeli, the local mafia boss Giuseppe Genco Russo captured the Italian troop commander and locked him up in the social club.

The Americans made both Vizzini and Russo mayors of their home towns. An Army lieutenant handed Vizzini the tricolour sash symbolising the mayor's office, and gave him and his men permission to carry weapons. The day after, the head of the local Carabinieri paramilitary police was killed in the town's main piazza.

CHAPTER ELEVEN

10 JULY: 0930-1640 HOURS

Aboard HMS *Tartar*, Repard couldn't afford the luxury of waiting to find out whether the three approaching aircraft were Allied
or enemy. Open fire first, ask questions afterwards, was the Navy
motto. As soon as they got within range he ordered the
destroyer's guns to start firing.

All morning he had been expecting an air or submarine attack
at any time, given the huge number of troop and supply ships
which were buzzing to and fro, unloading men, guns, ammunition and other supplies on the beaches. With every hour of clear
skies that passed, his edginess had increased as he kept asking
himself why things were so quiet.

The tension and the knowledge that he would get no second
chance if the planes were indeed enemy made him snap into
action as sharply as at the crack of a whip. Anything was better
than inaction at times like this and the thing that gave the best
relief was the old familiar drill – direction, range, load, fire. The
flak punched the sky with oddly shaped black clouds, but failed
to hit the planes. It was only as they sped away that word reached
Repard that the planes were Spitfires.

How many times, he asked himself, was the RAF going to scare
the pants off him? Didn't they know that, even in the English
Channel, any planes flying over a fleet without prior notice were
automatically assumed to be enemy aircraft? All too often
Spitfires came too close or turned suddenly out of the sun. He
had seen several shot down by British ships. If only, he thought,
they would realise that it was very difficult to recognise them
without binoculars, and that most men at guns didn't have any.

During the bombing of the island of Pantelleria a month

earlier, when they had an RAF group captain aboard, several F-W 190s dive-bombed the ship out of the sun. From the moment the group captain picked himself up off the deck when it was all over, he was as keen as anyone to shoot first and ask questions later. It was the first time he had been bombed, he told them. Unfortunately, it looked as if he had kept the story to himself.

Johnson's unit had reached fortifications at Piano Lupo six miles inland when in the early afternoon, Saladyga, a corporal with Polish blood from New York state, crawled up to where he was lying and tapped him on the left shoulder.

'Hey, Sarge,' Saladyga said cheerfully. 'Look behind you, back here. Look at those pretty tanks.'

Down a big valley to the north, some 2,000 yards away, a tank formation was heading towards the infantry deployed over various fields. Johnson thought he had never seen American tanks move in such a tight pattern, their coloured pennants flying gaily.

'Man, they really are beautiful. The ships must have off-loaded our tanks early,' Johnson said.

He was still admiring them when, now a thousand yards away, they started firing.

'Aw shit, they're not ours. Stay right where you are and dig in,' Johnson ordered as he reached behind his back for his entrenching tool.

He hacked at the earth to dig a foxhole as fast as he could and prayed quietly and quickly. His unit had rifles and pistols which would be useful if any of the enemy poked his head out of a tank. In north Africa, he'd been told to use his rifle butt to stop a tank dead in its tracks, but you had to get rather close to do that. All he could do for the time being was dig in and wait.

He promised himself that this time he would make a perfect foxhole. Usually his foxholes were too short for his six-foot-two-inch frame: he could lie down in them and get his butt in, but he'd have to bend his knees. This time he would make one deep enough to make sure the tanks couldn't squash him in it.

Johnson was still digging when Saladyga piped up. 'Let's surrender, Sarge. Let's surrender,' he said.

'You stupid son-of-a-bitch, you tell me how to surrender to a tank, and I'll do it,' Johnson snapped and carried on digging.

'Well, uuhhh . . .' Saladyga said.

'You can't, they got no place to put you, so they kill you. Dig that damn hole, and dig it deep,' Johnson said. He knew Saladyga would do as he was told, and wouldn't surrender. Saladyga obeyed orders, but they had to be clear. He had no sense of initiative; his aim in life was to sit down, relax and get by doing just as little as he could.

As he dug, Johnson threw a few glances at the tanks. They were German, Panzer Tigers. They zigzagged among the troops down in the valley behind him, their 88mm shells smashing into machine-gun positions, trucks, weapons-carriers and jeeps alike.

He saw the Panzers gun men down, run up on foxholes, lock their tracks and spin round and round until they had turned the man underneath into hamburger. Johnson didn't look for long. Every time he stuck his head out he risked having it blown off and he wanted to take it home with him, not leave it planted in Sicily. Besides, given that he might be next, he'd have been a damn fool to stare at what a Panzer could do to a man.

The tanks got closer and closer to the coast. Some people went crazy. A hundred yards from Johnson, a lieutenant stood up by the roadside, aimed a Colt .45 pistol, and shot at a Panzer as it clattered towards him. The tank swung off the road and squashed him. Fifty-six tons of machine against a human being. A hell of a mess about a yard wide. Something that looked like intestines had squirted out of the lieutenant's mouth.

Johnson thought of the lieutenant's mother. He was so close he could have thrown a rock at the tank and hit the damn thing. But all he did was press down in his foxhole, which still wasn't long enough. Johnson figured his spine was a very important piece of equipment, so he lay on his back. After a bit he took off his helmet and put it over his genitals, he felt more protected that way. 'You silly idiot, what a place to put your helmet,' he said to himself.

Johnson prayed: 'Our Father, who art in heaven, if You get me out of this I will be good. I promise.' Perhaps the Lord would hear him. Johnson's men were all quiet, save for Richards, an American Indian who had started chanting in his native tongue. Richards always did that under fire. The other thing about Richards, who was born an alcoholic and would die an alcoholic, was that he could find hooch. He would walk into a town square, stand and very slowly turn his head this way and that, and then he would make straight for a certain spot and, by God, there would be some wine or whiskey just where he thought there would be. Johnson was sure he could smell the stuff.

Johnson remembered the briefing on the ship. The officer had said Panzers were up in north-east Sicily and would take 'two or three days' to get anywhere near them. And instead here *were* the damn things, right here right now. The American artillery hit back, but it didn't hit much. Some American soldiers stood with their hands up. The tanks machine-gunned some of them, and rolled over the others.

Lying in his foxhole, Johnson felt the ground start trembling like jelly. He thought a Panzer was rumbling towards him and pressed himself down inside his foxhole. If it's coming right at me, I'll hop out and run. The shaking didn't stop but he couldn't hear a tank. So he glanced out and saw that a heavy cruiser had slipped in close to the coast, belching broadsides at the tanks. Its fifteen six-inch, automatic and high-velocity guns were cranking the shells out fast. Each time the shells struck the ground anywhere near Johnson, his foxhole shook. He had never before been shelled by such big stuff.

Whenever he dared to glance out of his foxhole, all he could see a lot of the time of a shell exploding was a column of fire, or just smoke and dust. He figured you could put a four-room house down the hole those shells made. Suddenly he saw a tank take a direct hit. He felt like cheering, but this was quickly muted by the thought that inside the tank was some mother's son, some woman's husband, maybe some child's father. He pushed the thought to the back of his mind. He wanted to feel elation, not pity.

Above the din of the cruiser's shells, Johnson heard the sound of aircraft engines. He looked up to see German fighter-bombers which, taking no notice of the troops ashore, were swooping down on the ships closest to the coast. They bombed a big LST (Landing Ship, Tanks) and a cloud of smoke and debris burst straight up into the sky. Johnson figured the bomb had dropped right down the elevator shaft, which was used for trucks and other heavy equipment. The blast must have fired men and equipment right up the shaft as if through the barrel of a shotgun. The ship burned in the water.

Earlier that day, at dawn, Snell had set down the wheels of the new Spitfire Mark IX with little elegance, but as the saying went, 'Any landing you walk away from is a good one.' He hadn't managed to get any sleep since his return and now at 1530 he was off again on his second flight on the day of the invasion with a four-strong section to patrol the beaches in the Gela sector.

He was glad to be back in his old Spitfire again. He had painted the white letter 'S' on the plane's side next to the registration number. It flew beautifully and was truly a wonderful aircraft. As he left Malta, he could see far below tiny fishing boats going about their business in the calm Mediterranean, oblivious to the war and to the new chapter that was being written that day.

The sight that awaited him as he approached the Sicilian coast, flying at 10,000 feet, was a very different one. The armada which he had flown over for the first time that night revealed itself to him – first a grey shield of staid warships forming a protective arc, shepherded by smaller and nimbler destroyers and corvettes darting among them, then an array of landing craft and smaller ships ferrying troops and equipment. And on the beaches, a jumble of men and vehicles of which Snell, as he swept past, could make neither head nor tail.

As his mission drew to a close, after more than an hour of to-ing and fro-ing over the beaches, Snell figured there was little chance of a good show today – the invasion had apparently scared off the Germans. After all that time with the sun beating down on the Perspex canopy, Snell was sure to have a terrible headache by the time he got back to Malta. All for nothing.

Suddenly on the R/T he heard someone call out: 'Red Section. Bandits at three o'clock above us. Angels 8,000. Tally-ho.'

Snell saw them. Diving out of the sun, eight Messerschmitt 109s plunged towards the beaches from 8,000 feet, preparing to strafe the troops. The four Spitfires swooped down, forcing the Messerschmitts to break off their attack. One pulled across in front of Snell, who got it in his sights and took a pot at it. One of its wings started smoking but to his dismay, it went on flying. Another Spitfire knocked down one of the Messerschmitts, then three of the enemy planes broke away and headed inland.

'Red Four here,' Snell radioed. 'Three 109s at ten o'clock. Am in pursuit.'

But the faster Germans, skimming at 200 feet over the rocky hillsides, had quite a start on Snell. At wide-open throttle, he latched on to 'Tail-end Charlie', as the pilots called the straggler in an enemy formation, taking as many pops at them as he could with his 20mm cannon. The Spitfire shuddered every time he pressed the firing button.

As the Messerschmitts sped on, further away now, Snell tried lifting the Spitfire's nose to increase the range of his ammunition. But the shells still fell short, simply thrashing around on the ground. Some thickish oil splashed onto Snell's windscreen – he must have pushed the engine too hard. He could still see clearly, that was the main thing. But the old Spitfire couldn't keep up, so he called off the chase, and made a sharp turn to the right, to head back to the beaches.

He had scarcely come out of his turn when he felt several

pneumatic drills hammering abruptly into the armoured back of his seat.

'Christ!' he exclaimed, as he turned fast to see four Messerschmitts pulling up around him.

One Jerry got onto his tail and Snell threw his Spitfire into a new tight turn. Out of nowhere, another Messerschmitt appeared ahead of him, closing in for a head-on attack. Snell pressed his gun button but nothing happened. He was out of ammunition.

'Red Four here. Exhausted ammunition and being attacked by two 109s, heading for beach. Give me a hand,' he called on his R/T.

The two planes closed in on each other, with Snell flying at 400 mph. It seemed to him that they were almost exactly facing each other, propeller to propeller. He saw his engine take several strikes before he kicked the right rudder and slipped below the Messerschmitt. For an instant, as the enemy plane flashed by some fifty yards away, he had a clear view of its yellow nose, and the black crosses on pale blue wings.

Thick black smoke belched from his engine, tongues of flame danced towards the cockpit. The engine made a couple of banging sounds, and then petered out with a final *worp, worp* moan of complaint. Through the smoke, Snell scanned the ground which was only 200 feet below him.

'Red Four here. My engine's gone. I'm going to have to crash-land,' Snell radioed.

All he could see at first were hillsides and rocks and olive groves. No place to attempt a crash-landing. Then he spotted a single tiny flat clearing among the scrubby trees, a grassy field with a few stone buildings at the far end. The field was so small he quite expected to crash into one of the buildings, but there was nowhere else to go.

He forced his aircraft into a violent sideslip, hard left rudder and opposite stick to position her belly and the underneath of her wings against the wind, and slow her down as much as possible. He locked the straps of his harness, snapped down his flaps, cut switches, and coaxed his burning Spitfire down towards earth.

CHAPTER TWELVE
10 JULY: 1640-2200 HOURS

The Spitfire's speed dial indicated 140 mph. Snell braced himself in his seat, and shoved her belly hard into the ground at the very beginning of the clearing. It was the only way he could slow the plane as it hit the ground. As the Spitfire jolted down the field at breakneck speed, the propellers which had kept turning as he glided down ploughed through the field with a huge grating noise, throwing swirls of dirt and stones over the cockpit. Through the dirt, he could barely make out the stone buildings at the far end which loomed larger and larger.

To Snell's surprise, the Spitfire skidded to a standstill about twenty yards from one of them, a small farmhouse. Snell slid open the canopy of the cockpit, swung out and ran for cover. He had barely got inside the farmhouse when he heard a roar as a Messerschmitt dived, strafing it with cannon and machine-gun fire. Snell threw himself onto the floor and lay there, his arms over his head.

One thought kept running through his head: 'I must get back. I must get back.'

After a couple of attacks he saw that thick smoke and dust were blowing past the doorway. Snell knew the Messerschmitts would attack again, so he ran to hide in the next house a short distance away, taking advantage of the smoke which screened him from view. Inside, a dark-skinned peasant was huddling on the floor in a corner, among some bales of straw. Snell spotted an empty cattle trough made of stone and jumped inside it, thinking it would protect him from bullets and shrapnel.

He heard the Messerschmitt make several more approaches,

but no bullets or shells came near his refuge. The only damage he could hear was the sound of tiles falling off the roof. He thought the Germans would miss him but might kill an Italian outside by mistake. 'And so what, they're all enemies anyway, Krauts and Eyeties,' he said to himself. When the sound of the plane receded into the distance, Snell and the peasant got to their feet. Snell went outside and stared at his Spitfire which was blazing furiously, the flames licking their way down to the white 'S' for Snell on its side.

The peasant pulled at his sleeve and Snell turned back to him. He didn't speak any Italian so he took off his Mae West and pulled out the handkerchief-sized silk map of Sicily which was part of his survival kit, his eyebrows raised questioningly.

'Where are we?' Snell asked, pointing to a spot roughly a dozen miles north of Gela which he thought corresponded to his position.

The Sicilian jabbed a fat finger at the same spot but it was obvious he had no idea how to read a map. So Snell pulled out a large Italian lire banknote, one with plenty of zeros, and putting his finger to his lips and making various other gestures, tried to tell the peasant he had to get away quickly and that the peasant mustn't tell anyone which way he had gone.

But handing over the banknote had the opposite effect to the one Snell had intended. The Sicilian gave a great cry of joy and immediately ran outside, shouting at the top of his voice. Snell rushed out after him and watched in dismay as the man – waving the note in the air as if it were a flag – raced towards a group of peasants who had apparently appeared out of nowhere. Snell looked around him, trying to make up his mind where to run. His Spitfire was still burning. The 'S' had disappeared. He had to get far away from it, quickly. He made a dash for an orchard behind the farmhouse and ran as fast as he could, darting through the trees.

It was only when he paused for breath at what he thought was a safe distance from the burning wreck that the feeling of panic lifted enough for the realisation to hit him, hard – he was several miles behind enemy lines, and he was alone.

Tartar's alarm bells sounded a mid-afternoon warning as Repard watched twenty Junker 88 bombers break up their formation and start to dive out of the sun. The aircraft had approached from Sicily and it seemed to Repard that they were forced to change their course to dive over the grey barrage balloons which floated over the supply ships anchored between the coast and the destroyer.

'Barrage, barrage, barrage,' Repard shouted. He wanted to throw up a wall of flak ahead of them, hoping the big black marks in the sky would frighten the pilots and make them pull away early or at least put them off their aim.

He kept his binoculars trained on the planes as they flew over *Tartar*'s own balloon, but when he saw a cluster of bombs drop like rain practically over his head he forgot all about the aircraft and stared, hypnotised, as the greyish bombs loomed bigger and bigger and more and more frightening. They seemed to be straddling the ship and as the seconds went by and time was concertinaed, he held his breath and kept asking himself: 'Will they hit us? Why are they taking such a long time?'

The cluster looked to Repard like an assortment of old iron, ranging from things shaped like tar-barrels which turned over and over as they fell, to more ordinary-looking bombs. He could see very well that some would fall over and a few short, but there were several he wasn't so sure about. The thought flashed through his brain that one of the bombs in particular – the one glinting the most brightly in the sun – was going to drop right through his binoculars.

There was nothing else for him to do except watch the bombs. The aircraft wouldn't be returning, it was clear they had dropped all they had.

Faintly, through the noise of the bombers, Repard heard the Captain calling: 'Full speed and hard-aport.' His eyes were still glued to the bombs. He was convinced that the destroyer had bought it.

With a great booming and crashing sound, a huge sheet of water leapt up all around Repard, higher than the destroyer's mast, pouring onto the tarpaulin which covered part of his platform, and splashing down his neck. The destroyer shook as great pillars of glistening foam – the red and black heart of the explosions visible at their core – climbed into the air, blotting out the horizon. Repard felt as if he was sitting on top of a water-spout, surrounded by volcanoes.

As the aircraft flew on and quiet returned, Repard picked up the telephone to the men in the transmission station below decks. He had learnt from the Captain how important it was to keep men as informed as possible about what was going on in combat zones. There was nothing worse than being stuck in the bowels of the destroyer, not knowing what the sound of firing in the distance meant, or what had shaken the ship. Messages from the bridge were always delivered in a calm manner: 'This is the Captain speaking, I want to bring you up to date . . .' The messages were always brief, but reassuring – the familiar voice meant that things were all right, they were unfolding as the bridge had expected.

Repard made an effort to sound as calm as possible. 'It's all right, chaps. They missed us,' he said.

Snell walked briskly, furious at having been shot down. He was determined to fly again the next day, and it was obvious that his best way of achieving this was to head south and find the Allied troops.

He was wearing his tropical outfit – a light tan cotton shirt, tan trousers and a pair of brown German boots, reaching halfway up his calf, which someone had stolen. Thank God the RAF didn't impose as rigid a discipline as the Army, he thought – no one at the squadron insisted on pilots flying in their uniforms, so he had no wings on him, no insignia at all. That left him free to risk walking, as long as he kept off the roads.

He climbed up a hill, hoping to get a glimpse of the coast where the Allied troops had landed. But his view southwards – he had two compasses with him – was obscured by another hill, so he decided to climb that one too. He hadn't walked very far when several Focke-Wulf 190s started flying up the valley. Snell hid behind some bushes in case they were looking for him. He looked at his watch, saw it was 1730, and memorised the time and the landscape. 'Now I know where the buggers are, I'll come back here tomorrow evening with a section, and sort them out,' he promised himself.

Just as he was emerging from the undergrowth at the top of the next hill, he heard orders being shouted in Italian and saw soldiers being marched up and down near some tents. He made a mental note that this spot was another good candidate for strafing. Deciding that going any further in daylight was too risky, he retreated into the scrub, found an isolated place where he could hide among some bushes and sat down to wait for darkness. He would reach the Allied beachhead that night.

He tried to rest. He felt tired, having been up since his 0300 mission, more than fourteen hours ago now, and knew he would need all his strength for the night ahead. As he waited, he made an inventory of what had now become his escape kit. The weaponry first: only one gun. The regulations were that he should carry the Smith & Wesson .38-calibre revolver which the RAF had given him, but without telling any of his superiors he'd swapped his with an American officer for a Colt .45. Snell collected guns as souvenirs, and he preferred the Colt because no one else had one in the squadron. It was semi-automatic and cowboys had once used it. But he only had two clips of ammunition.

In the pouch-like pockets of his trousers, he had various things to keep him going – emergency rations, Wrigley's chewing gum, a great big hunk of nutritious chocolate, a pack of Maltesers, boiled sweets, and some vitamin tablets. He also had a packet of Gold Flake cigarettes, and something much stronger – Benzedrine pills in case he needed to stay awake for a long period.

He still had water in his bottle, so he swallowed a Benzedrine pill. He knew it would be good for only a few hours, and afterwards he would collapse from exhaustion, but right now he needed the extra strength. He just wanted to keep going.

He found he had his Log Book with him – he'd forgotten to leave it behind. He'd already used part of his Italian money but he also carried some gold coins which he and his friends called 'gooley money'. They were to be used in case you were shot down over north Africa, and an Arab wanted to cut off your testicles. Snell didn't think much of the coins. There was nothing to stop an Arab taking the money and cutting them off anyway. At least he was in no such danger in Sicily.

The last of the Panzers vanished over the brow of a hill and Johnson emerged from his foxhole. He was drained and thirsty but he had nothing to drink. He and his men started walking among the casualties, trying to work out who was dead and who was alive. The men pulled the bodies off the road so that they would not get run over before Graves Registration could do their work. Fat flies had already got to them, buzzing in and out of the open mouths and crawling over the wounds.

The corpses were beginning to smell like the German poncho Johnson had found one cold night in the desert before a morning attack. He'd pulled the poncho over his head, started to get warm, and then noticed the smell. The warmer he got, the stronger the smell. He realised it must have been taken from a dead man, and Johnson knew all too well that nothing stank more than a dead human being. Johnson took the poncho off. But moments later he put it back on again, and kept it on despite the smell; the night was cold.

'We'll get those sons-of-bitches tomorrow. They'll pay for it,' Richards said.

Saladyga walked towards a body, sat down on it and started to munch his way through his C-ration. Johnson could never get used to Saladyga doing that. Johnson had once asked him: 'How the hell can you sit on a dead man and eat?' Saladyga had replied: 'It's softer than sitting on the ground.' Johnson could think of no answer to that. He guessed that was why when they were in north Africa together he'd never let Saladyga go drinking with him. That attitude towards corpses threw Johnson off.

He would never think of sitting on a body. He'd sat in a few foxholes with dead men though, and he'd talked to them. 'Hey, you hot?' he'd ask. 'Yeah' – Johnson did the replies too. They'd made him feel less lonely, and besides a dead man wasn't going to argue with you the way most of the live ones did. Johnson had got to the point where the only people he cared about were the five old-timers who had been through north Africa with him.

Whenever a replacement arrived and started talking about his family, Johnson would move away. He didn't want to know that stuff, he didn't want to think of the replacement as a person. Johnson would have liked to not even know his name. He would cut the man short and tell him to follow one of the old-timers, to do exactly what he did. The first seventy-two hours were the most dangerous: that was when the new recruit would pick something up, open a door, or stand around when the mortar dropped, asking 'What's that?' until he found out and by then it was too goddamn late. If he followed the old-timer, he would probably live. If he didn't, he would probably die. Johnson knew the war was changing him; he was becoming a sorry son-of-a-bitch.

He expected that after the tank attack his unit would want to lick its wounds, try to regroup and get back into some kind of shape. But an officer came up to him. 'General Allen's orders. Sock hell out of those damned Heinies, before they can get set to hit us again,' the officer said. The attack was to start at midnight.

'What we gonna attack with?' someone asked. There was no need to gesture towards the hundreds of bodies still lying all over the place. The Army commanders are up in heaven, Johnson thought, they've sent out officers as disciples to tell us what to do.

'With what you got. The whole Division. We're going to kick enemy arse while he's sleeping,' the officer replied.

In his destroyer's gunnery director, Repard watched through his binoculars as the white hospital ship with its cargo of men wounded in that day's landings dipped over the horizon some eight miles out to sea. All day she had steamed slowly backwards and forwards, stopping every now and then to embark the wounded from landing craft which ferried them to her from the Sicilian beaches. Dusk was falling, but she was as generously lit as a Christmas tree – a great, handsome ship with the look of peacetime – and Repard could still see the brilliant red cross on top of her which stood out like a beacon against the dark horizon.

Abruptly, long bursts of tracer bullets sped through the sky towards the hospital ship. Repard couldn't see the enemy aircraft, but from the angle of the tracer he could tell it was clearly flying low, very close to the ship. One of the look-outs on Repard's destroyer must have seen the tracer too, because moments later it swung away from the nearby coast and, full steam ahead, began to race towards the hospital ship.

With the distance still too great to call his guns into action, Repard saw a great flash and a cloud of sparks billow up into the sky – the enemy plane must have come round again, swooped down over her, and dropped its bombs. The lights on the big red cross went out. The destroyer powered on towards the hospital ship as day turned into night.

CHAPTER THIRTEEN
10 JULY: 2200–2400 HOURS

Snell left his hiding place soon after darkness had fallen. He walked as quietly as possible, tiptoeing over rocky areas and keeping far away from any roads. After barely half an hour, as he followed a narrow path up a hillside, he saw the silhouette of a man whom he could just make out thanks to the half-moon coming up above the horizon. Snell froze in fear.

The man, apparently a sentry, had his back to him and didn't move, so Snell crept back down the path. Several hundred yards down, he realised he had no alternative but to cross a large open meadow, within sight of the sentry. So he picked up a long stick, and hobbled slowly across the field, stooping like an old man, hoping the sentry would think he was a peasant on his way home. No one challenged him.

He had been walking for a couple of hours, snapping into his old peasant act when he had to cross open areas, when he saw a stone hut with a large tree nearby. He slowed down, debating how best to avoid the hut. Some ten yards beyond the tree, he spotted the outlines of two men in crouching positions.

A fraction of a second later bright orange flashes and loud retorts told him they had opened up on him with their rifles. He pulled out his Colt .45 and fired back as he ran to take cover behind the hut. 'Those cheap Eyetie rifles,' he thought – Jerry rifles wouldn't make such a noise, and such give-away flashes. His body protected by a wall of the hut, he fired another few shots but then came under fire from another soldier, whom he couldn't see. He had only one round left in his gun and expected to be hit at any moment.

The knowledge that he was trapped made his mind race. '*Kamerad!*' he shouted.

A BRUTAL FRIENDSHIP.
Benito Mussolini and
Adolf Hitler greet each
other at a meeting on
the Brenner Pass on 18
March 1940. Initially a
model for Hitler, Italy's
Duce was soon to play
second fiddle to the
Führer.

THE MAN WHO NEVER WAS. The body of the man named Major William Martin by British Naval Intelligence, complete with uniform and briefcase, on the eve of a bold secret mission to deceive Hitler and Mussolini.

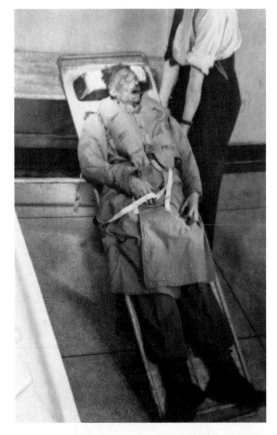

MAJOR MARTIN'S UNDER-WATER COFFIN. The steel container in which the corpse, packed in dry ice, was placed aboard the submarine HMS *Seraph*.

FORTY-EIGHT HOURS TO THE INVASION OF SICILY, the biggest amphibious assault man had ever attempted. At the Tunisian naval base of La Pecherie, tanks wait to board a tiny part of the armada which will soon set sail across the Mediterranean.

INTO THE UNKNOWN. An apparently posed photograph, showing a British soldier about to go ashore. Tucked into his pack is the *Soldier's Guide to Sicily*, a pamphlet with basic information on Sicily distributed to the invaders.

JOSEPH ROSEVICH, private secretary to Lieutenant-General George S. Patton. Rosevich believed that Patton's fiery and coarse speeches to the troops were an act the commander put on, part of a Jekyll and Hyde transformation to motivate the men.

LIEUTENANT-GENERAL BERNARD MONTGOMERY (*centre*) **AND PATTON** (*right*) **MEET AT A LANDING FIELD AT CASSIBILE, SOUTH-EASTERN SICILY.** This was after the invasion to plan operations and, in Patton's case, to ensure that the man he perceived as his rival did not steal his thunder. With them is Major-General Alexander Richardson, Chief of Staff to their superior, General Sir Harold Alexander.

DAVID REPARD, a Royal Navy sub-lieutenant on HMS *Tartar*, in charge of directing fire from the destroyer's guns. Traumatic experiences in combat at sea had taught him to devise his own made-to-measure survival kit, which included a lifejacket from the Merchant Navy he wore even when sleeping.

REPARD AND HIS GUNNERS IN ACTION. HMS *Tartar*, a 2,500-ton destroyer, puts up an anti-aircraft barrage with her 4-inch guns to ward off enemy aircraft. Repard called the gunnery director, the platform from which he directed fire, his 'draughty nest'.

PREPARING FOR COUNTER-ATTACK. A soldier digs in on a Sicilian beach as the unloading of men and equipment begins.

DAVID FENNER, a lieutenant leading a platoon of the Durham Light Infantry. He joined the army when he was eighteen, despite being under call-up age. Eager for more responsibility than the rank of private or lance-corporal gave him, he steadily worked his way through officer training and commanded respect from his men.

LIVIO MESSINA, a second lieutenant commanding a signals platoon in the Livorno Division. Indoctrinated at school about the achievements of Mussolini, he believed the war would allow Italy to show its greatness. A string of defeats however shook his faith in the Duce.

PRIMOSOLE BRIDGE, Sicily's most hotly-fought river-crossing. Despite its romantic name – 'Primosole' means 'first sun' – the bridge was the scene of a long battle as it stands on the main road leading northwards to Catania, Sicily's second city at the foot of Mount Etna.

THE LATEST INVADERS.
Sicilians watch a British
tank in Pachino, in the
south-east of the island.
Despite their island's
long history as a land of
conquest, Sicilians gave
the Anglo-American
troops a mostly warm
welcome, chiefly because
of widespread hostility
towards Mussolini's
regime.

'*Chi va là?*' (Who goes there?) one of his foes shouted in Italian.

Snell suddenly thought of speaking in French. '*Je suis un ami. Ne tirez pas!*' (I am a friend. Don't shoot!) he cried.

Still holding his gun, he put his hands up and walked towards the Italians, explaining in French – a fair amount of it picked up from meals with Arabs in north Africa – that he was a friend of Italy and fighting on their side. He knew his French wasn't very good, but there was a chance that the Italians, who looked as scared as he felt, would speak worse French. In what he hoped were self-assured tones, he described himself as a Vichy French officer. Could these gentlemen tell him where his unit, or alternatively the enemy, was? As he spoke, Snell returned his gun to its holster with a bit of a flourish, and left his hand resting on it.

He apologised to them for 'the misunderstanding' and thanked '*le bon Dieu*' (the Good Lord) that things had not turned unpleasant. The Italians who had moments earlier been trying to kill him offered their apologies in French which was barely better than his.

'*Quel dommage!*' (What a pity!) said a corporal, who headed a section of eight men. He asked if Snell was thirsty, and handed him a bottle of wine.

'*Santé,*' (Cheers) Snell said, before taking a swig at the bottle with his left hand – he kept his right on his gun. The wine tasted rough, but Snell wasn't going to start complaining. He wanted to stay friends. He was so thirsty he was tempted to ask the corporal to replenish his water-bottle, but that would almost certainly have given him away. So he took another swig, and passed the bottle back. The corporal drank to his health.

Snell explained that he had got lost. He hoped to find out how close he was to the Allies, or at least to the coast, but when he asked about '*l'ennemi*', he sparked off a confusing debate as the Italians offered their best guesses. Then they began to ask him questions, which he realised was testing his French beyond its limits. So, with as genial a manner as he could muster, he told them he had to be going, thanked them for their help, and said his goodbyes. Fighting the urge to break into a run, he walked away as slowly and as casually as he could. He had no idea whether he would get a bullet in the back.

When *Tartar* finally closed in on the hospital ship, the sea was so calm that Repard, his headphones off, could hear the screams long before he could make anyone out. In the light of the rising moon, he could see the black outline of the ship with its stern down in the water and an enormous hole amidships. Flickering lights – surely people, he thought – were already moving along her upper decks and there were more in the sea around her.

The hospital ship, the SS *Talamba*, was listing to starboard so the destroyer came to a stop on her port side, only thirty yards away which was as close as it could get. From his seat sixty feet up, Repard had a bird's-eye view of the ship which was lit up by the destroyer's signal lamp. The air, already noisy with the hiss of escaping steam, was filled with the shouts of sailors and the screams of wounded men. The sound of women's voices particularly unnerved Repard.

On board the *Talamba* people were rushing around, shouting orders as they tried to follow the evacuation drill. Medical staff – doctors, orderlies and nurses – were bringing up bandaged men from down below to the upper deck. The nurses went back down below again for more. They were doing their utmost without a thought for themselves. Repard imagined them struggling inside the ship as they lifted the wounded up the ladders that led from one deck to another.

From the upper deck men lowered the wounded, already wearing lifebelts, over the side, but several drowned because they were too weak even to float in the sea. Other casualties in one-man stretchers were attached to railings on the ship with lanyards to stop them drifting away. The stretchers, known as Neil Robertsons, were made of canvas and bamboo strips, and were wrapped so tightly around the patient that he couldn't move at all, as if 'mummified'. Each stretcher had a little red light. Rafts carrying more wounded and floating alongside were also attached to the ship with ropes.

One officer on *Talamba's* bridge reported that she was going fast. Repard could see that the quarter-deck was awash, the list becoming more pronounced every minute. People threw themselves into the water, shouting for help as they surfaced and struck out towards Repard's ship, whose seamen frantically lowered nets, Jacob's ladders and ropes into the water. Several of those who threw themselves in seemed to take for ever to surface and when they did they floated face down and made no movement.

Repard's destroyer did what it could. Officers shouted advice through loud-hailers. Sailors shouted to the swimmers, while others clinging to the Jacob's ladders struggled to get a grip on survivors slippery with a covering of oil and pull them out of the water. His stomach in knots, Repard wanted to help but he had to remain at action stations. He had witnessed attacks on ships in the past, but nothing had prepared him for such an outrage against wounded men, their medics and their nurses.

He picked up the telephone linking him to the destroyer's transmission station. There was one thing he could do: keep the men down below the water-level informed. They would surely worry about the destroyer stopping in enemy waters. As Repard described into the handset what he saw, he did his best to do so as briefly as he could, with a few phrases such as: 'There are people in the water,' and 'We're putting out lines for them.' His mother, an actress, was often extremely dramatic and he realised that his priority was to be as unlike her as he could and keep the men in the transmission station as calm as possible.

Calm enough to do their jobs, he thought, in case an enemy aircraft spotted the lights shining from the destroyer. *Tartar* would make an easy target. Not only was the destroyer a sitting duck, she was perfectly illuminated as well. But telling himself that aircraft detection at night was usually left to radar, Repard did not take his eyes off the scene below him.

Messina and the other officers of his regiment, some of them smoking, stood in the darkness at 2300 on the bare hillside near Gela, listening to their company commander, Lieutenant-Colonel Alessi, brief them on the next morning's attack.

'The Seventh Army of General Patton has landed,' Alessi announced, speaking in a tranquil tone of voice.

The name 'Patton' meant nothing to Messina.

Alessi continued, occasionally gesticulating with his right hand as his injured left one hung limply at his side: 'Unfortunately, we have to wait for the Hermann Goering Division which must come from eastern Sicily. So, again unfortunately, we will have to advance at 0600, when visibility will be good. Which means we will obviously be subjected to an enemy offensive.'

The officers listened quietly, and Messina's friend Nino Ciabattoni, a general's son with the build of an athlete, nodded calmly when told that he would lead a scout platoon. He had never been in combat before.

The officers' attitude, and the news that the Hermann Goering would be fighting alongside him, reassured Messina. The Hermann Goering was a famous unit, and its Tiger tanks boasted terrifying fire-power. The tanks would advance first, bearing the brunt of the Allied riposte, and the infantry would follow. Messina knew he could also count on air cover.

Alessi was finishing his briefing: 'Tomorrow, I will be at the head of the battalion. We must throw the Americans back into the sea.'

Talamba took several hours to sink

The sea around the hospital ship was heavy with oil and the air stank with it. Time and again Repard heard shouts from the water: 'I'm choking! For the love of God save me, I'm choking!'

A puff of smoke from one of *Talamba*'s three funnels and the sound of bulkheads shattering told Repard that the bowels of the hospital ship were breaking up, and soon she slowly began slipping into the water, stern first. She lurched drunkenly, and Repard feared for a moment that she would flop sideways and fall onto the destroyer, the two ships were that close.

She was going now all right and the water was a writhing foam. Sailors still aboard helped a nurse and several casualties into a lifeboat. As it was lowered down the side, a crew-member must have lost his nerve because one end of the lifeboat suddenly dropped down, throwing all the occupants save one, a nurse, into the oil-cloaked water. The nurse had managed to catch hold of a rope and dangled by the side of *Talamba*'s hull.

But the empty lifeboat, which hung vertically, swung in the swell like the pendulum of a giant grandfather clock. It swayed away from the hull of the hospital ship, paused for a fraction of a second and then swayed back, slamming into the nurse and crushing her against the hull until she too tumbled down into the water.

As *Talamba* slithered slowly backwards into the water, Repard watched all the little red lights on the one-man stretchers go out one by one. Many of the floating wounded were still tied to the ship's railings, and there was no one to untie them.

Repard was close enough to see the faces of two or three nurses who stuck their heads out of portholes near the stern, shouting for help. 'The poor devils,' Repard thought, 'they must have been down in the wards evacuating casualties, and now they're trapped.' The portholes were too small for them to get their shoulders through. They knew that they were going down with the ship and they screamed blue murder but there was absolutely nothing Repard or anyone else could do about it.

The bows rose cleanly out of the water, towering momentarily over the destroyer, and then *Talamba* slipped down backwards under the water with the clashing, grinding sound of metal against metal, throwing up bubbles as the boilers burst and sucking many

113

of the survivors who had managed to keep afloat until now down with her. As she vanished Repard felt the wash gently rock his destroyer.

Moments later, when he thought she was gone for ever, a funnel jutted a few feet out of the water, only to plunge back in again out of sight. Then there was silence over the patch of calm sea where the moon glinted only on oil and wreckage.

CHAPTER FOURTEEN

11 JULY: 0000-0330 HOURS

Snell felt a mixture of relief and anxiety as the sounds of battle became louder. After duping the Italians, he had reloaded his pistol and then used both the North Star and his compasses to guide him southwards. Flares floating in the night sky followed by streams of tracer bullets told him that he was close to the front line of the Allied advance. But these signs of fighting were so haphazard that he could discern no clues from them. As he searched for the coast road so clearly marked on his map, he noticed some tank tracks on the ground. He tried to guess the direction of the Allies from them but in the dim light couldn't make head or tail of them.

He came across a tarmac road, figured that it must be the coast road, and started to walk across it. He had gone only a few feet when he heard a deep guttural shout from the darkness beyond which made his blood run cold: 'Halt!' Then, another shout: '*Hände Hoch!*' (Hands Up!).

Snell could see the two Jerry soldiers ten yards away from him. They were standing beside what appeared to be a small concrete sentry box. Snell raised his hands just above his head, holding his pistol concealed in his right one. He thought that speaking English was the worst thing he could do, so he started with his poor French once more. '*Je suis Français!*' (I'm French!) he shouted.

The only reply was a tinkling sound as something hit the tarmac road a few feet away and rolled towards him. 'What the bloody hell . . .' Snell thought before realising what it was. He leapt sideways. The hand-grenade exploded just where he had been standing, but although the bang was deafening he was unharmed. He ran back across the road, two more grenades and several bullets narrowly missing him. He flung himself behind some long grass and lay there, waiting. Firing prematurely would give away his position.

Snell waited for a couple of minutes, but the Germans made no attempt to cross the road after him. Perhaps they thought he was dead? Snell started to creep back the way he had come. When he felt far enough away to stop and think, he figured that he was too far west of the Allied beachhead. Rather than risk following the coast road or the beaches which were sure to be heavily defended, he decided to head back inland, making a wide arc eastwards which he hoped would avoid meeting any more Germans.

He had barely set out on his new course when he came to a small track lined by three low strands of wire on either side which looked like small fences. He decided to cross but as he climbed over the first strands he accidentally touched one with his foot. Instantly, a burst of machine-gun fire sent bullets whistling by, uncomfortably close. After a short pause to gather his wits, he inched his way safely across. He felt exhausted. But he had got away from enemy soldiers twice – surely he would get to the beaches now.

At midnight, Johnson's 1st Infantry Division launched its attack on the Panzer camp. Johnson was dug in at a new position in an olive grove on a hillside. Down in the valley, a half-track armoured carrier loaded with ammunition and petrol was making its way along a winding road. He watched helplessly as a German mortar round blew it up. The explosion of shells and flaming gas was so great it engulfed not only the half-track, but also a tank and an ambulance next to it.

The German mortar and artillery fire went on and on. Johnson figured they must have thought they had hit the jackpot, some kind of immense target. His foxhole, as usual, was about half as deep and half as long as it should be, but although the popular wisdom was that you couldn't dig a foxhole while lying in it, he did just that. After an hour or so, the foxhole was fully as long and fully as deep as it should be. He'd even managed to hollow out a little cavity at one end to put his head in.

The shelling lasted about four hours. As General Allen had ordered, the Americans knocked the living hell out of the Hermann Goering Panzer Division, and got close to the Ponte Olivo airfield. It was the first time the American infantry had given a Panzer Division such a beating. German prisoners told their captors they would never have guessed at a night attack. The word went round that if the Americans hadn't attacked then, the Panzers would have pushed them off the beaches. Johnson gave credit for the victory to General Allen – 'Terrible Terry', as the men called him, knew just how far he could push his troops with a good kick in the backside.

In the small hours of the night, as soon as the Captain ordered a shift to a lower level of readiness from action to defence stations, Repard got himself relieved. He climbed down the ladder from his platform and hurried forwards to the mess decks, where the survivors from the hospital ship had been taken.

He had never seen the small mess decks so crammed with people. Many of the people on the hospital ship had been killed but *Tartar* had managed to pick up some 200 survivors. The air was thick with the smell of wet clothes, hot food and cocoa. As he walked among the survivors, sitting huddled in blankets, he was overwhelmed by the tender, motherly way the rough, unshaven sailors were caring for them. He knew the sailors as uneducated 'Jolly Jacks', and had punished several for some offence or other.

They were doing their absolute damnedest to help, handing out clothes, food and hot drinks. Many of those rescued wanted most of all to feel safe and the sailors reassured them, giving out human kindness in a way Repard found extraordinary. He knew that the sailors called officers like him 'the pigs aft', but that day he identified with them and with the poor devils they were helping.

The sight moved him nearly to tears and made him feel compelled to help in some way himself; he had never felt the urge to get personally involved so strongly before. It was so strange, it was like a pain inside him. Although he felt that as an officer he had no role to play on the mess deck, he thought there would be no harm in stopping to listen to the survivors talking to the sailors who were comforting them. One sailor, still dressed for action, was cradling a wounded man's head, his arms round his shoulders, trying to persuade him to drink some tea and not dwell on his ordeal.

'Where did you pick that one up?' Repard heard another sailor ask a soldier, pointing to the man's bandaged wound.

'I was in a glider and we landed in the drink. I managed to get my heavy pack off and swim to the shore but I got shot at on the beach. This bloody searchlight went on, and then I heard this great shell come in and the searchlight went out. We were only a couple of hundred yards away, but no one got touched,' the soldier replied. 'They operated on me on the *Talamba*.'

Repard guessed the searchlight was probably the one which he had fired at, and was relieved to hear there were no casualties. But he didn't say anything. Poor chap, he thought. The sinking of the hospital ship had thrown the soldier into the sea for the second time in twenty-four hours.

Snell had been walking for so long he thought he must be near the coast again by now. It was still dark and he could hear small arms fire but without any other clues he was unable to make sense of the battle going on. Ahead, a machine-gun suddenly opened up. He could tell from the tracer bullets that it was firing northwards. Shortly afterwards another machine-gun countered, firing south. The opposing forces seemed to be some 500 yards apart. 'God, that's wonderful. Surely my chaps are the ones firing north,' he thought. If he could only get to some Allied troops they would take care of him. He would be free again.

He walked towards what he thought sounded like an Allied machine-gun, and came to a small coppice. Careful to make as little noise as he could, he listened when it stopped firing and heard the snapping of sticks underfoot as men walked under the trees. He guessed the patrol was pulling back, and started following at a distance but soon lost track of them.

He was hurrying on, hoping to catch up with them, when he almost walked into some small piles of boxes which appeared to have been abandoned. He squatted down to feel the packages with his hands. They were sealed with some sort of waterproof covering. If there were any markings, he couldn't see them because the night was too dark.

Could these be Allied supplies which had arrived only a few hours ago? Or were they German or Eyetie? He walked on a bit, and came across some sandbags piled up high to form a shape which he recognised – a bay to protect an aircraft. Inside, he was stunned to make out a Focke-Wulf 190, a fighter-bomber, parked there. At the lunchtime briefing for his last mission, Snell had been told of an airfield very near to the coast which was liable to be taken at any time by the invading troops. This was probably it. Having seen the patrol head in this direction, Snell thought it likely that the airfield was already in Allied hands.

Trying to make certain, he virtually tiptoed around, staring into the darkness. He spotted the outlines of two helmets, and realised he was looking at two sentries standing under some trees twenty yards away. Snell hid behind a bush. He could hear them talking, but so quietly that he could not make out what language they were speaking. Judging by the shape of the helmets, they were Americans. Perhaps they were part of the patrol which had fired the machine-gun northwards, Snell hazarded. He looked at his watch: the luminous hands told him it was 0300. What the hell am I wasting my time for? he thought. I've been on the go for twenty-four hours, I might as well just come out and call them.

From behind the bush, Snell shouted the password he'd been given for the invasion: 'Desert rats!'

The answer should have been: 'Kill Italians!' But no answer came.

Snell tried again. 'Desert rats!'

Again, no reply. Bloody Americans, Snell thought, they've forgotten the password. Jesus, let's get it over with. He stepped out into the open and started walking towards the two sentries. He hadn't got very far when he heard the order, in English: 'Hands up!' Snell recognised the guns they were pointing at him. He had one in his collection. They were Schmeisser machine-pistols, and they were Jerry.

The German soldiers beckoned to him. He had no choice but to walk forward. He had never seen German soldiers before, except from the air. They looked young, and surprisingly ordinary. Once more Snell started speaking in French, telling them he was a friend and trying to persuade them to let him keep his Colt. But they made him hand the gun over.

A lieutenant appeared and marched him off across the airfield, the two sentries on either side of him. Seeing that there was no point in keeping up his pretence, Snell explained who he was, in English. The Germans' response was to order him to empty his pockets as they marched. Snell tried to prevent them from seeing everything he had, while pretending to be helpful. He pulled his silk map of Sicily out of his pocket and blew his nose on it, hoping they would dismiss it as just a handkerchief. Taking advantage of the darkness, he shifted things from pocket to pocket as surreptitiously as he could. He played around with his Gold Flake cigarettes. The Germans went through his pockets two or three times, but he managed to keep from them his silk map, a few lire notes, and one of his two compasses.

The group reached a low building, and halted. He could hear the noise of a battle less than a mile away, and a large gun was firing from the other side of the building. Someone flashed a dynamo torch on Snell, and asked him for his name, rank and number. Again the Germans searched him, and this time they found all his belongings.

An officer strode up to Snell, and spoke in English. 'You will sleep under guard in the room of the Kommandant tonight. Your personal objects will be handed back to you in the morning,' he said.

Snell nodded. He thought the officer seemed fairly pleasant, and felt reassured. He was marched round to the back of the hut, and saw the officer, carrying the Colt, enter what was apparently an underground operations room. He could now see the gun he had heard firing earlier. It was a Bofors gun, and it was banging away from a cliff which Snell estimated was 200 feet high at a beach a half-mile away. Snell's spirits lifted when he saw, illuminated by the light of the flashes from machine-guns rattling in reply, shapes of various sizes moving about on the beach. He could just make out soldiers racing up the beach and, out at sea, landing craft on their way in.

Snell felt so close to freedom. It would be a piece of cake to escape from here, go down to the beach that night, and hitch a lift on one of the landing barges returning to the ships. He had got away twice already. He would manage to get away again. Even if he failed, he was sure that he would be liberated by the troops before dawn. He knew the first thing he would do when he got back to his Squadron – he would fly back here, and get even with those who had shot him down.

Snell expected to be taken to his room, but no one moved. As he waited, the guards pointing their guns at him, he kept telling himself that he should never have walked up to the Germans so carelessly. Nor should he have been carrying an American gun. Together with his map of Sicily and his lack of uniform, it must have made him look suspicious. Snell cursed himself and his hobby of collecting guns.

CHAPTER FIFTEEN

11 JULY: 0330-0430 HOURS

After giving as much moral support and comfort to the survivors as he could by listening to their accounts, Repard, exhausted both physically and emotionally, made his way back to his cabin in the officers' quarters down aft. He wanted to change out of his weather-proof kit before having a stiff drink and something to eat in the wardroom.

He walked into his cabin and stopped short. Lying on his bunk under a blanket was a pale young woman, her dank hair spread across a blood-stained pillow. The top of her white nurse's uniform was visible above the blanket.

As soon as the nurse saw Repard, she began to fire questions at him. He noticed the wild look in her eyes. 'Is Mary all right? What happened to Lucy?' she asked.

'I'm sure they're all right,' Repard blurted out.

'And Jane? How is Jane?' the nurse said.

'Don't worry. There are several other girls on board, they're in other cabins and they're all right,' he said. It was obvious she was asking about fellow-nurses on the sunken ship, but Repard had no answers for her. All he knew was that very few had been rescued, but he couldn't tell her that. He guessed she was in her mid-twenties, a little older than him. He examined the cut on her head, found it wasn't serious and gave her some aspirin.

She went on asking about the nurses and her patients. 'Are they all safe? I know that all save one got into the water. Is he all right?' she asked.

Repard sat on the edge of the bunk, and did his best to re-assure her. He felt inadequate and struggled not to burst into tears. He felt as helpless as he had done three years earlier when,

as a teenage midshipman on a previous ship, he had been unable
to handle the distress of a sailor who had just learnt that his
entire family had been wiped out in a bombing raid. Repard had
made the mistake of handing the letter containing the news
directly to the sailor, even though its envelope was marked 'Via
the Captain'.

'Please don't let me go into the water again tonight, I don't
think I could stand it,' the nurse said.

'I promise you will never go in again,' he said.

She tried to smile. Repard found out from her that some 400
wounded men had been on board the hospital ship. He stayed
with her until she and the other survivors were transferred to
the Headquarters ship HMS *Bulolo* later that night. The destroyer
would not have been able to fight effectively with them on
board.

After the survivors left, he learnt that of more than thirty
nurses on the hospital ship, only six had been rescued. German
and Italian prisoners had also been on the ship, but none reached
the destroyer. Repard heard both officers and sailors say openly
that they would murder any German or Italian they could find.

Snell had been waiting for a half-hour when the German officer
emerged from the hut and said something to the two soldiers
guarding him. Snell noticed he wasn't carrying the Colt pistol
any more.

'You are now prisoner,' the officer said. Snell couldn't argue
with that one.

The officer ordered him to come with them, and keep his
hands up. Snell couldn't fathom where they were taking him. A
hundred yards away from the hut, the officer halted the group.

'Kneel down!' the officer ordered in English. The four men
were standing on a small patch of open ground.

'What for?' Snell asked.

'Kneel down!' the officer repeated, raising his voice.

Snell squatted down on his haunches, but did not kneel. He

turned his head upwards to look at the Germans, wondering what they wanted him to do. They stood about three yards away from him. One of them switched a torch on and shone a beam of blue light at Snell. It lit up the shining barrels of three Luger pistols which the men were levelling at him.

They were about to execute him. Snell sprang, and as he sprang he was almost knocked over by the force of a bullet which thudded into his right shoulder. It felt as if someone had given him a great big whack. As he ran on madly down a rocky slope which he hoped would lead him to the beach, Snell saw a great flash and heard an explosion so loud that he thought the Germans had trained the Bofors gun on him.

He slipped and fell heavily but he got up and ran on. As he fled through the night, sobbing, and tripping on rocks and boulders every few yards, he heard more explosions. He realised they were throwing hand-grenades at him and he could also hear bullets ping against nearby rocks and whine away into the distance. He lost his footing again, and stretched out his arms to cushion his fall. His right arm seemed to slip into a big hole. 'Hell, what is this big hole doing here?' he asked himself. He saw that he was jammed into a cranny between two boulders about three feet tall.

Snell was in too much shock to feel pain but he felt so weak that he didn't think he could stand up again. His right shoulder was mangled and bleeding like hell. He could feel the blood pumping away from what he guessed must be a severed artery in his shoulder and his armpit was slippery with the stuff. He realised that his arm was numb – that was why he had thought it had slid into a big hole. He knew he had been hit in several places but he didn't know where. More bullets pinged and ricocheted against nearby rocks. The Germans were about a hundred yards away.

'Christ, this is it. They're going to walk down here and put a bullet through my head,' he thought. He braced himself for the sound of hobnail boots and what would follow. He pictured the torch shining down on him, the pistol that would be held to his head. Snell was going to die. He was infuriated at the missed date with the blonde girl, the 'Jinx sister' in Malta. He pictured her waiting for him to turn up. He felt sorry for her but he was sure she had found someone else. He felt weaker and weaker. The blood would simply pump out of his body and he would die soon.

The Germans must have taken him for a spy. He suddenly remembered that in the breast pocket of his shirt, they had found a hard white pill. He'd bought it at a chemist's shop in north Africa. People there used it instead of shaving cream. It was a really clever little thing, you rubbed it against your face every so often and for a few days afterwards you only needed a little water to shave. Apparently it was invented by the ancient Romans. He planned to bring it back to England, where he'd have it analysed. He'd start a business, make a fortune. He'd completely forgotten that it was in his pocket. The Germans had probably thought it was a suicide pill, part of a spy's equipment.

He thought of home and his parents, of how disappointed they would be. One day he had been playing rugger at school, and sprained his ankle. Snell had tried to continue playing, and a housemaster, who was on the touch-line, had exclaimed: 'That boy's got guts!'

Snell decided he must show guts now, he must pull himself together. 'Bugger, I'm going to make one more go,' he told himself. He had nothing to lose. Twisting and turning to sit up, he found that his left arm seemed to be all right, although by the faint moonlight he could see bullet wounds in it. His right shoulder looked awful. 'Oh Christ, I'll be one-armed,' he thought. Instantly another thought came to him: 'Oh hell, it doesn't matter being one-armed if you're dead.'

Using his left hand, he managed to take off his blood-soaked shirt, and wrap it around his right arm in a tourniquet. Still with his left hand, he gathered up his limp right arm and folded both arms across his bare chest to support it. He looked back the way he had come. He saw the beam of a flashlight, and some soldiers. They were higher up the slope, near the spot where they had shot him. But it was too dark for them to see him.

'One more go,' he thought. His arms in a cradle, he stood up. Within a few seconds his eyesight failed him, and he hastily sat down again. His vision returned. He found the North Star and remembered he had to head south. He looked for a boulder in that direction, and found one a few yards away. He stood up again, more slowly this time, and stumbled to the rock, blacking out as he sat himself down on it. When he could see again, he realised he had moved all of three yards.

He forced himself to keep going, stumbling a few yards at a time, feeling weaker and weaker, the loss of blood making him lose his vision with every effort. His rests became longer and longer, and he lost track of how many times he failed to find a place to sit down and fell, his wounded shoulder scraping against the ground.

His whole body tense, Hahn sat out on the turret of his Panzer Tiger, scanning the darkness as the fifty-six-ton mass of steel rumbled cautiously down a mountain valley south of the town of Caltagirone towards the coast. Alerted in the small hours of the night, the men had taken only twenty minutes to strip the branches and netting off the Tigers, check their equipment and warm the engines, before setting off at 0400.

The Italian infantry which had been due to advance with the tanks had failed to turn up – no one knew why – so Hahn was obliged to sit outside to serve as an extra pair of eyes. Without the tank's 100mm-thick armour in front of him, he felt vulnerable. He hated doing the job of the infantry. He wouldn't be surprised if the Italians had thrown away their weapons and fled.

Hahn's Tiger slowed down, the crew of the tank ahead signalling instructions only with hand gestures, as wireless exchanges could be heard by the enemy. Road-blocks placed by the Italians didn't delay the tanks for long as they were easily shoved out of the way. So much for the Italian defences, Hahn thought. He didn't think much of the Italians as fighters. The few Italian officers he had seen always managed to look elegant, but the soldiers wore old uniforms and their boots, like the rest of their equipment, were of bad quality. They looked weak to him and he felt he couldn't trust them.

Hahn wondered whether the enemy – he had heard that American paratroopers had been captured in the area – was waiting to ambush him behind one of the rocks that stuck out of the ground on the edge of the road, perhaps with a bazooka. He knew that if he or his companions spotted the enemy first, the Tiger's 88mm cannon would immediately wipe out the attacker. He believed with the faith of a convert to a new religion that the Tiger, with that gun and its armour, was the best tank of the war. The Tiger made him invincible.

The first time he had seen a Tiger, in December 1942 – it was still a secret weapon then and he had to sign a form promising not to reveal anything about it – he was astonished and thrilled. The floor under his feet had shaken as the Tiger rumbled past the room he was in. It was nearly twice as big as the Panzer III tanks he had used in Russia seven months earlier. There, Hahn had seen companions killed by anti-tank guns or by artillery, with wounded soldiers in tears as they lost blood. One man lost an ear, and suffered severe burns to his hands when his tank caught fire. A driver had lost his leg when a mine blew up under him.

Now he would go into combat for the first time since Russia. There he had been simply a loader, the man who did the dirty work placing the shells in the breech and who couldn't claim any enemy targets destroyed. But since then he had been promoted to the role of gunner and that gave him the right to start keeping a tally.

CHAPTER SIXTEEN
11 JULY: 0430–1100 HOURS

When the dawn came Snell felt the last of his strength was going. He had stumbled on over the rocks, blacking out again and again, but had somehow failed to find the beach. Up a slope some thirty yards away, he spotted a small outpost with soldiers moving about and tried to identify them as friend or foe. He couldn't, but he hoped to God they were Allied. Whoever they were, he must get to them before he collapsed. He dragged himself up the slope, covering only a few yards before, his arms still folded, he tripped and fell on his face. He could not get up again.

Turning his head, he saw that the people were coming towards him. When they came close, Snell saw to his disgust that they were Germans. After all that bloody effort, back to square one, he thought. Surely they wouldn't try to shoot him again. They didn't say anything to him, but rolled him over on his back and put him on a makeshift stretcher. They carried him to their outpost, which Snell realised was part of the airfield he had stumbled across that night. Far from heading towards the beach as he had planned, he had simply skirted the airfield. All that pain and effort, for nothing.

As he lay in the stretcher, which had been placed on the ground, an officer came up to Snell and bent over him. Snell recognised him as the officer who had led the firing squad a few hours earlier, and left him for dead.

'The Kommandant has ordered you to be shot. What is your last request?' the officer said in English.

'I wish to see the Kommandant. Why on earth are you going to shoot me?' Snell asked.

'For spying on the aerodrome,' the officer replied.

'But I'm not a spy, I gave you my true identity last night. I am an RAF pilot. I was shot down in my Spitfire yesterday afternoon about twelve miles north of here. If you look for my Spitfire, you will find it,' Snell said. He saw three large German soldiers approach, rifles slung over their shoulders. My execution squad, he realised, his stomach tightening.

'And if you look in the papers that I had in my pockets you will find a Log Book with my name, rank and number on it,' Snell continued.

'The Kommandant says you are a spy,' the officer insisted.

'I want to see the Kommandant. That is my last request,' Snell said.

'Wait here,' the officer said before marching away. Snell was in no condition to do anything else.

The three soldiers stood awkwardly around the stretcher, avoiding his gaze. He saw little hope of a last-minute reprieve, and regretted that he had not let himself die peacefully during the night instead of straining himself almost to breaking point in such a futile endeavour. How would they shoot him? The easiest way would be to do it where he lay, in his stretcher. How convenient, they could then use the stretcher to carry his body wherever they wanted to get rid of it.

Then he saw a tree nearby, and guessed that for appearances' sake they would probably prefer to prop him up against it, and shoot him there.

After a few minutes the officer returned. He was pushing some cigarettes into a packet which looked familiar to Snell – it was the packet of Gold Flake cigarettes which had been taken from him that night.

'All right,' the officer said as he tossed the packet onto the stretcher, and lit a cigarette for him.

Snell felt overwhelming relief. They're human after all, he thought. The officer, apparently embarrassed by Snell's predicament, suddenly asked: 'You came from Malta?'

Snell nodded. The officer must have known already, as all fighters came from there.

'What squadron are you?' the officer said.

'I can't answer that,' Snell said.

The officer gave him a small smile. 'All right. You will go to a hospital,' he said.

The officer lit a cigarette and put it in Snell's mouth. But try as he might, Snell couldn't muster the energy to pull on the damn thing.

Messina followed closely behind as Lieutenant-Colonel Alessi, smoking a cigarette and carrying a riding-whip, crested the hill at about 0730. The Hermann Goering Division had failed to appear, but the Italians had launched their advance all the same. Suddenly, spread out before them lay the town of Gela. Perched on a hillock on the coast, it was some four miles away across recently harvested wheat fields where the yellow stubble shone in the morning sunlight.

Behind Gela, from horizon to horizon, the sea was black with ships. Awed, Messina figured there must be hundreds of them. They lay still and tranquil in the water, the furthest some two miles from the coast.

Messina exulted. 'Lieutenant-Colonel, what good are we going to do in Gela? It's full of our ships!' he exclaimed.

'Would to heaven that were true. Those are all enemy ships,' Alessi said.

Messina was astonished. 'Where are our ships then?' he asked.

'They're not here,' Alessi replied.

Despite his dismay, Messina kept on advancing. The love of the Motherland, the fact that he had been brought up to admire Italian military heroes of the First World War and other battles, drove him on. He did not even consider pulling back.

He worried about the asphyxiating heat, the weight of his backpack, and the difficulty he was having getting his men to advance in proper marching order. He thought of his family in

Naples. The advance progressed down the hill and on towards Gela in fits and starts, with Messina fretting more and more about the time lost, as the later it became, the more clearly the enemy could see them.

Enemy bombers flew over the troops, heading inland. Messina couldn't work out why the planes didn't attack them. Messina asked himself where the enemy was, and when he would start firing. He felt like a man who knows he is to be slapped down by a landslide, and examines everything around him to work out when it will come. He looked at the men marching next to him, and saw that their faces were pale and tense. His face must be the same.

He had been advancing for an hour and was halfway across the plain when he heard the whistling sound of a huge shell above his head just before it burst somewhere behind him. Even before he had thrown himself onto the bare earth among the prickly stubble of a wheat field, yet more shells came over. Messina squirmed on the ground, trying to offer as little of himself as possible to the avalanche of fire. Under the violence of the shells, the land around him seemed to boil, like water in a saucepan.

Raising his head for an instant he saw flames burst from a cruiser out at sea like the popping of fireworks and realised that he was under attack both from artillery in Gela and from the ships beyond. 'Flesh against steel, men against ships,' he thought as his body began trembling uncontrollably. Smoke billowed through the air as the explosions set the fields alight. His throat felt parched but his water-bottle was empty. He scanned the skies for Italian planes and the sea for Italian ships, but saw neither.

The plain offered no shelter. He was on a stretch of land as flat as a billiard table with no dry walls, no trees, no shrubs of any kind, not even the prickly pears which seemed to grow everywhere else in Sicily. Ideal terrain for tanks, he thought, but there was no sign of those which were due to go in alongside the Hermann Goering Division.

There were no other soldiers nearby. Instinctively, he began to crawl forward towards a railway line where his friend Ciabattoni and his scout platoon should have deployed. Messina wanted to check that his friend was all right and see if he could help him – but mainly he wanted to be with someone he trusted. There was nothing worse than being alone in the middle of that shelling.

In the early morning, Montgomery came ashore near the town of Pachino on the south-east tip of Sicily and set off north-wards to reach Syracuse. Riding in the car with him, apart from the driver in the seat next to him, were his aide-de-camp Henderson and Admiral Lord Louis Mountbatten, accompanied by his staff officer.

Shortly after the car reached a long narrow village, they heard the *rat-tat-tat* of machine-guns and the roar of an approaching aircraft. Swooping down the main street behind them was a Messerschmitt which was shooting at all the vehicles in its path. As the driver sped on, all the other men in the car except for Montgomery threw themselves down. Montgomery continued sitting ramrod straight and did not even turn his head to look at the aircraft.

The car reached a fork and turned right just before the Messerschmitt reached it. The plane veered down the left-hand fork. Feeling sheepish, Montgomery's companions recovered their composure.

Montgomery discovered that the Eighth Army had not only captured the whole of the Pachino peninsula and the town of Avola, but had also seized the vital port of Syracuse, still intact. The British had taken a thousand prisoners. One Italian lieutenant from a coastal division had continued playing cards and drinking wine with his platoon although two telephone calls warned him first that ships had been spotted off the coast, and then that enemy soldiers had landed on the nearby beach. He was badly wounded when Canadian troops assaulted his position.

That day, Montgomery wrote in his diary that the way he was

fighting it, 'the battle is simple and the enemy is being forced back by our relentless pressure. On my left the American 7th Army is not making very great progress at present, but as my left Corps pushes forward *that* will tend to loosen resistance in front of the Americans.'

Supreme confidence in his own superiority prompted Montgomery to start demanding that his superior, General Alexander, order the Americans to advance only a little into central Sicily and then hold firm against enemy action from the west. Then Montgomery, as he put it, could 'swing hard with my right with an easier mind'. He would use the Americans as a shield to his left, thus leaving him free to concentrate fully on pushing northwards parallel to the east coast.

Because no plan had been drawn up for the days following the invasion, Montgomery was free to request whatever he wished. But his suggestion amounted to demanding that Patton play a humiliating second fiddle to him and paved the way for a damaging rivalry between the two Allied leaders that was to overshadow the entire battle for Sicily.

Lying on his back in his own filth in a German tent, Snell drifted in and out of consciousness. After the decision not to execute him, Snell's stretcher had been placed on the back of an open truck. The truck took him on a painful journey to a field hospital where a doctor gave him a blood transfusion and sent him to sleep with chloroform poured onto a dirty rag. Coming to, Snell saw that his right arm had been strapped to his side and realised he had been operated on.

Afterwards, the staff pretty much abandoned him. No one helped him with his bodily functions and as he was too weak to get out of bed alone – he couldn't move his head or his arms – he had to use the bed he lay in as his lavatory. No one cleaned him or changed the sheets. Some American paratroopers shared the tent with him but they were too seriously wounded to be of any help to him.

The dressing on his shoulder started to smell but an orderly told him it mustn't be changed. They said his wound would heal faster if he just let the dressing rot away. The smell, the filth, didn't matter much to Snell. What mattered to him was surviving. He knew he wasn't far from the front line because he could hear firing quite close and the sound of tanks rumbling by. He wondered how long it would be before the Allies reached him.

CHAPTER SEVENTEEN
11 JULY: 1100-2400 HOURS

Messina made his way alone through the Gela plain, half-crawling, half-crouching. He stopped to brace himself every time he heard a shell anywhere nearby. The noise of the artillery and Navy barrage, combined with the stuttering of machine-guns, was so deafening he couldn't even tell whether an explosion was ahead or behind. He could hear the shouts of wounded men, but took no notice – training had drummed into him that the wounded should be left to stretcher-bearers, and that an officer's duty was to keep pressing forward.

Getting up and running was near-suicidal. He wished he was a mole, so that he could simply burrow into the ground and disappear. It took him an hour to cover no more than 800 yards. When he reached the railway line, he was relieved to spot his friend Ciabattoni after a long search.

Messina slowly got close to Ciabattoni. Shouting above the racket of the artillery, Ciabattoni explained that his platoon had been attacked by American Rangers. Several had been wounded or taken prisoner, but he had managed to escape to look for reinforcements.

'Listen,' he urged Messina, 'some of my men are in a bad way. We may not make it alive, but we must try to find some more people and get help for my wounded.'

Messina was so shaken he was ready to do anything Ciabattoni suggested. He knew that like him, his friend had never been in combat before, but Ciabattoni came from a military family and he would know what to do.

The artillery and machine-gun fire was so unrelenting it forced the two men, half-crawling and half-running, to seek shelter in a solitary farmhouse they spotted some 200 yards ahead, even though they knew it would take them closer to enemy lines. As Ciabattoni, still crawling, led the way to the farmhouse, Messina saw a little pool of brackish water. He was so thirsty by now that he hardly hesitated before risking a few gulps. It tasted salty and disgusting but he quickly swallowed another couple of mouthfuls before hurrying on.

They reached the farmhouse and Messina was able to stand up for the first time in hours, leaning against an outside wall out of sight of the enemy. He realised he was drenched in sweat and was so physically and mentally drained that he found it hard to stand.

Ciabattoni moved cautiously around the side of the house. He came back almost immediately. 'We've got to move. Now,' he urged.

'Why? We've got cover here,' Messina objected.

'Not for long, we haven't. Our coastal defences are inside the house, and they've got a heavy gun. The enemy could blow this place sky-high any minute,' Ciabattoni answered.

It was clearly too dangerous for them to go back the way they had come so they decided to make for a deep irrigation ditch which Ciabattoni knew ran close to a road leading into Gela. The ditch was wide enough to give good cover and was dry in summer. But to get there without exposing themselves to enemy fire, they would have to make their way through the barbed wire piled in coils to a height of some six feet which flanked one side of the house.

How absurd it was that this Italian defence should be stopping him getting where he wanted and not the enemy, Messina thought wryly. He gingerly picked his way through, the barbs catching on his shorts and shirt and tearing at his skin. Once free of the wire, he and his companion slid down the embankment on the other side. They had barely reached the bottom when they heard a big explosion behind them. They guessed a shell must have flattened the farmhouse.

Now on the edge of the Gela road, they could see the irrigation ditch running along the other side. Like all roads just outside the town, it was bound to be under American surveillance and anyone crossing was liable to be mown down by machine-gun fire. The two men agreed that Ciabattoni would go across first and signal to Messina when he should follow.

Ciabattoni darted across and he landed safely in the ditch on the other side but the Americans must have spotted him because they started raking the road with bullets at short intervals, obviously guessing that he might not be alone. During a pause in the firing, Ciabattoni signalled to his friend. Messina had almost reached the edge of the ditch on the opposite side when he tripped over the shoulder-strap of his map-case which was trailing undone and he went sprawling across the road. As he fell, he heard bullets whistle over him at what seemed like chest-height.

Ciabattoni reached out of the ditch, grabbed Messina by the trouser-belt and hauled him down to safety. The two men embraced silently and, hardly pausing for breath, they lit cigarettes to steady their nerves. Messina kept thinking that if the strap hadn't tripped him up, the bullets could have cut him in half.

At about midday, Rosevich marched up to the hilltop observation post and reported to Patton, who was staring through his binoculars at the fields and hills that stretched inland from the coast near the town of Gela. Perhaps it had a lot to do with the setting, so different from the desert Rosevich had endured for months, but Patton reminded him of the English country gentlemen he read about in novels. Patton's black orderly, Sergeant Meeks, a quiet guy who always refused to gossip about the General, certainly put in a lot of work getting the jodhpurs and the rest of the uniform perfectly pressed and the high boots gleaming.

Patton was grinning when he turned towards Rosevich. The General was in a jubilant mood because he was close to the front line. Rosevich figured he was a soldier who loved plying his trade, and who lived for war. On landing at Gela that morning, Patton had spotted some soldiers digging in right next to an ammunition dump where 500-pound bombs were piled high. 'If you want to save the Grave Registration a burial, that's a fine thing to do,' he had yelled at them, 'but if you want to live, you'd better find somewhere more suitable.'

Patton gestured for Rosevich to follow him into his tiny makeshift office which barely had room for two chairs and a desk. The two men sat down, and Rosevich opened his steno pad.

Before Patton could start dictating, the biggest explosion Rosevich had ever heard burst so close that he felt the room tremble. It almost threw him out of his chair. He looked at Patton, who sat with his hands raised in mid-air. Dirt had fallen down from the ceiling onto his helmet and his shoulders.

'My God, what was thaaaat?' Patton exclaimed, his voice a falsetto. He sounded shocked, and more than a little nervous. But in an instant he was his old self again. He stood up and brushed the dust off his uniform. He took off his helmet, and dusted that too. Patton looked over at Rosevich. Rosevich saw his eyes were shining and he was smiling: he was clearly pleased to be back at the front. Then the General marched out to find out what had happened.

Rosevich was surprised that Patton had, for an instant, dropped his guard and appeared almost afraid. He thought a general who so often quoted the motto 'Never take counsel of your fears' should show more control.

But he had no doubts about Patton's courage. Patton had repeatedly mentioned, both in letters and to fellow-officers, how much he would relish meeting Rommel for a private duel. Patton's wild plan was that both men would fight it out in tanks, in the same spirit as two medieval knights. 'Let me meet Rommel in a tank and I'll shoot it out with the son-of-a-bitch,' Patton had said. 'Winner takes all.'

Later that day, when Patton dictated his entry for the diary, Rosevich learnt that he had come under fire several times as he toured various command posts. Patton ended his entry with the words: 'This is the first day in the campaign that I think I earned my pay. I am well satisfied with my conduct today. Actually I was not much scared. God certainly watched over me today.'

Much later, Italian army commanders reported that they had intercepted a message from Patton sent by wireless at 1130, ordering the 1st Division to prepare for re-embarkation – they took it as evidence of how close to success the Axis counter-offensive had come. General Allen however dismissed this as 'nothing more or less than a lot of Italian eye-wash'.

The fire controller on the tanker from which *Tartar* was refuelling suddenly cut short the stream of obscene insults he had been throwing through a loud-hailer at his gunners, who had mistakenly fired at a squadron of Lightnings. Approaching fast were twenty Junker 88s in formation for pattern bombing, and *Tartar* and the tanker, as well as another destroyer and a merchant ship nearby, were all sitting ducks in the midday sun.

'Christ!' the officer exclaimed into his loud-hailer, his voice a blend of awe and fear.

Repard raced to take aim, aware that *Tartar* was the biggest target in the area. But the Junkers were coming from slightly astern, and he couldn't fire directly at the planes without shooting up the upper structures of both the destroyer and the tanker.

'Open fire when you can,' Repard heard the Captain, unflustered as ever, say in his headphones. Repard threw up a barrage on the side of the destroyer away from the tanker, reasoning that the aircraft would have to go through it when they pulled out of their dives.

The tanker's fire controller apparently had less time for niceties than Repard because his guns started firing towards the planes, shooting away most of *Tartar*'s RDF (radio direction-finder) aerial as the destroyer got under way.

When the smoke and water thrown up by the bombs cleared it looked as if nothing had been hit. But soon flames rose from the bows of a Dutch merchant ship, the SS *Baarn*. The crew abandoned her over the stern in a great hurry. Repard wondered what the haste was until a signal came to clear away as quickly as possible – the merchant ship was carrying dynamite.

An hour later she was blazing from end to end, derricks crashing down bent and twisted like hot sealing wax, and exploding ammunition sending tracers flying everywhere. *Tartar* fired a torpedo to sink her. The torpedo broke her back but it wasn't until more explosions tore her guts that she sank in a black funeral pyre of burning oil, the fire spreading over the water as fast as a gust of wind sweeps across a field of long grass.

In the early afternoon, Messina sat resting at the bottom of the irrigation ditch which was five yards wide, examining the cuts from the barbed wire on his legs and arms. The ditch was occupied by men of the Livorno Division, whom Ciabattoni had already tried to recruit for a new scouting foray. But they were under orders to hold the ditch, so Ciabattoni decided to venture out to find others. Messina could not muster the energy to follow him.

Shortly after he had gone, a sergeant-major crouching on the opposite side of the ditch, closest to the enemy, turned and called out to Messina: 'Please, come over here.'

The man was only five yards away. 'What for?' Messina asked, reluctant to move anywhere.

'I keep thinking about my family and it's making me feel low. I'd appreciate it very much,' the man pleaded.

Messina started to move across, telling himself he was in no state to give moral support to anyone. As he did so, an American jeep suddenly appeared on the road above them and a volley of machine-gun bullets thudded into the earth just at the spot where Messina had been sitting seconds earlier. A riposte by an Italian machine-gun which had been set up in the ditch made the Americans pull back.

Messina just stared at the spot where the bullets had struck. His parents must have been praying for him.

Moments later, an artillery shell burst close to the ditch and an officer who had been giving orders to a machine-gunner fell to the bottom of the ditch some thirty yards away – so woodenly he looked like a puppet. As the officer lay immobile on his side in the dirt, Messina saw there was earth where half his face should be: that side of his face had been blown away. The explosion destroyed the machine-gun, leaving the men in the ditch armed only with their rifles.

A mortar barrage began, so precise and intense it seemed to plough the length and breadth of the ditch, metre by metre. More men fell, those with any life still in them crying out for help or gasping for breath, but Messina could think only of saving his own skin. He hugged the earth, his face in the dust, listening to the whistling sound of each approaching mortar as the barrage swept up and down the ditch, like a giant hammer pounding the ground over and over again.

The three Lightnings dived down over the crest of a hill so fast that Hahn, standing on the back of his Tiger tank, saw them before he heard their engines. The column of Tigers could not have been more vulnerable: they had all stopped for refuelling. Hahn dropped the twenty-litre canister of petrol he had been holding, leapt down and crouched by the tank's tracks. There was no time for him to try to get under it.

He heard the bullets strike the road as the planes dived down once, twice, and a third time, and heard shouts from further up the column. He thought of the crude way the tankers described such moments – they said your rear end trembled and shook, and you could do nothing about it. How right they were.

In a few minutes it was all over. A tank driver who, like him, had been helping to fill a Tiger with petrol, was now fighting to stay alive. Bullets from a Lightning had set fire to a canister and the burning petrol had poured onto the driver. Another crew-member grabbed an extinguisher and managed to put the fire out, but the burning petrol had badly injured the man. A medic took him away. No one expected him to live.

The refuelling had to be finished and then, as fast as possible, the column got under way again. Hahn lowered himself through the turret and into his gunner's seat, just in front of the tank commander's. From now on, the tanks would advance with their crews all at combat stations. Hahn felt much safer inside his Tiger than out in the open where you could be hit by rifles or machine-guns. He felt so protected by the armour encasing him that he never bothered to wear his helmet. Besides, it was just too hot inside. Once, a couple of infantrymen had asked to take a ride inside the tank. But after only a short while they had shouted to be let out, complaining of claustrophobia. Hahn couldn't understand why they felt that way.

As the column advanced, the machine-gunner in Hahn's Tiger occasionally fired into bushes and trees, just in case the enemy was hiding there. Reconnaissance by fire, it was called.

Later that afternoon, *Tartar* had left the tanker and was under way again when a new wave of Junker 88s approached. This time, Repard had a clear line of sight to the bombers.

The first Junker he fired at fell apart in mid-air, and splashed into the sea in many bits and pieces to cheers from the ship's company. Repard shifted his guns' aim to another one, and this time the Junker's port engine caught fire and the plane glided down. 'They're going to hit the water, we don't really need to keep on shooting,' Repard thought as he watched through his binoculars.

But he didn't order his guns to cease fire. The plane landed in clouds of spray on the calm sea a couple of miles away. It stayed afloat. Repard saw two of its crew emerge and stand on one of the wings of the half-submerged plane as they apparently tried to help someone else out of the cockpit.

Repard made no move to stop his guns, and went on watching as the next four-inch shell smashed into the plane and the men disappeared. This time no one cheered, but he had no doubt that after the sinking of the hospital ship, a scene which was still vividly before his eyes, that last shell satisfied the ship's company. Everyone on board *Tartar* was ready to strangle any German bomber-crew they could lay their hands on.

Moments later, he felt awful about it. He could have stopped the guns. The plane's crew had survived the first salvo, and he killed them.

Repard wasn't new to what he himself called 'legalised murder'. When the Navy launched Operation Retribution in May as Germans and Italians evacuated Tunisia, Admiral Sir Andrew Browne Cunningham, known to his men as 'ABC', signalled to his fleet: 'SINK, BURN, DESTROY, Let Nothing Pass.' *Tartar* had spotted two merchant ships and opened fire within minutes, without any warning. The destroyer picked up some fifty or sixty survivors but, because she dared not stop any longer, the remainder were left to drown.

CHAPTER EIGHTEEN

12 JULY: 0000–1200 HOURS

Careful to keep their voices low, Messina and his friend Ciabattoni discussed their next move as they sat in the ditch shortly after midnight. Nightfall had brought an end to the artillery barrage and Ciabattoni had managed to slip back into the ditch not long after it ended, triumphant that he had been able to round up some thirty men.

Their elation was short-lived. The ditch turned into a death-trap after dark, when five American Sherman tanks stationed themselves in a field only some hundred yards behind them, apparently unaware of the Italians' presence. Any move forward that night would be sheer folly for Messina and his companions. And their rifles were no match for the tanks. The Italians were cut off.

Messina smoked although it was against regulations. He had pains in his stomach, his pulse was faster than normal, and he was shivering with a fever that had started in the evening. He kicked himself for drinking that brackish water earlier but kept quiet about his discomfort.

Thoughts of surrender ran through his mind. 'Are we going to give ourselves up?' he asked Ciabattoni.

'No, officers must never surrender, we have to go on fighting as long as we can. I'm going to try and get past those tanks. It's up to you to decide if you're coming with me or staying here. But remember you are an Italian officer,' Ciabattoni said.

Ciabattoni's appeal to his sense of duty shook Messina. He would have followed his friend blindly. 'Right, I'm with you,' he said.

Ciabattoni turned to address the soldiers in the ditch. Messina had always admired the way he treated soldiers as his equals, winning their respect and their friendship. 'Boys, you've got to decide for yourselves: you come with me and try and get past those tanks, or you stay here and surrender. It's up to you. If you're coming, get on my left; if you're staying, get on my right,' he said.

Messina noticed that Ciabattoni gave the men a choice rather than use his authority. Slowly, the men split into two groups, roughly half on each side of Ciabattoni. Each group wished the other luck, then Messina followed Ciabattoni as he climbed out of the ditch and started to crawl towards a gap some thirty yards wide which ran between two of the tanks.

Close to, the Sherman tanks looked enormous, giants of steel. Messina knew that in the American Army they were only considered light tanks but at twenty-one tons they were seven tons heavier than a medium tank in the Italian Army. He was surprised to see that the tank's turret was sealed shut. He could hear no sound from inside. The crews must be asleep, probably as exhausted as he was. He wondered if they had posted a look-out somewhere.

Messina crawled past the tanks and had just cleared another hundred yards when he heard shouts from the tanks. A machine-gun opened up. He saw the steel plate of an Italian mortar gun sticking out of the ground close by and raced to take cover behind it.

The machine-gunning lasted a few minutes. Messina and his companions waited for some time before setting out again, heading back through the fields they had crossed less than twenty-four hours earlier. No planes flew overhead, no artillery sounded. Messina felt he hadn't experienced such peace in weeks. He had yet to see an enemy soldier, he thought wryly, and he still hadn't fired his first shot.

At about midnight, Dakotas carrying 2,300 American paratroopers of the 504th Regimental Combat Team flew low over the water as they neared the Sicilian coast. The men were ready for a drop to reinforce the Gela bridgehead. Their commander, Colonel Reuben Tucker, had told his superiors that he feared so-called 'friendly fire' from the Allied fleet might greet the airborne force. Warnings had been sent to ships and onshore batteries.

In vain. When the Dakotas approached the fleet, flying as low as 700 feet, it was only half an hour after a German air attack had ended. Mistaking the Dakotas for German aircraft, the ships opened fire. The anti-aircraft barrage that followed claimed the lives of eighty-one paratroopers, and sixty pilots and crew-members. Out of the 144 aircraft, twenty-three were lost, and thirty-seven were heavily damaged.

Eisenhower later launched an investigation and an aide to Admiral Cunningham rather edgily explained to Army and Air Force officers: 'Will you, gentlemen, please remember that up to the present, any airship over our naval craft in the Mediterranean has been an enemy plane. And while the Navy is now in the transitional period, it is extremely difficult to impress upon all light-fingered gentry that there are such things as friendly planes flying over our craft!'

As dawn came and his Tiger tank sped through the silent countryside towards the battle he knew would come soon, Hahn simply had to urinate. It was impossible for him to leave his position at the Tiger's gun, so he did what the crew always did in such emergencies: he used an empty cartridge, which he would throw out as soon as he got a chance. In Russia, this technique had caused some aggravation on one occasion, when a full cartridge accidentally struck an infantryman marching alongside the tank.

The previous evening when his company stopped for repairs, he had come across a dead American soldier shot through the heart. Hahn went through his pockets. He wasn't interested in money, he was looking for a souvenir, or some cigarettes. The American ones were much better, and stronger, than the German ones, and the tank-crews were so short of cigarettes that they saved the stubs to make new ones. Hahn didn't find any cigarettes but he did find a pipe, which he took. There were several American dead in the area, but the Germans had left them where they were – there was no time to deal with them.

Shortly after dawn, under orders to reach Gela as fast as possible, the company's five Tigers entered a valley a mile short of the town of Niscemi. Hahn's tank was the last in the column, and he faced backwards, his feet playing automatically on two spring-loaded pedals as he rotated the turret slowly from side to side.

His tank commander Günther, who sat behind him, put a hand on his shoulder. 'Machine-gun ahead,' Günther's voice came through his headphones, above the noise of the engine and the tracks.

Pressing his face against the rubber frame of his glass viewfinder, Hahn swung the Tiger's gun round and saw that a machine-gun, some 400 yards away, was firing at him. With his gun already loaded with high-explosive ammunition – a shell one metre long – it took him only a few seconds to go through the drill of pinpointing the target and lining it up with the tip of an inverted 'V' in his viewfinder, using two small levers. He fired.

'You've hit them!' one of the crew shouted.

Machine-guns weren't big enough targets to be officially credited as hits – only tanks, armoured personnel carriers and anti-tank guns counted – but Hahn had achieved a direct hit with his first sally. He felt a flush of pride. This was only the beginning.

Repard was so shaken by the sinking of the hospital ship that he was relieved to hear that same morning that his ship had been ordered to tow its fellow-destroyer HMS *Eskimo* back to Malta. A bomb had burst in two oil tanks under a warhead magazine, and exploding detonators had ignited the flying spray of fuel. A sheet of fire burned to death whoever it touched, while a jet of flame like a huge blowlamp played for a time round one of the ship's guns, firing some ammunition. Nineteen men lost their lives.

The enemy failed to materialise as they sailed away from Sicily, so with *Tartar* at a lower level of readiness, Repard found the time to write a letter to his mother for the first time since the landings. He pulled out his wallet and extracted a strip of paper only an inch and a half long. The paper was tiny, but would get him into serious trouble if his superiors got to see it. Before leaving England, he had devised a home-made code with his mother and scribbled down details. A reference to 'meeting friends', for instance, meant that he had been bombed. 'Hearing from his uncle' meant he'd sailed in a convoy.

Repard was fully aware of the risk he was running. As an officer, he often had the job of censoring letters written by sailors and knew what could be said and what couldn't. But he was very close to his mother. His father had died when he was only eight, and he knew how much every bit of news from him mattered to her. He missed her, and wrote often. When she was running a canteen for night-duty gunners on Hampstead Heath during the Blitz, he'd written to tell her to be careful. She wrote back saying that she held a frying pan over her head and that kept the shrapnel off. After a few weeks, however, the strain proved too much for her and she moved to the countryside.

Repard knew that if he told her about the hospital ship she would be distressed, so he made no mention of it. Besides, he didn't have a codeword for what he had seen.

An hour before noon, eight miles short of Gela, Hahn heard his tank commander Günther shout: 'Enemy tank, nine o'clock! Armour-piercing!'

Hahn wheeled the turret round to his left as fast as he could. As he did so, the loader lifted an armour-piercing shell into the gun's breech. Hahn estimated the enemy tank – he recognised it as a Sherman from the pictures he had studied during training – was roughly 600 yards away. The Sherman must have intended to sneak up on Hahn's Tiger from the side, knowing that the armour was slightly thinner on the sides than on the front.

Hahn's shell smashed into the Sherman, which burst into flames. The hatch opened and a couple of men tumbled out. The thought 'my first enemy tank' flashed through his mind as he immediately began rotating the turret again, to keep looking for the enemy.

'One is already burning! Now we'll deal with the others!' he overheard Günther telling the company commander on the radio link.

Hahn fired again, this time at another Sherman a mile away – too far for the Sherman to attempt to penetrate the Tiger's armour, but the right distance for Hahn's 88mm cannon. The shell struck the Sherman at the base of the turret, immobilising it.

Forehead and cheeks jammed against his viewfinder, Hahn stared for so long at the blindingly white landscape that his eyes stung with strain. Occasionally the clouds of flame and dust caused by enemy artillery, mortar and anti-tank weapons made it impossible for him to see anything, and he could do nothing but wait for them to settle.

The barrage was worse than any Hahn had been through in Russia. Several times, through his headphones, he heard something thump against his tank, but he dismissed this as rocks or stones kicked up by the artillery shells.

As the battle dragged on, the temperature inside the tank rose higher and higher. Outside it was some 35° Celsius in the shade, but inside, Hahn estimated it must be between 50 and 60. The sun beating down on the thick steel armour, the heat from the engine and the gearbox, and the flames spitting out of the gun's breech as the last of the powder burned after each firing, all combined to turn the inside of the Tiger into a furnace.

The heat could not have been more different from what Hahn had seen in Russia. There, with temperatures of -30°, it was so cold in the tank that boiling hot tea would turn to ice within a few minutes. He remembered how ice crystals formed on the inside of the tank, his fingers sticking dangerously to the metal shells.

His shirt sodden, Hahn stripped to the waist. He was surprised to notice that he barely felt the heat from the flames which leapt, half a metre long, from the breech. It was so hot in the tank that not even a flame some eight inches from his face – so close that had he swung sideways it would have disfigured him – made much of an impression. In violation of regulations, Günther kept the hatch of the turret above his head slightly open, but this did little to change the air inside which was thick with dust, burnt powder, the stink of burnt petrol and sweat.

He would have given anything for a can of cool beer, or a thermos filled with ice-cream from the field-kitchen. He lit a cigarette. The air in the tank was so disgusting that a little cigarette smoke would make no difference, it might even make him feel better. Smoking inside the tank was of course against regulations, but most of the crew lit up whenever things got tough.

Spotting an armoured personnel carrier within range, he fired a high-explosive grenade at it. He watched the shell's path, traced by a powder similar to phosphorus which burned as it sped through the air.

The vehicle exploded, bodies and body parts jumping into the air. The grenade must have pierced the vehicle's armour and detonated inside. Poor fellows, Hahn thought. He could only too easily imagine his own fate if such a shell had entered his tank, perhaps dropping through an open hatch. That was the trouble with war; whoever strikes first, wins.

As he prepared to fire at yet another target, Hahn realised that the gun was not loaded. He turned and saw that his loader had collapsed with exhaustion. The man was the only one in the tank constantly on the move, continually lifting heavy ammunition. The others gave him some water and he lay on the bottom of the turret to rest for a time, while the wireless operator replaced him.

Rita stopped her playing in the street – she had no toys, and she had to invent her own games out of nothing – to stare at the bizarre procession passing by the end of her road. First a man, cradling some saucepans. Then a woman, dragging a heavy bag. More and more people passed: one woman was carrying a sewing machine, others blankets, chairs, desks, mattresses, camp-beds, cupboards and things which Rita couldn't identify.

She raced into the house where they had sought refuge three months previously to tell her mother. The family soon found out from a neighbour that the Germans had abandoned the school down the road and the locals were plundering it.

Rita's mother called out to her son Pippo: 'Go and see what you can find. You might get some pasta.'

But Pippo stayed where he was. 'I'm not going,' he said.

'Why ever not? Don't you know we're starving?' his mother asked. 'Look at all these God-sent things the people are carrying,'

'Mamma, those people are thieves. And I won't ever steal. I'd rather die of hunger,' Pippo protested.

Their mother didn't insist. She admired her son's principles, but the family couldn't live on principles, so she sent Rita's grandfather instead. The Fascists had set up a rationing system, but it was so inadequate and corrupt that food and just about everything else was in short supply. Rita's family couldn't afford the prices of the Mafia-run black market.

Her grandfather returned after a while with a bag almost as big as Rita. It was full of garlic. He insisted this was good for them, that it acted as a natural disinfectant for the body. Since he worked occasionally as a waiter, the family took his word for it. He hoarded his loot with great ingenuity. Whenever news swept through the neighbourhood that a police patrol was on the prowl, he would tie a rope round the bag and throw it behind the courtyard wall at the back of the house. After the police had gone, he pulled on the end of the rope to recover it.

Rita's grandmother, who had worn black ever since one of her children had fallen ill with a bad fever and died, laughed at her husband. 'Why do you bother going to all this trouble? You really think the police are going to arrest you for a bag of garlic?' she said.

The arrival of Rita's grandparents only a few days before meant that now a dozen people camped rather than lived in the tiny two-roomed house which had low ceilings, not a single window, no electricity and no running water. In the front room which gave onto the street the family ate and Rita shared a bed with her three sisters. They all washed in a tub in the courtyard. Because of the heat, they slept with the doors open in summer – in any case, they had nothing for thieves to steal.

Rita's father was still in jail after rowing with a policeman and the only source of revenue, apart from her grandfather's meagre earnings, were the roasted almonds wrapped in paper cones which her uncle sold in the street. Almonds grew plentifully on the outskirts of the city. The smell of his preparations tortured the hungry children but their uncle guarded the almonds jealously. Whenever she could, Rita would steal a few and hide them under the mattress to eat later. Once, her uncle refused to give any to Rita's mother when she asked for some, on the grounds that each paper cone had just the right number of almonds. Pippo pulled some coins out of his pocket, and bought some for her.

Every day Rita's grandparents and her uncle went out to search for food. They rarely found anything better than carobs, empty pea-pods, berries or chick-peas which the family roasted. Her grandfather would buy a few dried fava beans and Rita would have several for her lunch. For days after her grandfather came back with his haul of garlic, Rita had almost nothing but that for both lunch and dinner. She had to eat most of it raw because the family didn't have enough wood for the stove.

CHAPTER NINETEEN
12 JULY: 1200–2400 HOURS

Shortly after midday, Hahn's tank started down the hillside east of Gela and his viewfinder filled with ships. He felt overwhelmed. How could one company of tanks possibly take on all these battleships, destroyers and God knows what else?

He saw movement on the beaches and managed to hit a few trucks, his shells kicking the sand up into tall columns. He tried to fire at landing craft coming towards the beaches but he had a hard time of it, as the waves prevented him from seeing where his shells landed.

As he scanned the sea, he saw flashes from the guns of one of the warships and moments later heard the shells exploding behind him, too far away to be a threat. He thought it would be only a matter of time before the warship corrected the range. Hahn felt only relief when, more than an hour later, his company was ordered to pull back.

The company's strength was down to just two tanks. All attempts to contact the three missing tanks by radio failed. Hahn didn't stop to think about their crews – it was just Fate, and nothing could be done about it.

His Tiger had barely retreated a safe distance from the battlefield when the loud drone of its engine stopped suddenly. The driver couldn't restart the engine so Hahn clambered out, his limbs heavy with fatigue. The open air was so much cooler that he just stood in the road for a few moments, clearing his lungs.

He stared at his Tiger. On the side where his seat was, a shell which must have been fired by a Sherman had torn a gash diagonally across the turret. Stupefied, Hahn put his arm in the gash. It was so deep the armour plating was down to one centimetre in one place – a little more force and the shell would have penetrated inside to just where he sat. And yet Hahn hadn't even heard the shell hit the Tiger.

His fellow crew-members came up to stare at the turret. Hahn looked at them and burst out laughing. They looked like chimney-sweeps, their faces and bare chests black with dust and grime. Rivulets of sweat had traced greyish lines down their faces.

All over the tank, sheets of metal curled bizarrely. Parts of the tracks and the wheels had been shot away. Behind the turret, the metal box containing the men's change of clothes, food and other equipment was badly burned. Further back, a shell must have hit the engine's cooling system as water was leaking out onto the road.

Hahn started counting the marks of impacts on the tank. There were 108. He had done all he could in the face of an attack by both enemy tanks and artillery; his score, he estimated proudly, was about half-a-dozen tanks and armoured personnel carriers.

Snell lay in his hospital bed, unable to move his stinking body, the high windows rattling every time there was an explosion. The Germans had taken him on a painful ambulance journey away from the field-hospital near the Allied front line to a hospital in Catania. He was now in a ward on the lower ground floor. Judging by the sound of the explosions, he guessed warships were shelling the city.

The Jerry orderlies fed him, but no one gave him a bedpan here either and the filth stuck to Snell's skin, making the bed smell foul in the heat and giving him nasty sores. Infuriated at having been pulled back far from the front, Snell thought of slipping out of the hospital and hiding in the city until the Allies arrived. But he was too weak even to sit up, let alone get out of bed.

His neighbour, an Italian who had been amputated and whose stump was enclosed in a cage-like basket, started thrashing about in his bed, grimacing with pain. Snell shouted for help, again and again, until two Jerry orderlies appeared. One of them carried a syringe which Snell guessed contained morphine.

The orderly was just about to jab the syringe into the Italian's skin when the man went limp. Dead. The orderly pointed his syringe down the ward and squeezed. He squeezed so hard that the liquid spurted quite some way, and the end of the syringe flew off. The two orderlies burst out laughing.

'Christ, what awful people. And they're the ones who are supposed to be looking after us,' Snell thought.

In the early afternoon, Hahn and his tank's radio operator Eugen Grün, the youngest tanker in the company who had had his first taste of combat in the past two days, walked up to the farmhouse a little way from the road to find some water, each carrying two twenty-litre canisters for the Tiger's engine-cooling systems. Following his commander's order, Hahn clutched his pistol in his free hand.

The farmhouse looked a little like a medieval fort, with several towers flanking its low outer wall. Hahn knocked at the main door and tried to open it, but it was locked. He knocked again and again, as loudly as he could, until an elderly peasant, trembling with fear, opened the door.

'*Dove acqua?*' (Where water?) Hahn asked. He had picked up some Italian in Sicily.

The man turned and led them to a pump in the farmyard. Hahn was so hot and dirty that, pausing only to drop his canister on the ground, and put his pistol in its holster, he bent down over the cattle trough and let the cold, wonderful liquid splash down over his head. The tanks could wait.

Someone tapped lightly on Hahn's shoulder. He turned and saw a tall fellow wearing a light, desert uniform. The old peasant had disappeared.

'*Momento,*' Hahn said, thinking the man was Italian, and went on splashing himself.

Again, the man tapped on his shoulder. This time, Hahn saw the small Stars and Stripes flag on his uniform.

'An American,' the astonished Hahn called out to Grün as he tried furiously to work out how he could get out of this one. The American was apparently unarmed, while Hahn's pistol was safe in its holster.

Grün piped up: 'Ask him if he has some chocolate.'

Hahn did so, using the English he had learnt at school. It was only later that it struck him as a stupid request. The American, apparently nonplussed, handed them some chocolate, and the two Germans started munching away. Gradually, more and more Americans came out into the farmyard until there were twenty or so standing around. To Hahn, they looked much older than him, and he guessed they were paratroopers. There were probably more Americans elsewhere on the farm, which meant he and Grün, and the other nine Germans out in the road, were heavily outnumbered.

Hahn quickly thought up a plan. The Americans must see him as little more than a boy, so the more determined he appeared, the better. 'You must be careful. We have two Tiger tanks outside. You must help us camouflage the Tigers, otherwise your Air Force will bomb the area,' he said. He didn't tell them the tanks had broken down.

The Americans consulted each other, with the result that a dozen of them followed Hahn and Grün, helping to carry the canisters full of water back to the tanks. Hahn felt exhilarated that his enemy had agreed to a private truce. He asked himself who had taken whom prisoner, but he couldn't find an answer.

He reported back to Goldschmidt, his commander. 'There are more Americans in the farmhouse. I have brought these men here to help us camouflage the tanks,' Hahn said.

Hahn pointed out to the fascinated Americans all the hits which his Tiger had suffered, showing them how well the armour had resisted. Then the Americans helped him and the rest of the crews to cut down some branches to camouflage the tanks.

At Goldschmidt's request, Hahn led him to the farmhouse, escorted by a couple of Americans. They discovered there were a total of thirty Americans inside the farm. The Americans were friendly and offered them more chocolate, and cigarettes. In the stables, sheltering from the heat outside, two wounded Americans lay on the straw. Hahn realised the Americans had no medical staff with them, and knew nothing about first aid. He fetched some bandages from his own supply and helped to dress the men's wounds. He questioned the Americans, and worked out that they must have been manning the first anti-tank gun which Hahn had himself destroyed early that morning. He felt sorry for them, but not enough to regret firing at them.

The rest of the afternoon passed in a drinking session, with the Germans careful to drink as little of the farm's supply of Marsala wine as possible. Toast followed toast. 'Let's celebrate that none of us are prisoners,' Hahn said. Rather to his relief, the Americans drank to that.

Later, Goldschmidt took Hahn aside, and told him they should wait until sunset and then try to make their escape. In the meantime, the drivers would prepare the tanks for self-destruction with special charges. Hahn agreed without hesitation. He was ready to risk an escape. He trusted Goldschmidt who was a good commander, and he wanted to stay with his fellow-tankers. When no one was looking, he managed to pocket an American compass and a knife with a knuckleduster on the hilt. It looked more like a gangster's weapon than military equipment.

The chummy atmosphere was soured by the arrival of a medical officer with the rank of colonel. With Hahn acting as a translator, the colonel addressed Goldschmidt in stark terms as they talked in the farmhouse's kitchen: 'Don't think you can get away. It's hopeless. The front line has moved, so you're now thirty miles behind American lines. You must surrender.'

The colonel gave him a map on which the positions of both sides were marked.

'We refuse to surrender,' Goldschmidt replied. 'We will try to get through and return to our lines.'

'Surrender is your only alternative. The war is over for you,' the colonel insisted.

Goldschmidt was inflexible. He managed to negotiate a six-hour truce which would last until dusk. As Goldschmidt and the colonel said their goodbyes – even exchanging home addresses – they discovered a coincidence: the Americans were paratroopers of the 504th Parachute Regiment, while Hahn's Heavy Panzer Battalion was also the 504th.

The colonel got back in his jeep and the wounded men were lifted into it. An infantryman of the Hermann Goering Division, who had been found near the farmhouse, was also lifted into the jeep. In tears, he begged to stay with the Germans. But he was too badly wounded in the thigh to walk. Eventually he accepted that he would have to stay behind, reassured by the fact that he would be cared for in an American hospital. He wrote a letter which he entrusted to Hahn.

'Send this letter to my parents – that way they will know that I am still alive,' he told Hahn.

That evening, a groan went up from Fenner's platoon. 'Here's Webster with the orders, we're going into battle,' a private said. Webster, the company commander's runner, gave a big grin.

'All platoon commanders wanted at the company commander's order group, sir. The battalion is to attack just before first light,' Webster told Fenner.

Since landing two days earlier on the wrong beach, 5,000 yards off-target, Fenner had spent most of his time watching what seemed to be continuous air attacks on ships unloading in the Bay of Avola. His platoon had then moved north near the village of Solarino, where they sat in individual slit trenches, trying to keep warm.

Fenner learnt that the target, a unit of the Napoli Division stationed near farm buildings on a ridge, was some 2,000 yards away. It was too dark to get a look at the objective. Fenner asked about enemy artillery, and was told bluntly there wouldn't be any.

After he'd briefed his platoon, Fenner shared a tin of cold M&V (canned stew) rations with a sergeant, swigging the last of the rum he had been carrying for the past three days. The night was cold and no one had any blankets, but at least the rum warmed you a little. Around him, some of the men were asleep, while others lay with their eyes open, staring at the stars.

The only sound was that of men pulling on cigarettes. Fenner had heard that you could see the light of a cigarette from miles away, but he didn't believe it. Besides, it would have been impossible to stop the men smoking as they waited to go into combat.

As dusk fell and the time for their escape attempt approached, with the Americans still suspecting nothing, Goldschmidt took several of his men aside to promote them. He made Hahn a sergeant 'for bravery in the face of the enemy', giving him an epaulette which he had taken off his driver's shoulder.

'When you are made a prisoner, you will have the rank of sergeant,' Goldschmidt told him. Neither he nor anyone else thought there was much chance of the escape being successful.

When the sun set and the private truce drew to an end, Hahn and the rest of the crew members slipped away one by one out of sight of the Americans, several of whom were drunk. The two men who were due to blow up the Tigers were the first to go. Hahn made for the meeting place agreed with Goldschmidt, some 300 yards from the farmhouse. Shortly after he reached it, he heard the sound of explosions as the Tigers blew up. He felt a pang of regret as he pictured his wrecked tank, but because it was still classified a secret weapon there could be no question of it falling into enemy hands.

The explosions were so loud that the Americans in the farmhouse, convinced they were under attack, launched an artillery and mortar barrage. Hahn and the rest of the dozen-strong party could not have wished for a better diversion as they fled. The

Germans moved off in single file, with Hahn close to Goldschmidt as he would be able to answer in English if they were challenged by the enemy. Hahn felt no jubilation when they got a safe distance from the farmhouse, without any sign of the Americans pursuing them. He couldn't stop thinking about the long road ahead.

Using both the map which the American colonel had given Goldschmidt and the compass which Hahn had stolen, they headed north. Progress was slow through the hilly terrain, and not long after nightfall the men decided to rest. Hahn crawled under a bush and fell asleep.

CHAPTER TWENTY

13 JULY

Shortly before dawn, the slide-and-clack of bayonets being fixed, and the clicking of magazines onto Bren guns, told Fenner the men were ready to advance on the Italians holding the ridge near Solarino. He gave out the last of the rum left over from the landings – the men got only a spoonful each. He felt low and fearful, and much more comforting to him than the rum was the presence of men he considered friends around him in the darkness.

The order to move at H-Hour came as a relief. Fenner picked a star low on the horizon as his compass bearing. He had put ten pebbles into one of his pockets, and transferred one to his other pocket every few paces to help him measure out the thousand yards he was supposed to advance before launching the attack. But he soon lost count of the pebbles, and resorted to the simpler method of just counting his paces on the uneven ground, calculating that 120 paces were equivalent to a hundred yards.

Artillery fire opened up from behind. The top brass had at the last minute managed to get some fire support. The shells went whistling over the heads of Thirteen Platoon and the men continued to march on, walking so close to each other that a soldier could have put a hand out and touched the chap next to him.

They had made good progress when the commander of Charlie Company, Major Dominic Parker, stopped the advance.

'Right. Shake out into open order,' he ordered.

The artillery had stopped firing. The men spread out, and Fenner saw that they were practically all puffing away at cigarettes. 'Bloody hell, do the Durhams smoke in battle?' Fenner asked himself.

Just as the sun rose up behind him, the light played on the

bayonet as he held his rifle at the ready, blade pointing to the sky, ready to be lowered and plunged into the enemy. But he hoped that the enemy would have surrendered before things got to that stage.

Fenner caught sight of Italian soldiers on top of the ridge and his platoon swept forward across the field, the men whooping and opening fire as they went. The Italians fired back. A low stone wall stopped Fenner's advance. Ahead of them, Fenner saw three lorries and many Italians busy shooting.

Parker came up to Fenner and opened his mouth to say something. Fenner saw the major abruptly take a couple of steps back, as if punched backwards by an invisible fist, and guessed he had been shot. Fenner just couldn't see where he had been hit.

'Are you all right?' Fenner asked. It sounded absurd.

'Yes, I'm all right,' Parker replied.

Fenner moved behind the major to stop him falling and saw a tear in his shirt between the shoulder-blades. There was a small hole in the skin. Bits of flesh had been pushed outwards around the hole, but there wasn't much blood. The stretcher-bearers arrived before Fenner could shout for them.

Fenner got back to the job at hand, squeezing off as many shots as he could with his pistol. He watched in fascination as his Bren gunner, standing beside him, fired from the shoulder. Fenner saw the tracer pass over one of the trucks.

'Shoot at the truck,' Fenner urged.

The next burst set off an explosion in one of the lorries which burst into flames, showering debris over the Italians lying nearby. The gunner beamed in delight. Fenner went over the wall and saw a bunch of Italians surge towards him. Fenner kept shooting. He wasn't a very good shot but he saw one of them go down. The others ran on towards him, and one got to within three yards.

Fenner was wondering if he would have to use his bayonet when he suddenly realised the Italians were waving packets of cigarettes. They were surrendering. He stopped firing. One of the Italians offered him cigarettes – a peace offering.

'No thanks, I smoke a pipe,' Fenner replied in English. He got the words out and then realised how stupid they sounded.

He disarmed the Italians and told them to walk back towards the rear of the British lines. He made them carry the man he had wounded. He felt bad about having shot a soldier who was surrendering, but the Italians had failed to hold their hands up and there was no way of telling what they were up to.

Fenner's battalion took 400 prisoners that day. The Italians had proved themselves neither cowards nor poor soldiers and several light tanks had launched daring attacks. But his impression was that the overwhelming majority of Italians fought until you got close to and then they crumbled and gave themselves up. For all Mussolini's slogans he had seen daubed in three-foot-tall letters on the crudely whitewashed walls of Sicilian houses, such as 'Credere, Obbedire, Combattere', (Believe, Obey, Fight), 'Mussolini ha sempre ragione' (Mussolini is always right) and 'DUCE DUCE DUCE', it was obvious that the soldiers' hearts were not in the war. Many of them simply asked if they could go home now.

Hahn awoke and found himself under a bush in open countryside. He realised that more than fifteen miles separated him and his ten companions from the German lines. The sooner they got going, the better. He got to his feet, only to drop down to the ground immediately. Barely fifty yards away was a farmhouse with Americans milling around it.

After whispered consultations, the fugitives decided that it would be suicidal to attack as they had only a few pistols among them and the Americans were likely to be more numerous. The only way out was to go round the house, keeping a safe distance away and continue the march northwards. Hiding behind any available bushes and trees, they started crawling away from it in Indian file.

Hahn came across some cables leading towards the house. He decided they must be American communication lines, pulled out the knife he had stolen from the Americans earlier and cut through them. He enjoyed using an American dagger against the Americans.

The fugitives soon ran out of water and Hahn ate as many tomatoes as he could find as they were the only available source of liquid. They came across an abandoned farm, killed a chicken and tried to boil it, but the smoke from the fire drew artillery fire. They fled, Hahn tearing at the half-boiled chicken with his teeth and forcing the rubbery morsels down his throat as he ran.

'Goddamn!' Patton's voice, more high-pitched than ever, rang through the command post that warm evening.

Rosevich, sitting at his desk in the next room, couldn't help hearing the shout – when Patton was angry he didn't care if everyone knew it. Rosevich worried that perhaps he was the cause of Patton's anger and that Patton would storm out to vent his fury on one of his staff. The general mood at Headquarters always depended on that of Patton; everything revolved around him as if the staff were a swarm of bees.

But this time Patton stayed in his office, making telephone call after telephone call, his voice raised occasionally in anger. Rosevich heard him complain about a huge waste of precious time and about Montgomery stealing the show. Rosevich could always feel the dislike in Patton's tone when he talked about Montgomery. But it wasn't until Rosevich managed to question Patton's aide Colonel Charles Codman, a debonair Bostonian, that he found out what was upsetting his boss.

General Alexander, whom both Patton and Montgomery answered to, had ordered Patton to clear the Vizzini–Caltagirone road to make way for the British troops. It meant the Americans would have to return the way they had come before swinging north-westwards, a humiliating command. That would leave the way clear for Montgomery to reach the port-city of Messina in north-east Sicily. Patton was convinced that Montgomery had put Alexander up to this. Ever the keen horseman, Patton talked of a 'horse-race' against Montgomery. Rosevich couldn't see why Patton thought beating Montgomery mattered so much. To him, they were like prima donnas at the opera, always competing against each other.

Patton made no effort to disguise his resentment when he dictated his diary entry to Rosevich: 'Went to lunch at 1250. Generals Alexander, Cunningham . . . arrived at 1310 so I had to quit eating and see them. They gave us the future plan of operations . . . which cuts us off from any possibility of taking Messina. It is noteworthy that the Allied Commander of a British and an American Army had no Americans with him. What fools we are.'

Later, Rosevich told GIs who were also on Patton's staff about the General's anger and the race for Messina, and they all had fun imitating his voice. 'Goddamn!' they squeaked with as high a pitch as they could until their vocal cords ached.

When they'd calmed down, Rosevich asked: 'Are we fighting the Germans or Montgomery?'

'This isn't just about war, it's about ego. Patton wants to be Number One,' a friend said.

'Yeah. I guess Napoleon felt the same way,' Rosevich said.

As night came, the dilapidated forces of what used to be known as the Livorno Division began to pull out of the Mazzarino camp. The battle for Gela had failed, the Americans had advanced to the town of Butera further inland and the price paid in casualties was so high that the top brass had decreed the Division no longer even existed. Of its total force of 11,400 men, the Division had lost 214 officers and 7,000 junior officers and soldiers killed, wounded, missing in action, or made prisoner.

Messina had returned to Mazzarino on a truck to find the town emptied of its inhabitants who had pillaged the camp before seeking refuge in the hills. They had stolen his camera, the pictures of his girlfriends, his books and even his family letters.

Still weak after a short stay in the camp hospital recovering from his fever, he joined the men who set out under cover of darkness, as the Allies had supremacy over the skies, for the heart of Sicily. He found out that he was now part of what had been renamed the Livorno Grouping, but no one knew where they were headed. Superiors described the troop movement as 'a strategic retreat' but Messina, dejected and embittered, was convinced that the battle for Sicily had already been fought, and lost.

CHAPTER TWENTY-ONE

14 JULY

On the march inland towards Niscemi, refugees attached themselves to Johnson's unit and there was nothing he could do to shake them off. Most of the women, children and old men were from Gela, and they realised that as long as the invaders were unloading troops and equipment on the beaches, the area would remain dangerous. Johnson couldn't talk to them, so he couldn't explain that the best thing a civilian could do in war was get the hell away from anything military.

The rags they wore spoke volumes. Most of them were barefooted and some had fixed pieces of car-tyre to their feet with wire. Signor Mussolini, Johnson thought, had stripped them of almost everything they owned, and what they still had they carried in wicker baskets. A couple of women carried their babies wrapped in rags. One old man leaning on a stick led an emaciated jackass which pulled a gaily-coloured, two-wheel cart, typical of Sicily. Others had big rolls of bedding on their backs or on their heads.

The heat was worse than in the desert, because here it was moist, not dry. The late morning sun made the air so hot that Johnson felt he could taste it on his tongue and it tasted like brass. Perhaps the fact that he was waiting for an attack had something to do with that brass taste. Attacks always came sooner or later.

The glare from the sun made the men's eyeballs ache. Some tried marching head down and with their eyes shut, only opening them every few paces. As they all trudged inland, the fine white dust swirled up from the road. Passing supply vehicles kicked it up to tree-top height. It got into their mouths and noses, stuck to their skin and their clothes. Some tried to breathe

167

through their handkerchiefs. The sweat ran down the dust-caked faces of his buddies and Johnson thought it looked like mascara running down a woman's face when she cries.

They passed a couple of beautiful olive groves, but most of the Sicily they saw was dirt and dust, dust and dirt. It didn't seem to bother the locals. To make sauce for their pasta, they left pulped tomatoes on tables in the street, to dry in the sun. Dust and flies quickly became part of the recipe.

Shells hit the road, kicking up thick clouds. Johnson guessed immediately that they were from the crack of the cannon firing – 88mm artillery. He scrambled into a ditch, shouting: 'Fire mission!' to order his men to call in some shelling.

The refugees had no idea what to do. They started screaming and hollering and just sat down in the road.

Johnson beckoned furiously to the refugees closest to him. 'Come here, you damn fools!' he shouted.

A couple came. But most stayed on the road, and the shrapnel tore into them. It wounded one of the babies. Johnson tried not to look at the baby. It was the first time he had witnessed the effect of shelling on civilians. It meant something to him that these men, women and children weren't trying to fight anybody. All they wanted was to reach somewhere safe.

On one side of the road was a wheat field, and beyond that a line of trees which every so often bent sharply sideways as if kicked by a giant, each kick throwing up dust. The tell-tale concussion from the 88s told Johnson where to aim. He read off the wheat field's coordinates on his map, and gave the order for white phosphorus to be fired into the field. It burst into flames, belching smoke which he hoped would stop the shelling.

Johnson got lucky when his artillery hit what must have been a big ammunition dump, judging by the size of the explosion. A grey smoke ring drifted lazily up the hillside. It looked beautiful.

Repard was glad of the opportunity to stretch his legs on solid ground. The Captain had sent him ashore at Augusta on Sicily's east coast to replenish *Tartar*'s stores. Three days earlier, the port had surrendered quickly after a small fleet of German E-boats based there had destroyed its depot of torpedoes and supplies, before fleeing north. Their already weak will to fight sapped by such betrayal, the Italian troops manning Augusta's defences – among the strongest in all Sicily – had blown up their heavy coast guns, anti-aircraft batteries and fuel tanks.

Repard walked up to the port authority in search of the British officer in charge, whom he had known from Navy training days. A soldier indicated the officer's door. Repard knocked and went in. He found himself staring at the muzzle of a revolver pointing straight at him. The officer was sitting behind his desk, his hands wobbling as he struggled to hold the revolver steady.

Rooted to the spot, Repard managed to blurt out: 'Sir, it's David Repard. It's all right, sir. You know me. We met during training.'

The officer looked blankly at Repard for a moment, then put the gun down. 'Oh yes. What can I do for you?' he said.

Later, Repard was told that the officer had lost his nerve on the very first day he was due to set sail on the Hun-class destroyer under his command. He had arrived aboard in a flood of tears. Sent to recover ashore for several months, he was then given a planning post in Cairo and later the administrative job here at the port authority. Repard explained his business as briefly as possible, still shaken that he had come so close to being shot, and by a fellow-officer to boot.

With the help of a few peasants, who would have done anything for a few cigarettes, Repard picked lemons, grapes and almonds from the deserted countryside and sent them back to the destroyer. Before making his way back himself, he went for a swim and marvelled at the beauty of the clear, deep waters.

Young Sergeant George Mims came to Rosevich in tears. A tough, rough Southern boy, Mims had been Patton's driver for some time and Rosevich would never have guessed that he could break down like a little boy.

'I can't take what he's just done to me. I want to get a transfer to the front tomorrow,' Mims cried.

Bit by bit, Rosevich pieced together what had happened – Mims had made Patton late for a meeting and Patton had given him a dressing-down. But what upset Mims most was the fact that Patton had humiliated him by shouting at him in front of other people.

'He bawled me out. I won't stay any longer with that man,' Mims said.

Rosevich did his best to calm the sergeant down. He reminded Mims of how in north Africa Patton liked to let fly at senior officers and even fellow-generals and the way that even top brass would stand before Patton, hands shaking because they were so nervous. And they were tough, hard men with leathery skins, who had spent months and months in the desert.

'Patton expects people who work for him to be perfect all the time. He doesn't expect anyone to make mistakes. But it beats the front,' Rosevich said. Mims decided to stick with it.

Rosevich kept hidden his own fear that the same thing might happen to him, any day. He felt he had to do his absolute best for Patton all the time and he didn't know how long he would be able to keep going. What if the war lasted ten years? He would be an absolute wreck.

Johnson had shaken off the refugees by the time he got within sight of Caltagirone. He knew the Germans had probably dug in outside the town, but nothing had prepared him for the god-awful shrieking and whining sound which marked the start of the barrage of enemy rockets raining down close to him.

'*Neeeeow, neeeeow*' went the rockets, as they hit the earth in quick succession. It sounded like some machine dying of a terrible pain, six times over. He had no idea what this form of artillery was – nobody had briefed him about it. It was so strange that it terrified him. He felt as if the whole damn world was blowing up and that this time he was going to meet his maker.

'What in the hell is that?' Johnson yelled.

'Screaming Meemies!' someone shouted back. The rockets wailed and screeched as they flew through the air before punching the earth in batches of six at a time like mortar blows which shook the ground under Johnson's body. They didn't look very accurate but they covered such a big area they didn't need to be; they scared everyone and they claimed a number of casualties.

Knowing the Second Armored Division was close by, he radioed back to shout for tanks. Within ten minutes he spotted four clouds of dust powering down the hillside on a long straight road behind him. As they got closer, he saw they were Sherman tanks. Then he heard 88mm cannon and saw all four Shermans burst into flames.

Johnson and his men stayed put and waited. So much of war was just waiting.

'Goddamn, look at that!' someone shouted. An American light tank was tearing down the hillside.

Johnson watched with dismay. If the Shermans couldn't handle the 88mm cannon, what chance did a light tank have? he thought. Their armour was only one inch thick. But the light tank raced on down, the 88s crashing all around it. It sped into the valley and vanished.

'You see that? That's pretty slick,' Johnson said.

Out came another light tank, then another, until half-a-dozen of them had raced down the hillside and reached the valley safely. Charging in and out of ditches, darting behind buildings and then out again, they succeeded in crushing the German positions. None of them got hit. Johnson and his men lay on the ground watching, so tickled pink by the antics of the light tanks that they laughed like a bunch of idiots.

Johnson didn't feel like laughing later that day when an officer ordered him to turn back the way he had come. His 1st Infantry Division must leave the road clear for Canadian troops led by Montgomery. Previously allocated to the Americans, the road had suddenly been given to Montgomery so that he could continue unhindered his drive towards Messina on the north-east tip of the island.

Johnson was incensed. He wouldn't have minded giving up the road to an American outfit but this way he felt the GIs who had died on the march inland had died for nothing. His Division had fought for every foot of dirt in Sicily and now it had to pull back and start out on a big circle through the mountains at the heart of the island, towards its ancient capital, Enna.

All to make way for Montgomery. Johnson and his men detested him. 'That little wormy son-of-a-bitch ought to come here and then we'll kill him too,' one of his men said.

CHAPTER TWENTY-TWO

15 JULY

Described by one acquaintance as 'an insignificant being, with an upturned nose, two bright little black eyes, a pale face and thin lips', Claretta Petacci had become infatuated with Mussolini as a teenager, writing letters and poems to him in which she called him 'Divine Being'. She was in her early twenties, and married, when she became the favourite mistress of the dictator more than twice her age after approaching him at the seaside resort of Ostia outside Rome.

Early in their courtship, Mussolini summoned her mother to his office at Palazzo Venezia and asked her point-blank: 'Madam, do you permit me to love your daughter?' The answer must have been to Mussolini's liking because Petacci's husband, a pilot officer, was promptly despatched to Japan.

Her devotion to the Duce was remarkable. Virtually every afternoon, she left her sprawling villa in northern Rome in a taxi, and made for a prearranged location where a motorcycle and sidecar sent by the dictator awaited her. Hidden from view in the sidecar, she was then taken to an apartment next to his office in the Palazzo Venezia, where she would sometimes wait for as long as six hours for what was often only a brief encounter.

A stenographer at the Interior Ministry recorded one particular conversation in which Mussolini professed his love for Petacci. 'I love only you!' the dictator told her. 'The perfume of your kisses stupefies me, destroys me! When I look into your eyes I read the bottom of your soul! The world vanishes, I forget everything and everyone! . . . I want only our kisses, nothing else counts!' It was a declaration of love 'from a schoolboy to his first love', the stenographer commented, very different from the tone the Duce adopted with his other female conquests.

At 0035 on 15 July, Mussolini picked up the telephone and dialled Petacci's number.

'Goodnight,' Mussolini began. At the Interior Ministry, a stenographer was, as always, taking down the conversation.

'How are you, Ben dear?' Petacci asked.

'How should I be? If you mean my ailments, as usual, or worse. As for the rest, well, best not to speak of it!' he said.

'You must get a grip on yourself. You've overcome many other crises; you'll see that this time as well . . .'

'The fact is that I have never found myself in such circumstances before, whether physical or moral!'

'Do it for our love, Ben! You'll see that these will be momentary trifles.'

'They aren't at all trifles . . . Can't you see what's happening?' Mussolini asked.

'In the life of a man like you, there are always ups and downs. But you are too alone. You should perhaps talk to someone. Even people you least expect may be able to give you advice,' Petacci suggested.

'You don't realise that, even in my last speech, I made some stupid gaffes. I said things which didn't even make sense.'

'You mean the one about the "water-line"?' Petacci asked. In his speech, Mussolini had promised enemy invaders would be stopped on the 'water-line', when what he had meant was the tidemark on the shore.

'There! You too, like all the others, you mock me! I have become a laughing-stock for everyone with that damned word! I will go down in history not as the Duce of Fascism and the founder of the Empire, but simply as the "water-line"!' Mussolini said.

'Let's not exaggerate, Ben dear. I only said that because I didn't know which speech you meant; I had no wish to make fun of you. My love, how can you possibly think that I, who love you so much, could be as cruel as that when in fact I care so much about you?'

'Forgive me, my dear; but you must understand what a state I'm in. And anyway, it's the truth. Most Italians don't see things the way you do.'

'It's just an impression you have,' Petacci reassured him.

'Unfortunately, I know that's not the case. I have in front of me various reports which show I'm right. I'm not inventing things: the phrase has become common knowledge and it's bandied about as a joke, precisely by those very same people who came to applaud me at Piazza Venezia. Even the forces of repression, which used to spring into action if they heard just one word which they thought showed disrespect for me, now just issue a report. That's a really bad sign!'

'Let's hope that, at least this time, you are mistaken,' Petacci said.

'I know men well!' Mussolini told her.

Hahn and his companions marched down the road towards Caltagirone in the moonlight, singing obscene songs. The sounds of artillery behind and ahead of them told them that they were now in no-man's-land. After two days and nights, Hahn would soon be back with his unit and safe at last. Thinking of the long letter he would write to his parents, he wondered just how much the censors would cut.

The road led them down the hillside to a small bridge over a shallow river in a valley just below the town. Just as the men were about fifty yards from the bridge a flashlight on the other side was switched on, its beam blinding them.

'Don't shoot, we're Germans!' they shouted.

The reply from across the river was in German: 'Take cover!'

Seconds later, a big explosion ripped through the night. It seemed to send the entire bridge flying up into the air. Hahn cowered as blocks of stone rained down, splashing into the water and thudding into the ground.

The night became quiet again, and another shout came from across the river: 'Come over now!'

Unharmed, Hahn and the other fugitives picked their way

across the remains of the bridge. As soon as his men had got to the other side, Goldschmidt gave vent to his anger: 'You stupid idiots! Why did you blow up the bridge in front of us? You could have killed us! Who are you anyway?'

He found himself facing an agitated sergeant in charge of a unit of engineers of the Hermann Goering Division. Ignoring Goldschmidt, the sergeant ordered his men to surround the new arrivals and hold them at gunpoint. They must be Americans, he said, and should be shot on the spot.

'Don't be so stupid! No American would come down to the river like that. And besides, you must have heard we were singing German songs,' Goldschmidt retorted.

Neither the tank-crew's protests, nor the pay-books which they pulled out of their pockets, could persuade the sergeant that they were indeed Germans. He had them lined up against a wall. After all he had been though, Hahn thought, his own side was going to shoot him. But the still furious Goldschmidt insisted on speaking to the sergeant's superior and, after some heated exchanges, finally managed to make his compatriots accept the truth.

Fenner always avoided disgusting sights and made a point of averting his eyes from scenes of carnage. Over the past twenty-four hours alone he'd looked away when the pilot of a German Stuka fighter-bomber dropped down to earth like a rocket, his parachute on fire. Another time, he'd walked in the twilight past a reeking mess of burnt metal, paint and flesh which was all that was left of a half-dozen bombed Bren gun carriers. He didn't see the point in staring at things like that.

But there was nothing he could do to escape the stench which greeted him that afternoon at a junction close to Primosole Bridge. The smell hung heavy in the stifling air as something ahead blocked his column's advance. It was very different from the usual scents of wild sage, thyme, rosemary and other herbs which filled the air as tanks and other vehicles rolled over them.

On either side of the road flies were feasting on the twisted, lacerated bodies and carcasses of men, horses and mules. Nearby lay wrecked pillboxes and smashed signposts. The spot, named Dead Horse Corner, had first been the scene of an attack by RAF planes on an Italian unit and then of battles pitting the British against the Germans.

Fenner could hear the sound of fighting less than a mile further on. He supposed nobody had time to bury corpses. When there was any fighting going on, the first thing you did was dig a hole for yourself. Never mind about the chap who didn't need one any more.

As the platoon marched on, some ambulances – the men called them blood wagons – passed by, coming from the opposite direction. In one of them, Fenner saw a German, a corporal of the Panzer Grenadiers. He looked pretty sick and had a label hanging from his neck which Fenner knew would give his condition and medication.

The news spread quickly among the men. 'Aye, aye, Jerry's arrived,' a private said.

Ahead, Fenner heard, a long battle was being fought for control of Primosole Bridge which lay at the southern end of the Catania plain. After the British had captured the whole of south-eastern Sicily in just three days, the top brass saw the bridge as the key to the advance northwards, because it carried the road from Syracuse to Catania. Beyond it lay not only a major airfield but also Catania's industrial port.

Primosole had already changed hands several times. British paratroopers of the First Parachute Brigade – their aircraft fresh targets for friendly fire from the Allied fleet as they flew in – had seized it first on the night of 13–14 July. They overcame not only Italian and German forces which were well-entrenched there, but also German paratroopers who had been dropped in the very same area a few hours earlier. The British got off to a good start and managed to dismantle explosive charges set by the Germans to destroy the bridge but a counter-attack then swept them off it.

In the morning hours before Fenner's arrival, a battalion of the Durhams, the 9th, had attempted to retake the bridge. Many drowned trying to cross the river by the bridge, weighed down by their heavy packs of equipment and 200 rounds of extra ammunition slung around their necks. Those that got across fought hand to hand with the enemy but the attack failed. The British lost more than a hundred men.

Soon, Fenner thought, it would be his turn to cross that river.

Making as little noise as possible as they moved through the night, Johnson and his men inspected cave after cave in the mountains west of Enna, looking for Italian or German troops who might be hiding there. The caves worried Johnson because they were ideal hiding places for the enemy – they would be able to hear and see him first, and could easily surprise him with a bullet out of the darkness.

Johnson was just emerging from one he had stopped to check when he heard something he hadn't heard since landing in Sicily – music, and a woman singing. It seemed to come from another cave up ahead. He clambered over some rocks towards the sounds, his men following. No one said anything. There was no need to; they knew you checked anything out of the ordinary, and this certainly was.

Light danced on the rock wall at the wide mouth of the cave. He walked into a vast cavern and then stopped in his tracks. A beautiful young woman whose long auburn hair reached almost down to her waist and gleamed in the flickering light of a bonfire, was singing solo. A few civilians, one of them playing the accordion, sat around the fire, listening. They were refugees, he guessed, but they looked happy and safe.

The woman stopped singing when she saw Johnson and his men. She looked scared, so Johnson tried to reassure her with hand gestures. His men quickly searched the cave, found no sign of any soldiers and sat down by the fire to get a bit of a rest.

No longer afraid of them, the girl started to sing again, both Italian and American songs. Johnson couldn't take his eyes off her, or tear himself away from the sound of her voice. When he did look around him, Johnson suddenly became aware that the cavern had filled with several dozen American soldiers. All of the dirty, mean, gun-toting soldiers were staring at the woman. He must look just like them, he thought. And like them, he drank her in.

Bathed in moonlight, Sicily looked peaceful from the top of the ridge overlooking Primosole Bridge. Fenner, wondering when the order to attack would come, scanned the fertile plain which stretched seven miles from the River Simeto below him to Catania. The city clung to the slope of Mount Etna and, filtering out from the top of the volcano, he could see a little white plume of smoke.

What with the view and the shade from trees overhead, it was a lovely spot. The Luftwaffe personnel from the airfield closer to Catania obviously thought so too, judging by the large tent, empty bottles of German beer and odd bits of uniform they had left behind. Fenner wondered if they had brought their girlfriends here for a bit of a frolic. It was far enough from the airfield to be safe during bombing raids.

The only downside was the mosquitoes. Fenner and his men were forced to wear long trousers all the time even though the cloth made their legs clammy with sweat. One soldier quipped that anyone outside his net after 1900 would be lifted by the little blighters and carried away.

Nothing moved on Primosole Bridge itself, 1,200 yards away. Its name meant 'first sun' in Italian, but there wasn't anything attractive about it at all. A web of iron girders 400 feet long, it was flanked on Fenner's side of the river by a concrete pillbox, into which a British glider had smashed.

To the left, the countryside was flat with plenty of cover for the Germans Fenner knew were hiding there – thick vineyards stretched for a quarter of a mile along the road that ran as straight as an arrow to Catania. To the right were more vineyards, a small wood and then marshland which spread towards the coast just over a mile away. To cap it all, poplars, eucalyptus trees, shrubs and hedges grew on either side of the road as far as he could see.

Fenner was grateful for the fact that he wouldn't be venturing into that battlefield tonight. Another battalion, the 8th Durhams, had been picked to launch an attack in the small hours and artillery observers were milling about in the open on top of the ridge and on its forward slope, choosing their vantage-points.

Fenner's platoon was resting on the same ridge. Private Ben Dickenson, at the age of only thirty the oldest man in the platoon, goose-stepped up and down clad in a Luftwaffe greatcoat he had found lying about. Dickenson, a thick-set Liverpudlian with a broad accent, was a very good soldier – Fenner had told him he could become a sergeant, but he was happier as a private – and the self-appointed company clown. His antics caused great laughter, the padded shoulders going down a treat.

'Aye, aye, spiv!' the men shouted.

Fenner didn't feel like laughing, and put a stop to the mock-parade. There was a good chance the Germans might see them from across the river, and start shelling at any time. He told his men to keep out of sight.

A senior officer sent Fenner to make contact with the Durhams' 9th battalion, which was on a slope to the east. He came across two soldiers, grey-faced with fatigue and stress. He was surprised to see how exhausted they looked and listened quietly as they told him what they had been through: a forced night move through hostile territory, followed by a daylight attack, and then a German counter-attack which had driven them back and pinned them down in the open under fire from 88mm cannon and a new type of machine-gun, called the Spandau, which fired 1,200 rounds a minute. The soldiers hadn't slept in two days.

CHAPTER TWENTY-THREE

16 JULY

From his trench, which was so narrow and crammed with soldiers he had to sit with his knees up, Fenner couldn't see anything of the battle raging over a thousand yards away across the river below him as the Durhams' 8th battalion attempted to recover the ground lost the previous morning. But next to him crouched an artillery officer who kept up a running commentary from the moment the shelling began at 0050.

'Heavy artillery starting,' the gunner said as the British guns boomed before the troops attacked.

Then, an hour and ten minutes later: 'That's the artillery finished, you should hear the small arms fire now.'

On cue, Fenner heard the sounds of the infantry coming to grips with each other: the bursts from tommy guns and machine-pistols; the slow tap of Bren guns and the sheet-ripping sound of the faster Spandau machine-guns; and the crump of grenades. He pictured the men fighting at close quarters among the vines.

Some time into the attack, shells started dropping on the ridge where Fenner's battalion was spending the night. He cursed his fellow-soldiers for walking about so carelessly a few hours earlier – they had clearly given away their position to the Germans. But he was relieved to see that only about a third of the shells exploded and those that did failed to cause any casualties.

Fenner hadn't been given any orders yet but he was as sure as night follows day that his turn would not be long in coming. There were no other fresh troops around. Later, Fenner heard a rumour that the shelling was from a big gun on a train which ferried it in and out of a tunnel, some six miles away.

＊　＊　＊

Halfway through the morning, the chaplain came up to Messina and two fellow-officers as they stood by the side of a road skirting a broad valley north of Enna where the River Dittaino ran. During the day, the Italians spent most of their time resting and hiding from the enemy. They moved at night, sometimes on foot, sometimes in trucks, Messina's sense of shame quashed by the realisation that if he didn't keep retreating, the Allies would catch up with him.

The Italian Army could not have been in greater disarray. Many Sicilian soldiers had abandoned their uniforms and were now dressed in civilian clothes, ready to rejoin their families. Others had returned home from the mainland on the pretext of joining the battle in Sicily, but as soon as they reached the island, they too went home to find their loved ones.

Messina gave the chaplain a warm welcome; he hadn't seen him since the eve of the defeat at Gela on the coast.

'Have you received absolution?' the chaplain asked.

'Yes, Father, you gave it to us before we went into combat,' Messina replied.

'Well we have a bit of time now, why don't we renew the holy service? We should pray for our friends who are no longer with us,' the chaplain said.

Messina nodded readily. He and his companions took turns to kneel down before the chaplain. Messina confessed a couple of sins to do with girls and some oaths. His companions were within hearing distance, but the sins he described briefly were so minor he felt no embarrassment.

'I absolve you of your sins, my son, in the name of the Father, the Son and the Holy Ghost,' the chaplain intoned as he touched Messina's forehead with holy oil from his little phial.

'Amen,' Messina replied.

The chaplain was about to take his leave when three trucks suddenly braked hard in a cloud of dust just opposite them. The doors of the trucks' cabins swung open and men jumped out, shouting as they ran to the far side of the road: 'Planes, planes, planes!' One yelled that the trucks contained ammunition.

The only shelter near enough was a small dry ditch at the roadside, so shallow it could barely contain Messina and his three companions. Somehow an order of precedence was established in a few fractions of a second, with the result that the chaplain lay at the bottom of the ditch, with three men as flat as they could make themselves on top of him. For some reason – perhaps because he was the youngest – Messina ended up on top of the pile. His body was virtually level with the surface of the road, only a few yards away from a truck loaded with ammunition.

Five 'redheads', or Spitfires, bore down on the road, machine-guns rattling as they tried to hit the trucks. Messina could feel the gust of hot air as each Spitfire swooped past, flying about a hundred feet above ground. He stayed as still as possible, squashing his face down in the nape of the man underneath him.

He felt bizarre. It was as if his mind had detached itself from his body, and he was looking down on it from several dozen feet in the air. Uncle Antonio, who had died fighting in Albania, and Saint Anthony, whom his family venerated, were both there in the ditch with him too. With the coolness of a surgeon observing a patient, he saw his body shake with fear as the bullets struck the road.

Messina heard the boxes of ammunition in the truck close to him begin to explode. Shells destined for anti-aircraft guns burst in all directions as the Spitfires pulled away and vanished.

The rain of ammunition slowly came to a stop. Messina got to his feet and he and his friends hugged and kissed each other on the cheeks effusively. The drivers of the trucks kept apologising, as if they had been responsible for the attack. The chaplain emerged from the ditch, and smiled at Messina. Messina smiled back, and cracked a couple of jokes.

But for a whole half-hour, he couldn't stop his body shaking. He had felt fear before, especially when he had crawled through the artillery barrage near Gela, but then he had been able to control – even analyse – his fear. This time was different. Now he knew the real meaning of fear. His nerves were shattered and the thought that his life hung by a thread began to torture him.

As he'd expected, Fenner received a warning to be ready to attack under cover of darkness. Since launching its attack the night before, the 8th battalion had managed to secure a small bridge-head on the other side of the river. But the Germans launched a hefty counter-attack, and Fenner heard the battle drag on through the long, stifling day. The men fought hand-to-hand as Durhams crept up on Germans hiding in the vineyards and bayoneted them.

Fenner and his men were to pull out of their positions on top of the ridge that night, drop down the side of the hill, and advance towards the river in single file. His company would be the second of three companies in the lead.

After fording the river to the left of 8th battalion's position, the men would line up on the bank and then move forward to capture a sunken road which had become known as Spandau Alley. It did not feature on the maps and had given a lot of trouble to the British because of the machine-guns which gave the road its name. The plan was so simple it seemed the most obvious one possible and Fenner approved of simplicity; he felt that in battle simplicity was essential.

'Get as much sleep as you can,' a senior officer told Fenner.

When Fenner got back to his men after receiving the orders, he found that a battery of Priests – 105mm self-propelled guns – had started pumping away from behind him. So much for getting some sleep.

In the hour before midnight, Fenner and his men got ready to abandon their position overlooking Primosole Bridge. He did his best to push fear and worry to the back of his mind and concentrate on the job.

A sergeant came up to Fenner. 'Sir, Morris has left,' the

sergeant said. Morris was a good soldier, a platoon veteran, wounded in both El Alamein and Gazala.

'How do you know?' Fenner asked.

'We think he's hiding in some caves behind the battalion area,' the sergeant replied.

What a nuisance, Fenner thought. This was no time to send out a search party. Fenner would report the news later. It wasn't a complete surprise; Fenner had censored a few of Morris's letters home and it was clear the man was under strain. But Fenner would never have guessed that he would desert only minutes before a battle.

Fenner saw Morris's rifle lying by his slit trench, and picked it up. He decided to take it into battle with him. For one thing, it was a more effective weapon than his own gun, even though it was the same model the British had used in the First World War. Anyone wandering around on a battlefield with a pair of binoculars around his neck, a map-case slung around his shoulder, and no rifle, was sure to be recognised as an officer and shot at by a sniper.

To the north-west, closer to Mount Etna, the sergeant-major singled out Hahn: 'You've been promoted for bravery, you do the job. Take a truck, go to Gerbini airfield, and bring back as many of the bombs the Luftwaffe has left behind as you can. We can't let them get into enemy hands, our engineers will blow them up.'

Hahn nodded. Although he had been awarded the Iron Cross, Second Class on his return to his Division, he didn't feel particularly brave. He'd got the distinction for destroying enemy tanks, taking prisoners, and escaping through enemy territory. But he hadn't taken any prisoners – the Americans at the farmhouse were so numerous it would have been impossible. He comforted himself with the thought that his father, who had won the Iron Cross, First Class during the First World War, would be pleased for him whatever the precise circumstances.

As he'd lost his tank, the award didn't stop Hahn being reduced to the status of infantryman. He was appointed to head a platoon, but disliked the infantry so much he didn't see it as promotion. He'd trained as a tanker, and tankers were part of an elite whose commanders were mostly aristocrats, not like run-of-the-mill infantrymen. Besides, he would be virtually naked on the battlefield, vulnerable to all the bullets and shells and shrapnel whistling about.

Thankful that Günther, his guitar-playing former tank commander, had volunteered to accompany him, together with half-a-dozen private soldiers, Hahn set out for the airfield west of Catania at night in a seven-ton truck. They drove past the last German outpost and continued as slowly and as quietly as they could, headlights out, to the airfield some 300 yards further ahead in no-man's-land.

They found the bombs easily enough, piled high in big wooden crates. Carrying a machine-gun, Hahn clambered up one pile and, perched on top, acted as look-out while the others lifted crates into the truck. As the men worked, at a snail's pace as it seemed to him, Hahn reflected ruefully that he would have been much safer in his tank. This was a typical 'Himmelfahrt', a mission which could easily send him heavenwards. One machine-gun burst into the pile of bombs and off he would go.

CHAPTER TWENTY-FOUR

17 JULY

Shortly after midnight, as Fenner picked his way down a dry ditch under the clear starry sky, one of some 300 men in single file, he reached out with his left hand and took hold of the leather scabbard which dangled from the waist of the soldier in front of him. It was the best way he knew of ensuring he stuck to the zigzag route they had to follow.

It was impossible to walk straight because of the corpses strewn on the ground. Fenner recognised the uniforms of both British and German paratroopers and infantry, many of them burnt, like the vegetation all around them, by phosphorus bombs and tracer bullets. One completely blackened corpse sat upright on the side of the ditch, staring sightlessly at Fenner as he struggled past. Fenner saw that even the face was black, before he remembered to turn away.

Once near the river, and finding a clear patch of ground, he sat himself down to wait for the signal to cross. Everyone was very quiet; he could hear bullfrogs croaking in the burnt-out reeds. Fenner had no girlfriend to think about, so he simply concentrated on the mission ahead.

'Fix bayonets.' The order passed among the men.

'I never use it, why should I bother to fix it?' grumbled Dickenson, the regimental comedian. He got a subdued laugh. Then, having expressed his opinion, he too pulled his bayonet out of its scabbard and fixed it. It was still dark, but no one needed to see to fix a bayonet. Rifles and machine-guns were cocked.

Shortly before H-Hour, set for 0100, Fenner got up and started making his way down to the edge of the river, through reeds and more bodies. He reached the river-bank, slid down and – holding onto a wire stretched across the river as a guide – he slid into the water.

His feet sank at once into mud and it was hard work to keep going. The water reached up to his chest but its gentle, cool flow was refreshing. There was no sound from the other side of the river. He couldn't see the bridge but knew that it was further down to his right. After wading through some thirty yards of water, he scrambled up the bank on the other side and through more tall reeds. He lay flat with his platoon, waiting for H-Hour. Spandau Alley, the sunken lane with its row of machine-guns, was some 400 yards further on through vineyards.

H-Hour was still several minutes away when someone said: 'What are we waiting for?'

'Let's get stuck in,' another voice echoed.

The men got up and started to walk quickly through the closely planted vines. Each man was only some five feet away from the next one. Fenner was vaguely aware of the enemy some-where ahead firing at them. He glimpsed some isolated Germans running away, but he didn't get a chance to fire a shot. Some snipers seemed to be firing from behind the olive and heavily laden lemon trees dotted among the vines.

Fenner kept on going as the Spandaus in the sunken road opened up, spitting blindly as their gunners couldn't see the British in the dark. Red, white and green tracer swept past Fenner at knee height. Bullets ripped through the vines, scattering the leaves and pulverising the bunches of grapes. Shattered orange trees gave off a bitter-sweet smell. Several men were hit but the line of infantry kept advancing.

A little further ahead, the British walked straight into an artillery barrage. They halted abruptly and threw themselves to the ground. Several of the men cursed – they had come under fire from British artillery before, and they were sure the guns firing at them now were British too.

'When I get out of this, I'll do those bloody gunners!' Dickenson shouted. He got another laugh.

Fenner thought Dickenson was a little optimistic. Shells were dropping all around them. One gun fired its shells at precisely the same spot, in the middle of the company, with great regularity. They threw up a lot of earth, but no one was hurt. At least the barrage silenced the Spandaus.

When it lifted, the company got up as one man and rushed forward again. Fenner had only been running a few seconds when he was brought up short by a hedge of cactus and prickly pears. The dagger-sharp leaves and needles scratched him as he forced his way through to find himself on the edge of Spandau Alley itself. Below him in the sunken lane, a group of Germans stood with their hands up.

Fenner's platoon had taken eight prisoners, six of them injured. He looked around and saw that the Germans had dug slit trenches on one side of the lane. They had placed their Spandau machine-guns there, creating fields of fire through the cactus and prickly pears which grew closely together, three to five feet high, and afforded perfect cover.

Cratered with shell holes, the place was littered with German parachute equipment, torn blood-stained clothing, belts of ammunition and broken rifles – and British and German corpses. Fenner's men took the prisoners' weapons, made them sit down, and handed cigarettes around to calm them down and stop them causing trouble.

There was no time to lose. The platoon must set up defensive positions as the Germans could counter-attack at any moment. Apart from the pop of small arms fire, things were quiet in Fenner's area but he could hear the sound of battle from further east. As the men assembled, Fenner realised about a third of his platoon was missing, but refused to let himself stop to worry about what had happened to them.

In the first light of day, he got out his entrenching tool – a pathetic instrument, he always thought – and started scraping away at the ground. He saw that several of the soldiers had managed to get hold of the ones the Germans carried, which were much more efficient. They were soon digging in at great speed, shovelling the earth which was soft and dark as if full of soot.

One of the prisoners, who were all paratroopers, could speak quite good English and announced that he was Austrian. 'Funny how so many Germans suddenly become Austrians when we catch them,' Fenner thought to himself. They must think being Austrian was more acceptable but to Fenner it made no difference at all.

Dickenson called out to Fenner: 'Sir, there's a German who wants to know whether he'll be sent to Canada now that he's been captured. He's going on and on about it.'

'How the Hell do I know whether he's going to be sent to Canada?' Fenner said. Obviously a chap who looks far ahead, he thought.

At about 0800 with the sun already making the stink of Spandau Alley stronger than ever, Captain Glass, the company commander, told Fenner he was going to try and make contact with the company on their right, and was going to take a couple of chaps with him.

Glass hadn't been away long when shooting started up again. The noise was coming not from further ahead where he knew the German front line was, but from behind him. He guessed they must be Germans overrun by the British advance who were now desperate to move back, cross the front line and rejoin their units. Well hidden in the vines, they were full of fight. Fenner and his men did their best to tackle them by snap shooting and immediately ducking out of sight but the Germans let fly as soon as they made the slightest move. Fenner saw they were paratroopers dressed in camouflage smocks, their faces covered by veils of green netting.

Suddenly, he spotted a group of Germans coming up the sunken lane towards him, from the direction in which Glass had gone. They hadn't seen the British. Fenner's platoon opened up with everything they had, including rifles and submachine-guns, but the Germans kept coming. Fenner had found a German Schmeisser machine-pistol and he fired as much of the Germans' ammunition back at them as he could. He was usually a good shot but because everyone was joining in he had no way of telling if he had hit the attackers. He heard the sound of screaming coming from the group and then they slowly put their hands up.

Fenner's soldiers moved among this fresh batch of prisoners, confiscating their arms. There were twenty-eight Germans in all, many of them wounded in the torso and arms. Fenner looked away when his men confiscated the Germans' watches. He knew this was wrong but they were his friends and reprimanding them was out of the question. Besides, stealing watches from prisoners was standard practice, as the British Army was so stingy they couldn't afford to buy any. And everyone having a watch made sentry duty run smoothly.

The prisoners sat quietly, several of them eating their way through the small packets of cheese they carried with them. A private handed what looked like bits of rag to a big blond figure, a typical Aryan with blue eyes. They were badges of rank, and the blond German fixed them back on his shoulder. He must have taken them off earlier, thinking it would be easier for him to escape if he hid his identity as a lieutenant. Moments later, another of the prisoners also put his badges back on his shoulder. Two lieutenants captured, Fenner thought, that's pretty good going.

Captain Glass turned up, beaming. He had spotted the Germans in good time and been able to take cover until they passed. He was delighted his company had dealt with them quickly.

A private called to Fenner. 'Look at this, sir,' he said, holding out a handful of what looked like small white tickets which he had found as he went through the pockets of several of the prisoners.

Fenner looked closely, and saw that the words printed on them were in French. 'Madame Pauline', read one of them, and underneath, 'Mademoiselle . . .' with a space for the young woman's name to be filled in. The names Fifi and Zouzou had been pencilled in many more times than any of the others.

A couple of the Germans explained that the tickets were from brothels in Marseilles. The Germans had flown from the South of France three days earlier, and the tickets were for customers to book the girl they wanted. Even the price was scribbled against each name. As soon as word got round, Fenner's men stood about laughing and the Germans joined in. Fenner laughed too.

At the usual noon military conference in the Wolf's Lair, his advanced headquarters at Rastenburg in East Prussia, Hitler turned his attention to the Italian theatre.

The news from Sicily did nothing to lighten the gloomy atmosphere in the Wolf's Lair, a complex of drab wooden buildings and bunkers on the outskirts of a dense forest of fir and pine trees. Buried beneath six feet of concrete, it reminded Hitler's own interpreter, Schmidt, of the fable of the wicked witch. Mussolini's son-in-law, Count Galeazzo Ciano, had been struck by 'the sadness of that damp forest and the boredom of collective life . . . There isn't one spot of colour.'

The Sicilian invasion had come just as Hitler was forced to call off Operation Citadel, an offensive against the Red Army at Kursk, after history's biggest tank battle. The German losses had handed the Russians the initiative, and Hitler feared the fighting in Sicily might force him to send reinforcements from the Russian front which needed all the men he could muster.

Addressing the conference, the Führer informed his military chiefs that he had 'personally meditated' on the best course to follow in Italy. The biggest problem, he told them, was general demoralisation in the Army. If only a few units were affected, he said, it would be possible to appeal to their sense of honour and to offer them medals as a reward.

But there was no denying that the entire Army was in a state of collapse and only 'barbaric measures' could save the nation. A directory, a tribunal or a court-martial must be set up in Italy with the task of 'eliminating undesirable elements', Hitler concluded. He found it impossible to believe that everything in Italy could go to the dogs so quickly.

The Führer resolved that he must talk to Mussolini as soon as possible. Only if the situation in Italy could be radically reversed and traitors eliminated, he concluded, would it be worthwhile for Germany to send more troops to Italy.

In the meantime, the German commanders on the ground in Sicily were ordered to redouble their efforts to fortify their hold over the north-east of the island and keep the way open for an evacuation to the mainland, should the need arise.

The battle for Primosole Bridge was over by lunchtime. A senior officer sent Fenner off to locate B Company and he found himself wandering through scenes of devastation on a battlefield which stretched over only a few acres. The three Durham battalions had suffered more than 500 casualties and together with over 300 German dead, their bodies, or what was left of them, lay haphazardly among the crushed grapevines, gnarled trunks of ancient olive trees torn to shreds, amputated poplars and eucalyptus trees and smashed guns and other equipment.

Lacerated British and German bodies often lay so near each other it was clear the men had fought at close contact. Fenner could tell from the stripes on their uniforms – black pips on a red background – and from their black cap badges that many of the dead were from his own 6th battalion. Two stretcher-bearers had been shot and wounded as they carried an injured soldier. The soldier lay dead on the stretcher. Flies gorged themselves on the wounds.

On Primosole Bridge itself British tanks had crushed British soldiers as well as the enemy in the rush to get across as quickly as possible. Twenty-two Germans had been gummed to the melting tarmac after British paratroopers set their vehicles alight with a two-pound Gammon bomb. Their cargoes of petrol and ammunition had blown up in the explosion.

Just below the bridge, a dozen or so rifles had been stuck into a small mound of freshly dug earth. Helmets and berets rested on top of the rifles. Over both the dead and the survivors hung a pall of white dust, and the horribly sweet smell of death.

It was the worst carnage Fenner had ever seen in such a small area. Veterans who had served in his battalion since the fall of France in 1940, who had been through Gazala, El Alamein and Mareth, told him that they too had never seen so much slaughter and destruction in so small a space. The toll at Primosole was so terrible that the British and the Germans took the almost unheard-of decision to organise a temporary ceasefire, allowing each side to collect their wounded. Germans and British shouted to each other, showing the enemy where their casualties lay.

The exhausted Durham survivors, sweating heavily in the heat, spent much of the rest of that day tidying up the battlefield. Little rough wooden crosses, made from British ration boxes, sprouted here and there. Close to Spandau Alley, later renamed Stink Alley, soldiers dug a mass grave. Twenty men from Fenner's battalion were buried there, a chaplain conducting a makeshift service. Fenner's battalion lost a total of 120 men and another battalion, the 9th Durhams, lost a hundred. Many of the 300 or so German dead were simply pushed into their slit trenches and covered with the earth they had themselves dug up before dying.

PART 3

THE DOWNFALL

18–25 July

CHAPTER TWENTY-FIVE

18–19 JULY

Hitler's abrupt summons on 18 July to an 'urgent' summit conference, which must take place the following day, profoundly irritated Mussolini. To his son-in-law, Count Ciano, Mussolini complained that he was sick of 'being summoned by the sound of a bell. That's how waiters are summoned.'

Mussolini, whom Hitler had initially admired as a model and praised for his 'superior intellect', hated to be reminded just how much his fellow-dictator had outshone him. In one attempt to emulate Hitler, the Duce had copied the German goose-step, which he considered 'the greatest spectacle in the world'. During one military parade, he rushed from his podium to the head of a column and goose-stepped along to the amazement of onlookers. But the new marching step led to a propaganda disaster as his soldiers, lacking the long legs of the much taller Germans, produced what one Italian marshal described as 'a ridiculous show of mechanical dwarfs'.

In their most recent meetings, Mussolini had been subjected to tirades by Hitler which lasted several hours. Anxious to ensure that the Duce would not be verbally crushed by Hitler yet again the following day, his military chiefs pleaded with him to be forceful. With an Allied invasion of the Italian mainland expected any moment, they urged him to insist that Italy had no alternative but to repatriate the thirty-six divisions he had spread across the Balkans, the Aegean Sea and the South of France. It would be impossible, they told him, to withstand an invasion of the mainland with only the thirteen divisions currently deployed in the country.

Mussolini's Chief of Staff, General Ambrosio, stressed that

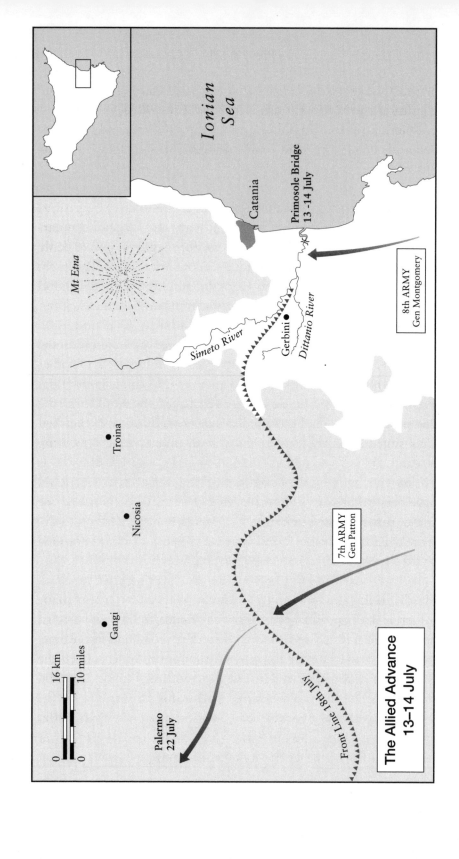

Ionian Sea

Catania

Primosole Bridge
13 -14 July

8th ARMY
Gen Montgomery

Mt Etna

Simeto River

Gerbini

Dittanio River

Troina

Nicosia

7th ARMY
Gen Patton

Gangi

16 km

10 miles

Palermo
22 July

Front Line 18th July

**The Allied Advance
13–14 July**

he must make clear to Hitler that the Italian military was in no condition to resist for long. Sicily could not be defended without German help. Mussolini promised to be firm, and agreed to demand that Hitler send reinforcements to both Sicily and the rest of Italy.

Hahn stared in amazement and grabbed his machine-pistol as 600 yards or so in front of his trench bare-chested figures wearing shorts started running around in crazy zigzags. He suddenly realised that a dozen enemy soldiers, Scots from the Black Watch, or the Argyll and Sutherland Highlanders – his superiors didn't know which – had emerged from their trenches not to attack but to play an evening game of football.

Over the previous few days, Hahn had got accustomed to the ridiculous sound of bagpipes from the enemy trenches on the other side of the Gerbini airstrip, which was little more than a flat meadow. By some tacit accord, the last two hours or so of the day were always quiet, the war as if suspended before the sun set. This suited Hahn well as it was a good time to have something to eat.

The Germans could have shot the players but what would have been the point of doing that? The more Hahn watched the game, the more it struck him as a perfectly normal thing to do. If he'd had a ball, he found himself thinking, he and his men could have played too.

Hardly in the best of moods, Mussolini waited for Hitler's plane to arrive at Treviso airport north of Venice on the morning of 19 July. He had arrived there earlier that morning from Rome, flying his plane himself for part of the journey. He noticed the gloomy attitude of the Italian Air Force officers and troops who had been lined up as a welcoming party for Hitler.

At 0852, the big Focke-Wulf Condor plane carrying Hitler appeared. It made one large sweeping circuit of the airport, as was usual, but then began to make a second.

'Why on earth is he going round again?' someone wondered.

Baron Hans Georg von Mackensen, Hitler's ambassador to Rome, explained: 'It is three minutes to nine and the arrival is fixed for nine o'clock precisely.'

The Condor landed and Hitler emerged, shuffling as he walked. One of the waiting Italians thought he looked older: the stooped figure was 'like a dead larva; there was something unreal about him.'

Mussolini greeted Hitler effusively – Hitler reciprocating in a cooler manner – then the two men got into a car bound for the nearest railway station. They would not have much time together. The Führer was due to return to Germany that same afternoon, and much of the two leaders' time would be spent travelling to and from the venue chosen for the talks: a seventeenth-century villa at the foot of the Italian Alps, an hour away by train and car.

On his arrival at the Villa Gaggia, Mussolini found himself leading his guest through an SS ring of steel which encircled the sprawling mansion. The villa itself was such a maze that it felt to him like 'a nightmarish labyrinth of large and small rooms'. He had expected to be alone with Hitler but instead the two leaders were joined in the ornate ballroom by a host of German generals. As one of the few Italians present commented later, this was 'humiliating and offensive'.

For an hour Mussolini sat in silence on the edge of his armchair which was too wide and too deep for him, his hands clasped on his crossed legs, while Hitler, documents piled up on his lap, delivered one of his notorious monologues, justifying more than ever before Mussolini's description of him as 'a gramophone with just seven tunes and once he had finished playing them he started all over again'.

The concept of total war, Hitler explained at length, meant that 'not one inch of conquered land' could be abandoned. Raw materials everywhere, from northern Norway to the Balkans and from the Ukraine to France, were too vital as was the need to keep the war as far as possible from the Fatherland.

Much of what Hitler said was simply lost on Mussolini. The Duce prided himself on his German and he refused to use an interpreter but in fact it was barely fluent enough for a simple conversation.

At noon, Mussolini's private secretary, pale-faced, entered the ballroom and, apologising for the interruption, walked up to the Duce and handed him a piece of paper. Hitler paused.

Mussolini read the note out loud, translating it into German: 'At this very moment, Rome is undergoing a violent air raid.'

Hitler showed no reaction. For a time no one spoke. It was the first time that Rome had been bombed since the beginning of the war.

'I want detailed news,' Mussolini said to his secretary.

'I've already tried. But in Rome the telephones are disconnected. Communications are down,' the secretary said.

'Persevere,' Mussolini said.

The secretary left the room and, after another short silence, Hitler began to speak again.

The Führer's voice became more and more strident as if he was addressing a large crowd. His glare fixed on Mussolini, he branded as 'inept and cowardly' the conduct of Italian personnel, both in Sicily and the rest of southern Italy, for failing to prevent the destruction of fighter-planes on the ground.

The Axis must decide whether it should actually fight in Sicily. 'If we do, we will have to bear all the consequences of our decisions in a fanatical spirit. If we do not want these battles, every man we send to Sicily will have been sent in vain,' Hitler said. The alternative was to fight the decisive battle on the Italian mainland.

Mussolini still sat in silence, enduring Hitler's delivery which he had once compared to that of 'a biblical prophet'. Every so often, in a nervous tic, the Duce would stroke his aggressive-looking chin with his right hand. Sometimes he also reached behind his back with his left hand, and pressed a place where he was apparently feeling discomfort. Occasionally, he breathed a long sigh.

His secretary reappeared, and the Duce virtually tore the slip of paper from his hands. Interrupting Hitler, Mussolini read aloud, in German: 'The violent bombardment continues; some 400 aircraft flying at a very low altitude; suburbs and also buildings in the centre seriously hit; scant reaction from anti-aircraft batteries.'

Hitler resumed his oratory. He announced that as soon as the winter was over he was going to use 'two new weapons' against the British. He said he preferred not to give any details, but added that the British would have no means of defending themselves.

Mussolini, as he confided later, felt his own will-power ebb away as he listened to Hitler and began to wonder whether they might not both be slightly mad.

For a full two hours after that, Mussolini endured Hitler's monologue. The Führer's speech had turned into a denunciation of Italian cowardice. His solution was to execute every soldier and every officer who deserted their Army or Navy battery while there was still so much as a single shot left in the entire unit. It was 'a problem of training'.

'What has happened now in Sicily must not be allowed to happen again!' Hitler exclaimed.

Trapped in his armchair, in which he shifted uneasily, Mussolini had twice passed a handkerchief over his face – a gesture which struck his staff as odd, as he rarely sweated. He appeared to be in pain.

Five minutes short of one o'clock, a tall and elegant German aide-de-camp walked stiffly up to Hitler and whispered something in his ear. Carried away by his own words, Hitler went on speaking as if he had heard nothing. The Axis was going through a difficult period, he said, but everything would be certainly overcome if all countries, and chiefly Italy, demonstrated firmness of spirit and an iron will to resist and to fight.

After five minutes, the aide-de-camp again approached and whispered into Hitler's ear, with robot-like respect. The Führer stopped speaking and looked displeased. The Italians thought some important and urgent piece of news had arrived. But in fact the news concerned lunch; the meal had been scheduled for one o'clock, and since German protocol considered Hitler a guest of Mussolini, his staff had intervened to ensure the timing was respected.

After a brief lunch, Mussolini met his advisers. They were dismayed when he immediately told them: 'I am very upset to be away from the capital at such a moment. I would not like the Romans to think . . .' The Duce's only concern was simply his fear that the people of Rome might think that he had known about the raid in advance and had arranged his meeting with Hitler on purpose.

One of Mussolini's advisers dared to suggest to him that he might consider extricating himself from the war – with Hitler's consent – but the Duce reacted impatiently.

'Are we willing to cancel with a single stroke twenty years of regime? To destroy the fruits of such long and hard labour? To admit our first military and political defeat? To vanish from the world stage? What would Hitler's attitude be? Are you perhaps thinking that he would leave us free to do as we please?' Mussolini said.

Mussolini had one last chance to take a stand with Hitler when the two dictators took the car and train again back to the airport. The Führer had urgent business to attend to in Germany and Mussolini was anxious to return to Rome as quickly as possible. In the car, Hitler talked on and on, gesticulating wildly while Mussolini sat with a sullen expression, head bowed. The Duce, his patience wearing thin, told his driver to go faster.

During the journey, Hitler informed Mussolini that the submarine war would begin again with 'new means' and that in late August an airborne force would be launched against London. The British capital, Hitler said, would be 'wiped off the face of the earth in a week'. Mussolini did not even hint at the possibility of Italy bowing out of the war if Germany agreed. Later, he claimed to have obtained a pledge from Hitler to send all the reinforcements Italy needed. Hitler's interpreter Schmidt described the meeting as 'one of the most depressing I have ever taken part in'.

At the airport, as Hitler prepared to climb back into his Condor, Mussolini, shouting to make himself heard above the noise of the engines, called after him: 'Führer, we are fighting for a common cause!'

As the Condor rolled down the runway and took off, Mussolini kept his right arm lifted in the Roman salute until the plane disappeared from his sight.

Ten days after enemy forces reached his country's shores, the Duce, the man who had brought Italy into the war, had lost the chance to stave off defeat. His very political survival was at stake.

CHAPTER TWENTY-SIX

20-21 JULY

On arriving at his office in the Palazzo Venezia in Rome at 0700, Mussolini telephoned his mistress Claretta Petacci. As had become the norm, a stenographer at the Interior Ministry transcribed their conversation.

'Good morning, my dear,' Mussolini said.

'Ben, dear, I was worried, how did it go?' Petacci asked.

'Couldn't have been worse. With the Allies in Sicily, the massacres which have begun on the capital, rebellion in the air, and all the rest, I really don't know how I'll cope. While I was talking with that megalomaniac, I got the news that they were bombing Rome. I left immediately, by plane, and from far away I saw smoke from the fires. Were you afraid, my love?'

'Very much. It was like Hell, and several bombs fell not far from us. Damn them! What did he do?'

'He was courteous, as usual, but he made it clear to me that he didn't want to give me the weapons, given the timing and because our soldiers are unprepared for his new weapons. He would have agreed to let me have them on condition that his men use them, which would amount to establishing a force of occupation on our territory, ready to intervene when necessary. You understand I couldn't accept such humiliating conditions.'

'And so?'

'And so, all that can be done is wait and see.'

Mussolini's faith in Hitler's secret weapons was boundless. Back in Rome as fires started by the bombing raid lit up the sky across the capital, Mussolini had talked to his teenage children Romano and Anna Maria. He told them about the hidden workshops where the Germans manufactured what he called 'flying bombs' – V-1s and V-2s. When they were deployed, he told them, the enemy would be caught in a death-trap. The 'flying bombs' became the two teenagers' favourite topic of conversation.

Johnson was so exhausted he overslept with the result that he got separated from the bulk of his Division which had already left for Enna. Washing never took long. Everyone was rationed to two canteens of water a day, so a wash meant little more than wetting the tips of his fingers and wiping them over his eyes to soften them up because in the mornings they'd be crusty with dust and gunk. He called over his driver Spendolini, and together they set off towards the city of Enna to catch the others up.

They couldn't see any troops – neither friend nor foe – as they approached the walled town so they drove on through its outskirts and into it. The town was so deserted it felt spooky. With its big white star on the bonnet, the jeep was an obvious target. Johnson hoped that the Division was up ahead somewhere.

'I don't know whether we should go on or not,' Johnson said.

Spendolini, who had been a middleweight champion boxer in the Army before the war, drove on. He was usually slow to work things out – he had a room temperature IQ in Johnson's eyes. They threaded their way into the town's centre, an empty warren of narrow paved streets.

Great place for an ambush, Johnson thought. That might be the last thing I'll ever think of, he told himself. He held his tommy gun ready.

The jeep turned a corner and Johnson tensed. A row of armed figures stood in the middle of what looked like the main piazza. The jeep slowed and then stopped. A man wearing a black suit with a tricolour sash draped round his torso – he must be the mayor – called the men to attention and launched into a speech.

Johnson and Spendolini had no idea what the mayor was saying. But no one was shooting at them so they sat and watched. The men were a mix of police and soldiers, some fifty in total.

The mayor gesticulated a lot. Johnson had heard that if you cut off an Italian's hands, he wouldn't be able to talk.

The mayor finished his speech. The Italians marched forward, one at a time, and laid down their weapons in a pile. Johnson and Spendolini exchanged glances. The men were surrendering. This was their chance. They drove right up to the mayor. Johnson didn't salute or say anything. He and Spendolini loaded the jeep with all the weapons from the pile, while the mayor and the men stared. The job finished, the pair drove off, waving goodbye as they went.

'We got us enough trade material to last us for a while,' Johnson said as they drove on, bound for the far side of town.

Shortly after they caught up with their battalion just outside Enna, they learnt that it had conquered the town at 0900 that morning, 20 July. The battalion commander called for Johnson.

'Gimme those damn guns,' he ordered.

Johnson tried to hold a couple of pistols back, but the mayor had apparently reported the precise number of weapons and Johnson lost the entire haul.

That evening as Mussolini changed at his Roman residence, his maid fastening the buttons of his collar, his wife Rachele reported the results of her latest investigation into the men she was convinced were plotting his downfall.

When she first saw Mussolini, Rachele, the daughter of peasant smallholders, had been impressed by what she described as his 'eyes like fire'. He had lived up to that first impression, even pulling out a pistol and threatening to shoot himself when he demanded that her parents allow them to marry. Now fifty-one, Rachele had lived with him for the better part of three decades but she had never become part of his public world. She rarely ventured out of the Villa Torlonia where the family lived, but she was a power to be reckoned with because her well-placed spies kept a careful watch on those she saw as her husband's enemies.

Unperturbed by the maid, whom she trusted completely, Rachele announced that she had received extremely serious warnings of plotting by their son-in-law, Count Ciano. She was always convinced that Ciano was her husband's worst enemy. She hated his playboy attitude to women and his indiscreet infidelity to her daughter Edda. She had once told an SS colonel that he had 'brought unhappiness into our family'.

The plump-faced Ciano's marriage to Edda, Mussolini's favourite daughter, in 1930 had been arranged by the Duce, keen to inject some noble blood into his family. Since then Ciano had speedily reached the top of the Fascist regime: first as the head of Mussolini's press office, then as propaganda minister. He was only thirty-three when Mussolini made him foreign minister – the youngest in Europe. Ciano, who liked to see himself as the Duce's heir apparent, even imitated the dictator's public posture – chest stuck out, hands on hips, legs astride.

But reports began to reach Mussolini's ear that Ciano opposed the alliance with Nazi Germany, was daring to complain about him in golf club chats and, after the bombing of Leghorn, his home city, had gone so far as to rail in public against 'that crazy tyrant who wanted this war'. In February, Mussolini had sacked him from the foreign ministry, demoting him to the post of ambassador to the Vatican – a job Ciano welcomed when writing in his diary because 'more than ever, the future is in the hands of God'. The day after his dismissal, a jubilant Goebbels branded Ciano 'a scoundrel and a despicable traitor, without precedent in history'. Like Rachele, the Nazis were convinced that Ciano was her husband's worst enemy.

Rachele was sure that Ciano was not the only plotter. Fascist party chief Dino Grandi, whom Mussolini had made president of the Fascist Chamber (the lower house of parliament), was also an enemy, she believed. So was Marshal Pietro Badoglio, the head of a royalist faction who, she claimed, tapped all telephone calls made at their home.

'But Rachele, it's the American tanks which worry me, not Badoglio's tapping or other people's intrigues,' Mussolini protested.

Unabashed, Rachele assured him that Giuseppe Bastianini,

under-secretary at the foreign ministry and another traitor in their midst had released passports to several prominent Fascists without his knowledge. She knew the names, she said.

Mussolini snapped that she was the schemer.

In front of her husband, Rachele promptly picked up the telephone and called Bastianini. She told the official what she knew, listed the names of those involved and added that she had informed her husband.

Mussolini grabbed the handset from her and cut the call short.

The Duce and his wife had clashed repeatedly over her demands to wipe out this 'traitor' or that. Her nagging infuriated Mussolini so much so that he once complained to his eldest son Vittorio: 'According to your mother, I am surrounded by traitors, spies, saboteurs and weaklings. Do you think it's useful to execute forty generals, decimate regiments and jail ministers?'

Over the years, Mussolini ignored virtually all the considerable evidence Rachele accumulated. With typical bluster, he explained to his family that he had long ago chosen for himself the motto 'Live dangerously'. As an old soldier, he added, he gave the following order to his followers: 'If I advance, follow me. If I retreat, kill me. If they kill me, avenge me.'

Mussolini had other reasons for disliking Rachele's investigations. As well as probing Roman politics, her parallel police force had unveiled several of her husband's extramarital affairs. She did not hesitate to confront him with her findings but in the end, she always forgave him. 'Of all your father's women,' she once confided to their son Romano, 'I was jealous only of those whom he thought about often. The others didn't interest me.' Strangely enough, her network had so far failed to reveal the existence of the mistress who meant the most to Mussolini, Claretta Petacci.

For two days, Snell had been lying on a bunk in a large ward aboard a hospital ship, with only the sky to look at through the window. Near him was a delirious British soldier who had a bullet lodged in his head and barked out orders as if he were still on the battlefield. 'Look out, here they come!' and 'Bring up the tanks, bring up the tanks!' he would keep shouting until, exhausted, he fell asleep. He died as the ship sailed on.

Before Snell was carried aboard, he had felt the full glare of the Sicilian sun beating down on the truck jolting him up the coast road. Mount Etna was a black and foreboding mass to the west, its white smoke the only sign of movement in the oppressive sky. Lying on a stretcher in the back of the truck which was open to the sky, Snell had oozed sweat and had fought hard not to lose consciousness. When he finally reached the port-city of Messina, the locals jeered at him as he was carried to the quayside. He spent that night in the open, grateful for the respite from the daytime heat. A woman saw him lying there in the dark and gave him some fruit juice. The drink was delicious, but more than the physical relief what affected Snell was the compassion in the woman's gesture.

Aboard the ship, which had big red crosses painted on the sides, a sophisticated German officer came one day to lecture Snell who was trapped in his bunk: 'You will see. The war will be over in six weeks and we shall win. And you will be our prisoner.' He looked so confident that Snell didn't feel like arguing. He hadn't the energy anyway.

It was some time before Snell found out he was bound for the Tuscan coast. He found out from the nurse who brought him food – she didn't clean him up, even though dysentery soon made his bunk a mess and gave him more sores. She told him he was being taken to a prison hospital in Lucca. She had a small map in the back of her diary, and showed him where Lucca was, near Pisa. Quickly, Snell memorised a route from there to the Swiss border.

CHAPTER TWENTY-SEVEN
22–23 JULY

Over the past week, Patton had manoeuvred swiftly to change an order, initiated by Montgomery, that he should limit his efforts to merely protecting the British flank and head into the centre of Sicily, in order to cut the island in half. Patton could see no glory in this and, following the example set by Montgomery, he decided to exploit the lack of an officially agreed blueprint for the Sicily campaign. What he wanted, and what he obtained, was permission from his superior, General Alexander, to seize Palermo – the name of the island capital was so well-known across America it would make front-page news.

For several of his senior officers, Patton's fixation on Palermo made little military sense when the bulk of the Axis troops were blocking the Allies in eastern Sicily. General Bradley wrote that conquering Palermo was meaningless in the strategic sense, adding that there was no glory in 'the capture of hills, docile peasants, and spiritless soldiers'. Major-General Lucien Truscott, commander of the 3rd Infantry Division and the man whom Patton entrusted with the task of taking Palermo, believed its port was of no use at all to the Americans.

But nonetheless Truscott did as he was told and set off from the southern coast on the hundred-mile journey across inhospitable terrain, with mountains as high as 4,000 feet or more towering over narrow roads and hairpin bends. He reached Palermo in four days thanks to 'the Truscott trot', a marching pace of up to five miles an hour which the Major-General, complaining that the legions of ancient Rome were faster than his men, had imposed on them during long foot-journeys in north Africa.

On 22 July, planning to make his triumphant entry into Palermo that evening, Patton raced towards the city in a jeep. The drive felt like a victory parade to Rosevich, who was part of Patton's convoy, because troops who recognised the General as he passed saluted and waved. But in the middle of the countryside, the jeep was held up for some time. Rosevich could only see the back of Patton's head, but he could guess how impatient the General must be feeling. Everyone knew Patton had no time to lose.

Word came down the convoy that a mule was blocking the road. Rosevich saw Patton's jeep swing out, its outsize, three-star pennant fluttering in the wind – Patton believed that it was good for the troops to see his flag flying all over the front. It headed towards the front of the column of troops and vehicles which was beyond a bend in the road, out of sight.

Less than a quarter of an hour later, the convoy started to move again. As his jeep crossed a narrow bridge, Rosevich saw what looked like a dead mule lying in the dried-up river bed, with the smashed wreck of a gaily coloured cart. He learnt that the mule had refused to budge, despite the combined efforts both of its owner and of several soldiers. Exasperated, Patton had driven up to the cart, broken his stick over the peasant's back, and ordered the mule shot and pushed off the bridge with the cart.

Shortly after 1730, the good-looking and debonair Dino Grandi, one of the most senior figures in the Fascist party, entered the Duce's office at Palazzo Venezia, a cavernous room with a twelve-metre-high ceiling originally built for Renaissance popes. His large, bulging eyes cold with disdain, his face tense, Mussolini greeted Grandi curtly.

Mussolini prided himself on the harshness of his stare, once boasting to his son Romano that its effect 'when I want, is the same as if I had forced my visitor to stay standing'. Another favoured tactic was to make his ministers and generals run the twenty yards from the door to his desk.

Mussolini had good reason to be angry with Grandi, who had made the most serious challenge to the Duce's authority since he had taken power in 1922. In a motion which Grandi wanted Fascist party chiefs to discuss, he called for Mussolini's dictatorship to be dismantled and for power to be returned to parliament, government ministers, and other bodies as the law and the constitution laid down. He also urged King Victor Emmanuel III – 'for the honour and salvation of the Nation' – to take back the command of the armed forces from Mussolini, who had seized it in 1940. Mussolini had read the motion for the first time that morning and thrown it onto his desk, branding it 'unacceptable, inadmissible and vile'.

The forty-eight-year-old Grandi, a young officer in the First World War, had for years been a firm Fascist and a loyal servant of the Duce, speculating humbly in a tribute to him: 'What should I have been if I had not met you? At the very most, an obscure provincial lawyer.' But Grandi disliked the alliance with Nazi Germany from the outset, and his tour of duty as ambassador to London in the mid-1930s had confirmed him an Anglophile. Churchill held Grandi in high esteem. After Italy's entry into the war, Churchill believed Grandi was the only man who could replace Mussolini and bring about a separate peace with Britain.

A friend had pressed Grandi not to present the motion, arguing that Mussolini would have him arrested and the Germans, if they became involved, would have him shot. But Grandi had persisted nonetheless. To his mind it was the only way of persuading the King to depose Mussolini – if the King failed to do so, however, Grandi's efforts would be in vain.

As soon as Grandi walked up to his desk, Mussolini, who had remained standing, began to reprimand him: 'Your obscure and ambiguous attitude towards the war has prompted a profound reaction among Fascists and in the party leadership, and that means severe measures must be taken against you.'

Grandi refused to let himself be swayed and decided to place all his cards on the table. To the Duce's face, he said all he thought about Italy's plight: the only solution was for Mussolini to give up spontaneously all his powers and entrust them to the King. 'It is the only way you can still serve the nation,' Grandi said.

As Grandi spoke, Mussolini continued to stare fixedly at him, his face sullen as he fidgeted nervously with a pencil. Grandi believed he was taking only a limited risk in speaking so openly, because Mussolini knew what he thought already. He expected a violent reaction from Mussolini, but none came – the Duce let him speak without interruption.

When Grandi stopped, Mussolini asked in an icy tone: 'Have you finished?'

'I have finished,' Grandi replied.

'Well then, you should know a few things which you will have to fix firmly in your mind and on which I invite you to reflect when you will leave here,' Mussolini began. The war was far from lost, he told him, and soon 'extraordinary events in the political and military field' would reverse the course of it.

'I don't yield powers to anyone. Fascism is strong, the nation is with me, I am the leader,' Mussolini said. 'It's true that there is much defeatism around, inside and outside the regime, but that will be dealt with as it deserves as soon as I judge the moment has come.'

He dismissed Grandi: 'You may go.'

As Grandi left the room, Mussolini thought to himself that the former minister was 'already on the other side of the barricade'. But he agreed to have the motion placed on the agenda for a meeting of the Fascist Grand Council scheduled to take place two days later. It would be the first time it had met since the start of the war, even though it was on paper the supreme governing authority of the regime. The meeting was due to discuss the possibility of the Grand Council taking a greater role in ruling the country. Council debates in the past were regularly punctuated by participants standing up to shout 'Long live the Duce!', and rarely ended in a vote. Invariably, Mussolini simply interpreted the Grand Council's recommendations as he saw fit.

* * *

In the early morning of 23 July, Rosevich wandered down the long corridors of the former Royal Palace in Palermo, marvelling at the faded beauty of the ornately decorated rooms. Although it was bright outside, much of the palace was in semi-darkness, the windows closed and the scorching sunlight kept out with thick curtains. The air smelt musty.

Patton had arrived in Palermo late the previous night and made straight for the palace, which he had chosen as his new headquarters. Rosevich had to hand it to Patton – who else would requisition a summer palace dating back to the Saracens as his Sicilian headquarters and sleep in the King's bed? Rosevich reflected that the choice of the palace reflected not only Patton's high opinion of himself but also his strong sense of beauty – something he hadn't expected to find in a general. That sense showed in his dress, his bearing and in the way he liked to talk about the art he had seen in museums he had visited.

Rosevich had spent the night in a room far away from Patton's marble-panelled apartments. The room which had previously belonged to the King's chauffeur was spartanly furnished, but Rosevich had a real bed and that to him was plenty luxurious in itself.

Parts of the city outside the palace gates had been destroyed by bombs but inside the royal home only time had damaged the furnishings – the rich carpets were faded and worn, the oil paintings darkened, and ugly patches stained the mirrors in their carved golden frames. In the biggest room, 140 feet long and 60 feet wide, parts of a fresco of the Labours of Hercules were missing. The vastness of the palace impressed Rosevich. The only thing he could compare it to was the Capitol in Washington, which his father took him to see when he was a boy.

When Rosevich parted a curtain and opened a window, light and the sound of water flowing in the fountains flooded the room. A vast garden full of orange and lemon trees stretched out below him. Nothing stirred in the sultry air and Rosevich basked in the illusion that the war was a long way away.

He was soon put to work by Patton who was the hero of the hour. As Patton had fully expected, American newspapers praised him for seizing the first great European city from the Nazi-Fascists and he made no attempt to hide his elation. In one diary entry, Patton described how all the people in the streets of Palermo had applauded his arrival and how most of the Italian prisoners had saluted him and then clapped. 'War is lots of fun – I like it more all the time,' Patton dictated.

Messages of congratulation poured in and Rosevich filed them away in the green metal cabinet which had accompanied Patton from Fort Benning, through north Africa, and into Sicily. The cabinet was as tall as Rosevich and was getting heavier and heavier to shift. President Roosevelt sent a signed picture, Churchill a telegram. General Alexander radioed his 'heartiest congratulations'.

Montgomery sent a note. 'Many congratulations to you and your gallant soldiers on securing Palermo and cleaning up the whole of the Western half of Sicily.' Montgomery said he would be very honoured if Patton came over to visit him. They could then 'discuss the capture of Messina'. Patton predicted he would have a tough time with Montgomery – he was more than ever determined to win what he called the 'horse-race' for Messina against his British rival and he had already given orders to his troops to strike out eastwards along the coastal road towards the city.

Unknown to Patton, on 22 July the bulk of the 29th Panzer Grenadier Division had sailed across to Sicily from the mainland, its objective to cut off the northern coast road to Messina. Had the Americans, instead of making for Palermo, started down that road earlier, they would have found the way clear.

After a four-day sea journey, an ambulance took Snell through flat countryside. He realised precisely where he was when he spotted the Leaning Tower of Pisa. He felt elated to see a landmark he recognised but this was quickly followed by sadness at the knowledge that he was in Tuscany, far to the north of the Allied invasion.

On his arrival at PG 202, a prison hospital in Lucca, not far from Pisa, Snell discovered with delight that the orderlies were fellow-Brits. They cleaned him thoroughly, the first time anyone had bothered since he was shot down two weeks earlier. Snell would never have suspected that warm water and clean sheets could give him so much pleasure.

An Italian doctor listed the wounds he found on Snell's body. One or two bullets – it wasn't possible to tell precisely which – in the right shoulder had shattered it. One bullet between the fingers of the right hand ripped the skin away. Two bullets lodged in the left arm. One bullet grazed his left hip, and another came to rest close to his spine. There were fifteen pieces of grenade all over his body, one of which severed a nerve on his left wrist.

Snell watched when the doctor operated once more on his shoulder, using a local anaesthetic. He could see everything reflected in the metal structure of the light above his head. When the doctor peeled back the dressing which had not been changed since Sicily, the smell of rotting flesh made Snell's stomach turn. A piece of bone was sticking out of his shoulder. The Germans at the field-hospital had set his arm wrong. 'We'll fix that,' the doctor said. With what looked like hedge-cutters and making a grating, crunching sound, he severed the bone.

PG 202 was a hospital within a prison, well-guarded by Italian soldiers. But as soon as he got there, Snell started to hoard all the concentrated foods he could lay his hands on, ready for any chance of escape he might have. He scrounged a binocular case off an army officer and packed it carefully with Horlicks Malted Milk tablets, Marmite cubes, treacle and chocolate among other things. Many of these were items he kept back from his share of the invalid Red Cross parcels which arrived at the prison. Snell also laid by a store of sulphanilamide anti-bacterial ointment and a supply of dressings for his wounds.

His recovery wasn't helped by the hospital diet which was both dull and frugal. The nuns cooked rissoles for both lunch and supper day in, day out. Whenever he could, Snell made himself a Benghazi roll, the prisoners' speciality – bread filled with anything that could possibly be edible, then rolled up, tied with string, and boiled.

But he was young and strong-willed, and he was soon able to stand and then walk. He started exercising in the ward every day, his right arm in a sling, and then in the prison garden. He walked just a few minutes along the garden path at first, then for longer and longer until he lost count of how many laps he made every day, going round and round. He exercised morning, afternoon and evening. He was confident that an opportunity for escape would come and he wanted to get fit in time.

Snell spent much of his time either resting, or playing poker with the other British and American prisoners in the hospital. They had very little money between them, but that didn't stop them playing endless rounds. One American prisoner, Dan Coffee, a tank commander, had been sitting in his tank when a shell hit. The explosion sent objects flying around the small space inside, and a screwdriver ended up in his neck. The doctors bungled the operation, cutting through his vocal cords by mistake.

Snell got on pretty well with all the prisoners, but there was one British Army major, Peter Lewis, whom he disliked from the outset. Both of them had been wounded in Sicily, and both had big moustaches. They had nothing else in common and kept arguing, even during poker games, over which of the two forces – Army or Air – was making the more vital contribution to the war. Their fellow-prisoners kept telling them to shut up.

CHAPTER TWENTY-EIGHT

24 JULY

On the day set for the meeting of the Fascist Grand Council, Mussolini had been up for a short time when he heard a knock on the door of his room. His wife Rachele came in, immediately asking: 'Is this evening's meeting really necessary?'

Mussolini looked surprised. 'Why? I expect it will be only a friendly discussion. I don't see why we shouldn't hold it,' he said.

Incensed, Rachele burst out: 'Friends! Is that what you call that group of traitors who surround you, even that Grandi? Don't you know that no one has been able to track him down for days now?'

Mussolini tried to persuade her there was no danger in holding the Grand Council and that he would deal with Grandi when the time was right, but he left for his office without managing to convince her and spent the whole morning there, apparently oblivious to several warnings of plots against him. Twice in the past few days alone, the Fascist party secretary, Carlo Scorza, had dropped hints, muttering about 'something fishy, very fishy indeed', but Mussolini had paid no attention. Confident that he had nothing to fear, Mussolini assured a friend that whenever the plotters surfaced, he would get rid of them 'in ten minutes or at the most a couple of hours'.

The dictator who liked to boast he held twenty-five meetings a day was convinced that nothing could escape his control – and certainly not a rebellion from within the Fascist party.

That afternoon when Mussolini took his leave of Rachele after lunching with her at home – something he did only rarely – she tried one last time to make him open his eyes to the danger she believed lay ahead. Just as Mussolini's driver was closing the door of the official Alfa Romeo to drive to Palazzo Venezia and the Grand Council meeting, Rachele shouted after him: 'Have them all arrested, before the meeting starts! The Militia will soon do it for you. You know you can count on them.'

Mussolini ignored her.

The road to Gangi curved to the right and Johnson and his men started shooting as soon as they spotted the Italian soldier. He was near a tree on the edge of the road.

'Hold on, he's praying!' Johnson shouted a moment later. He had seen that the Italian was kneeling with his hands joined in prayer under his chin, his forehead resting on the trunk of the tree. Johnson didn't want to shoot someone while they were praying. It didn't feel right.

Johnson and his men stood there, guns pointing at the Italian as they waited for him to finish praying. Johnson would shoot the Italian when he stopped praying. The Italian didn't move. They waited some more, then Johnson sneaked up to him, ready to shoot.

As soon as he saw the Italian's pale face he knew the soldier was dead. There was a small pool of blood on the earth in front of him, between his knees and the base of the tree.

The Italian had gone down on his knees to pray and some-one had shot him. Johnson figured that Italians or Germans had ordered the execution because to his knowledge his unit was the first Allied one in the area. Johnson didn't lay the Italian down but left him praying there by the tree.

Mussolini strode into the Hall of the Parrot shortly after 1700. Scorza, party secretary and a former member of a murderous blackshirt gang, called out: 'Salute the Duce!' Grandi, Ciano and the twenty-six other most senior figures in the regime stood up, their right arms raised, to give their leader the Roman salute. Mussolini considered it 'more hygienic' than a handshake.

Outside the dry, dusty sirocco wind from the Sahara was blow-ing and, although it was daylight, the heavy blue curtains had been drawn across the chamber's great windows. The air inside

A STREET-BY-STREET CONQUEST.
US Army jeeps roll through the mountain town of Pollina, near Palermo. Narrow alleys, typical of many Sicilian villages, and offering plenty of cover for retreating German and Italian forces, often made the Allied advance slow and perilous.

TONY SNELL, a Spitfire pilot with the RAF's 242 Squadron. As a teenager, he joined the Local Defence Volunteers at his home town of Tunbridge Wells and, with a .22 pistol and a pitchfork, spent many happy nights watching from the bell-tower of the local church.

FROM WHEAT FIELD TO RAF FIELD. Peasants watch a Spitfire coming in to land on a newly-built airfield. Within days of the invasion, the RAF was building rudimentary landing strips in Sicily to give its planes a longer range into enemy territory.

THE FAMILY OF RITA FRANCARDO, a nine-year-old refugee living in Catania. The photograph taken in 1936 shows, from left to right: Pippo, Nina, Tina, their mother Maria, Anna and Rita.

MEN OF THE ROYAL MARINES dash through rubble in the shadow of Catania's cathedral. Widespread looting broke out when the Germans abandoned the city.

WATCHING AND WAITING. American soldiers monitoring enemy defences as they lay siege to Troina, Sicily's highest town and a key bastion on the German line of resistance. The photograph is by the legendary Robert Capa, who one year later made his name with blurred but powerful pictures of D-Day in Normandy.

ALFRED JOHNSON, an American sergeant, leading a forward observation unit to guide artillery fire. He joined the Army at the age of sixteen, forging his parents' signatures on the recruitment papers. He soon regretted it, but when he appealed to his father he was told: 'Son, you made your bed, now you lay in it.'

FROM A FORWARD OBSERVATION POST, a German officer seeks out the advancing Allies. As the Germans retreated, they exploited the Sicilian landscape, especially the hilly and rocky terrain, to keep harassing the Allies with artillery and sniper fire.

PURSUING THE ENEMY. Near Troina, a peasant indicates which way the German troops had gone. This picture, the best-known of all photographs of the Sicilian campaign, was also taken by Capa.

WERNER HAHN, a lance-corporal serving as a gunner in a Panzer Tiger Tank of the Hermann Goering Division. Hahn, whose mother was a painter, chose to enlist in the tank regiment, believing its reputed speed and daring would give him a chance to shine on the front line.

THE WRECK OF A GERMAN MARK 3 TANK stranded in the town of Centuripe, central Sicily, after two days of street fighting from which the British 78th Division emerged victorious. German tank crews invariably chose to blow up their vehicles rather than let them fall intact into Allied hands.

THE FORUM WHICH SEALED MUSSOLINI'S FATE. The Duce (*far right*) presides at a session of the Fascist Grand Council, attended by his dictatorship's highest-ranking dignitaries. Debates were invariably punctuated by shouts of 'Long live the Duce!'

THE DUCE IS OUSTED. Sicilians vent their frustration after years of war, misery and oppression under Mussolini. Portraits of the Duce in all Sicilian towns and villages were pelted with eggs, tomatoes and rotten fruit.

BRITISH GRAVES in a field
near Primosole Bridge.

the room was already hot and close. The Fascist dignitaries took their seats, sweating inside the party uniform Mussolini had ordered them to wear for the occasion – black safari jacket, and grey-green shorts and boots reaching to just below the knee.

Mussolini himself wore the light-coloured uniform of commander of the Militia. His imposingly solid table and chair had been placed on a platform draped in crimson velvet, which enabled him to physically dominate the others present. Concealed under the tabletop in front of him was a small button which would instantly summon the Militia standing guard outside. The Duce could place all the dignitaries under arrest at any time he chose. Squads of blackshirt Fascist militiamen and police officers were stationed along the ornate staircase in the corridors of the Palazzo Venezia and in the courtyard.

Arrest for any of the dignitaries present would be followed by prison, or worse. The last prominent politician to defy Mussolini, opposition leader Giacomo Matteotti, had been stabbed to death in a car by blackshirts in 1924.

Several of the Council members, aware of the risks they were running, carried a gun. Grandi, who was virtually convinced that he would not emerge from the Palazzo Venezia alive, had two hand-grenades. He hid them in his safari jacket pockets. Some of the Fascist leaders had been to confession that morning.

Mussolini, a stack of papers piled up on the table in front of him, remained sitting as he began to speak in a calm, almost distant, tone of voice. The 'absurd hypothesis' of an invasion on Italian soil had become fact, he said, and now 'the real war had begun'. As a result of the invasion, all the factions hostile to the regime had coalesced against him and spread demoralisation even within Fascist ranks.

'At this moment I am easily the most disliked and, in fact, hated man in Italy,' he said.

In Sicily, only two weeks after the invasion, there were already 70,000 prisoners, including five generals and an admiral. Mussolini went on to give a list of those he held responsible: 'The Sicilian people, who instead of resisting have welcomed the invader; our troops, who did not fight; but above all the commanders of these troops, who were unable or did not want to inspire courage and confidence among their soldiers.' Tens of thousands of soldiers and seamen had abandoned their uniforms and were strolling around in Sicilian cities. But he, Mussolini, had ordered that anyone who left their post should be executed by firing squad.

Mussolini, who until now had spoken with his head buried in his notes and documents, suddenly looked up, his face illuminated by a harsh white glare from a wheel-shaped chandelier above him. Giuseppe Bottai, one of the Fascist chiefs, commented afterwards that it was as if a mask had fallen, exposing the expression of a man resigned to a final reckoning.

'Defeatists' claimed that there was no popular support for the war, but this was irrelevant. 'If a war is successful it is popular; otherwise it is not,' Mussolini proclaimed.

If the Grand Council wanted to speak to the nation, he ended, it must address the following issues: 'War or peace? Surrender at discretion, or resistance to the bitter end?'

Outside, behind the thick curtains, the sun was setting. The last rays of the day barely reached the room. Mussolini's speech had lasted an hour and a half, and Grandi noted that his tone was as usual 'absent, scornful and hard, as if he were making a special favour to those who had the privilege of listening to him'.

The jeep braked close to Johnson and his men, who lay in a field by the roadside, glad of a break. 'How far to the front?' a colonel shouted from the jeep.

Johnson recognised the colonel; his name was O'Connor. Three years earlier when Johnson was a new recruit in Vermont, O'Connor had given him permission to go home for Christmas. Johnson was thinking of going AWOL at the time and word reached O'Connor who asked him to give his word 'as a Southern gentleman' that he would return. The description had impressed Johnson, whom people usually called 'you goddamn dumb rebel' because he was the only Southerner in his battalion. Even at roll-call, Johnson was just 'damn rebel'. He promised O'Connor he would come back and come back he did.

Johnson straightened up, pointing up the road. 'Top of this hill right here,' he said.

'What ya all doing laying here, resting? I'm gonna take a look,' O'Connor said.

'Sir, don't go over that hill. There's a machine-gun nest over there. He'll get you,' Johnson said.

O'Connor was unshakeable. 'Well it's my job to go up and see what kind of shape the front's in,' he said. 'Go ahead,' he told his driver.

Johnson saw the jeep go over the brow of the hill barely fifty yards away, then heard the machine-gun. He sneaked up to take a look. Both O'Connor and his driver were dead. Afterwards, Johnson wondered whether O'Connor had recognised him. He decided the colonel probably hadn't because otherwise he would have realised that Johnson would not lie to him.

The sun had set by the time Grandi's turn to speak came. Elegant and dignified, his goatee beard perfectly trimmed, the man who had written the motion defying Mussolini launched an indictment against the Fascist dictatorship, while all the time shrewdly proclaiming his loyalty to and respect for the Duce.

Grandi's impassioned speech held his entire audience in thrall. He denounced 'the killing of Fascism' and the way Mussolini had 'nazified' Italy.

Criticising the 'Mussolini of uniforms, of choreographic parades no one believes in', Grandi suddenly grabbed the bottom of his uniform jacket with both hands and exclaimed: 'Free us, Duce, of this ridiculous jacket and the cap with the eagle, and leave us only the old black shirt!'

A few minutes later, Mussolini abruptly shifted his position, and leant forward in his chair, his chest almost touching the edge of the table. He pressed hard on his stomach with his left hand

– as he often did when nervous tension gave him stomach cramps. His expression – a mask of great attentiveness – did not change.

'This is not about saving ourselves, nor about saving the regime or the party. This is about saving Italy,' Grandi concluded. 'Let all factions, even ours, perish as long as the Motherland can save itself.'

No one had ever dared make such an attack on the Fascist regime in front of Mussolini. In the heavy silence that followed, the leaders of that regime – who for two decades had subscribed to its motto 'The Duce is always right', turned towards their mentor, expecting him to cut short the debate.

Mussolini said nothing. Nor did he summon the Militia. The dictator, whom newspapers worshipped as an 'incarnation of God', simply called for another speaker.

In the whole six hours of speeches that followed, Mussolini, his face a dark mask, did nothing to stop speaker after speaker level criticism at him. Only one of the Fascist figureheads spoke vigorously against the move to strip him of his military command.

Even Mussolini's son-in-law Ciano spoke against him, emphasising in a calm voice the occasions on which the Nazis had humiliated their Fascist allies. The invasions of Belgium, France and Russia, he revealed, were all launched before the Nazis informed Rome. Now there was no hope of victory, Ciano argued, so Italy must surrender.

Mussolini, angry eyes fixed on his son-in-law, looked according to one observer as if he were masticating a string of silent curses.

Twice Mussolini, unaccustomed to such criticism – he liked to boast that he needed only to press a bell to create a cheering crowd – threatened his rivals. 'I allow you to speak freely tonight, but I could have you arrested,' he said at one point and later: 'I see among you people who betray me.'

Shortly after 2300, Mussolini finally acted. With the pretext that it was late, and many speakers had yet to take the floor, he suggested that the meeting be adjourned to the following day.

The ploy was an obvious attempt to prevent the Council from voting on Grandi's motion and win the Duce more time.

Before Mussolini had finished proposing the adjournment, Grandi sprang to his feet, noisily pushing back his chair. 'Ah no!' the usually unflappable Grandi exclaimed in a hoarse shout, only to instantly recover his composure. 'Forgive me, Duce,' he apologised. 'From this room we must emerge with a decision.'

After a pause, Mussolini announced: 'The sitting is suspended for twenty minutes, after which the discussion will resume and we will put it to the vote.'

Mussolini stood up and strode out of the room. In that moment, as Grandi later recalled, he feared that Mussolini would not return. Instead, he expected the blackshirt Militia to burst into the room. The Duce's strange silence, he thought, was like the calm before a storm.

CHAPTER TWENTY-NINE
25 JULY: 0000–1300 HOURS

As Rome – the city which Mussolini had once branded a 'centre of infection poisoning the whole of our national life' – lay plunged in complete darkness in case the bombing started again, some diehard Fascist veterans in the Grand Council rallied to their dictator's defence. One denounced what he branded 'defeatism, sabotage and treachery', while another had a drastic recommendation for the Duce: 'Bump them all off, immediately, and you will save the situation. Here one needs to be radical like Hitler and lance the abscess!'

Shortly before 0100, after all those who had asked to speak had done so, Mussolini took the floor one last time. His voice studiously steady, he warned his audience that there was no going back – ending his dictatorship would spell the end of Fascism and capitulation to the enemy.

Resorting to intimidation, Mussolini warned them in a detached tone of voice that the King might well accept Grandi's invitation to carry out his constitutional duties, but he might also hold Fascist leaders responsible for the current situation, and seize the chance 'to liquidate them all at once'. To press the point home, he drew a finger across his throat.

He predicted that when he went to see the King to report on the night's debate, the monarch would give him his personal support. Mussolini's last words were threatening: 'And then what will your position be? Be careful, gentlemen!'

The room went quiet. Mussolini's words astonished many of his listeners, and left them badly shaken. The confidence of several of his critics wavered.

Grandi's shout broke the stillness. 'This is blackmail,' he cried.

'The Duce has set before us a dilemma, that of choosing between our loyalty to him and our loyalty to the Homeland. Well then, I say to him, one cannot hesitate even for one moment, when the Homeland is at stake.'

Grandi's outburst eased some of the tension prompted by Mussolini's threat. But one after the other, the Duce's most fervent supporters protested their loyalty to him. One of them, General Galbiati, the Militia Commander, shouted: 'What will the battalions of blackshirts camped at the gates of Rome say when they learn what happened here tonight?'

Grandi turned to his neighbour, Marshal De Vecchi, one of the leaders of the columns which had taken part in Mussolini's March on Rome, and whispered: 'This is it.' De Vecchi nodded and under the table Grandi passed him one of the two hand-grenades he had brought with him.

But Mussolini did not call on the Militia. He was so confident that a majority of the audience had rallied behind him that he granted Grandi's request for a vote – the first time the Grand Council had ever voted on a motion. He was convinced that the vote would isolate his most vocal rivals, but perhaps his poor state of health as well as his customary over-confidence was affecting his judgment.

At about 0230, exhausted, their nerves on edge, the Grand Council voted on Grandi's motion by roll-call. When Ciano's name was called, Mussolini and his son-in-law, according to an observer, 'exchanged a long and penetrating stare'. Several of the plotters had urged Ciano, because of his family tie to Mussolini, to restrict himself to speaking his mind but not to vote. Regardless, he voted in favour of stripping Mussolini of his powers.

As the final vote was announced – nineteen in favour, seven against, one abstention – Mussolini got to his feet. His tone still dispassionate, he announced: 'You have provoked the crisis of the regime. The session is closed.'

The party secretary was about to call for the ritual 'Salute to the Duce' when Mussolini stopped him with an irritated gesture of the hand. 'No, you are excused,' he said before making for his office.

For the first time in two decades, Mussolini had suffered a humiliating defeat at the hands of his own Fascist party. The Duce gone, one of the party leaders whispered: 'Now they will arrest us all.'

More than an hour after the vote, Mussolini was still at the Palazzo Venezia. Before leaving to return home, he picked up the telephone to call his mistress Claretta Petacci at her villa in northern Rome.

'When did you finish?' asked Petacci.

'A short time ago,' Mussolini said.

'How did it go?'

'How do you think?'

'You frighten me!'

'There is little to be frightened about. We have reached the epilogue, the biggest turning point in history,' Mussolini said with his typical love of melodrama.

'What's the matter with you, Benito dear? I don't understand you.'

'The star has been obscured!'

'Don't torment yourself. Explain!'

'It's all over. You too must try and take cover!'

'And you?' Petacci asked, in tears.

'Don't think about me, just hurry!'

'But if no one knows anything?'

'You will know in a few hours' time.'

'It's just an idea you've got into your head.'

'Unfortunately, that's not the case.'

'And so?'

'Do as I say, otherwise things may get even worse!'

Mussolini struck a far more confident tone with his party secretary, who drove back with him to Villa Torlonia. He would see the King later that day, he announced.

As the car neared Villa Torlonia, Mussolini saw in the morning twilight his wife Rachele, waiting to meet him on the steps of the portico. She had been forewarned of his return. She hurried up to him and immediately guessed the night's outcome from the sombre and exhausted look on his face.

Without stopping to greet him, she asked: 'Did you at least have them all arrested?'

'I'll do it tomorrow morning,' Mussolini replied quietly.

'If it's not too late,' she murmured.

A little later, when Mussolini recounted the night's events, Rachele interrupted him only once – when he told her that their son-in-law Ciano had voted with the Duce's enemies. 'Him as well!' she burst out.

At an airfield near Syracuse that morning, Montgomery and Patton leant over a map of Sicily spread out on the bonnet of Montgomery's command car. Two weeks into the campaign, Patton had accepted Montgomery's invitation and flown over to meet him and discuss, as the Eighth Army commander put it, 'the capture of Messina'.

When Montgomery unveiled his plan, Patton was dumbfounded. Patton had come braced for tension with his opponent in the race for Messina, and yet here was his rival apparently bowing out. Montgomery suggested to Patton that the Americans, and not the British, conquer Messina. Montgomery also agreed that Patton should have both the coastal highway from Palermo to Messina, and a mountain road running further inland. Patton, as he later wrote in his diary, couldn't shake off the idea that Montgomery must be pulling a trick on him. As Patton wrote in his diary that evening: 'He agreed so readily that I felt something was wrong but have not found it yet.'

Montgomery had in fact been forced to accept the inevitable. Given his failure to pierce the German line north of Primosole Bridge, he had given up on his eastern coastal flank and instead launched what he called a 'left hook' to try to advance around the western side of Mount Etna. But four separate offensives had all failed to make progress as the Germans held fast to their defence line, and there was thus little chance for him of reaching Messina alone.

A spiteful-sounding Patton complained in his diary that no one gave him any lunch after the meeting, adding: 'Monty gave me a 5-cent lighter. Someone must have sent him a box of them.'

Rita's father smiled in triumph when he returned from his morning foray. 'Look what I've found,' he announced as he placed a paper bag carefully on the wooden table.

He had been released from jail a week earlier, after spending six months locked up after an argument with a policeman. He was frail and shabby, but despite his poor health he spent hours every day foraging across the city to find food, braving not only the German soldiers who struck him with the butts of their rifles when they caught him scratching through the rubble of food shops, but also the bombing raids and naval shellings which were becoming increasingly frequent as the Allies got nearer and nearer to Catania.

Rita's mother inspected the bag. Inside was a mixture of broken pasta, earth, small stones and shards of glass. Her father explained that he had found a shop whose front window had been shattered by an explosion. Other people had stripped it bare before he got there, but he found the pasta scattered on the floor among the rubble.

'Good, we'll clean it up,' her mother said.

Rita and her sisters started separating the pasta from the dirt. Her handsome teenage brother Pippo was nowhere to be seen. He usually spent most of the day at the shelter but would probably be back in time for lunch. At the first warning or explosion, he would drop anything he was doing and race for the shelter, even if it meant abandoning the pitcher he was in the middle of filling at the fountain.

Once, Rita had asked him why he always went to the shelter,

and why he stayed there all day, only coming home for meals. 'I go there because I'm scared. I don't want to die here, and at least if I go to the shelter I'm doing something to save myself,' Pippo replied.

He was always trying to persuade his mother and his sisters to follow him, but almost always they refused. 'The Virgin Mary and Saint Rita will protect us,' his mother told him.

Rita hardly ever went to the shelter. Usually she waited in the tiny house for a raid to end, with the whole family scattered around the main room, carefully keeping to the corners in the belief that they were safer than in the middle. As soon as the alarm sounded, Rita's oldest sister Anna, who was fifteen, used to put her nightshirt on and climb into bed. 'I'm going to sleep, that way I won't hear anything,' she would say. Twelve-year-old Nina would start singing. She said it made her feel braver.

As for Rita's youngest sister, seven-year-old Tina, she spent most of her days and nights under a bed, whether or not a raid was in progress. Her family had to pass her food to her. Rita, on the other hand, couldn't stay still. She would keep dashing to and fro across the room, until her mother called her over and made her sit down next to her. But moments later, Rita would be on the move again.

CHAPTER THIRTY

25 JULY: 1300–1500 HOURS

Rita's lunch that day was a banquet. After the pasta – which as usual was only half-cooked because there wasn't enough wood or even paper to burn for the cooking stove – the family feasted on meat her brother Pippo had brought and on unleavened flat bread made from chestnut flour. As usual, Tina ate under the bed.

It was the biggest and best meal Rita had ever had in that house, and she even managed to save a piece of bread which she wrapped in cloth and stowed away in a drawer for later. After they had finished, her mother stretched out on the bed to rest. She lay on her side, moaning softly because she was suffering from faint labour pains. They all knew that when the pains became stronger, she would have the baby at home, as she had done five times already. Rita's grandmother sat by the door which was open onto the street and started sewing. Rita fetched a brush and began to sweep the floor.

'I'm going to the shelter. Who wants to come with me?' Pippo asked. For several days, the sirens had hardly ever sounded in advance of an attack as Catania was coming under fire from both warships and heavy artillery close to the city.

His mother shook her head. 'I'm not feeling too well, you go. Papà will stay here with me. Ask your sisters,' she said.

Rita and her sisters all refused to go. They felt safer at home with their parents.

Pippo walked into the second room to go to the toilet to which was just a closed-off space in a corner. Moments later his grandfather called out to him. 'Hurry up, Pippo, I have to go too,' he said.

'I've finished, grandpa,' Pippo said. Rita saw him in the doorway between the two rooms, just about to go to the shelter.

She heard a whistling sound, but there was no time to wonder what it might be.

Moments later, she found herself in a daze and slowly realised that she was crouching on the floor. Clouds of dark grey dust swirled inside the room. At first she could hear nothing. She tried to pick herself up, but couldn't. She could move the upper part of her body, but she had the sensation that something was pulling her down every time she tried to get up. She felt no pain.

She reached out a hand and felt someone there. She couldn't see who it was, but as soon as she recovered her hearing she realised it was her brother Pippo. He was shouting '*Aiuto!*' (Help) and 'Where are you all? Where are you all?'

He must have fallen on his back. She wondered how. Then she realised that she was crying. Other voices were shouting for help. She made out the shape of her father as he groped his way towards her. He bent down, picked her up and took her out into the street where he set her down on a bench.

Rita looked around her. Across the narrow street, just where the front of their neighbours' house should have been, lay a mess of rubble and smoking dust. Her grandmother, covered in dust from head to foot, sat nearby, a towel wrapped around her right leg. Rita could see her grandmother had hurt herself, but didn't think it was serious.

Her sister Anna walked out of their house, which was still standing, into the street and Rita saw blood spurting from three different places on her chest. Their mother came to sit down next to Rita. She put a hand to her thigh which was splashed with blood. Her hand slipped into a wound before she realised what was happening. Then she stared at Rita.

'My love, my child, your leg. What happened to you?' her mother asked.

Rita looked down to see what her mother was staring at. The lower part of her left calf, just above her ankle, seemed to have decided to slip away from her. It was covered in blood but that hardly registered in her brain. Rita grabbed the part of her leg which was almost severed and did her best to put it back in the right place. She knew it was important not to make her mother worry about anything, because her mother was pregnant.

'Mamma, don't worry, it's just a scratch,' Rita said.

A neighbour lifted Rita up in his arms, her foot dangling uselessly, and started running down the street. In her shocked state, all she could see was the man's head and his blond hair. Everything else seemed blindingly white. As he ran, the neighbour kept saying to her, 'Don't cry, don't cry. We'll be there soon. We'll soon be at the hospital.'

Rita held on to him as tightly as possible, and kept on crying. 'Help me, Papà,' she said, talking to him as if he were her father. 'Help me, I'm dying,' she said, although she felt no pain.

She was only dimly aware of the sound of explosions as shells continued to rain down. The neighbour darted in and out of doorways to seek some protection, jolting her, and she pleaded: 'Gently, Papà. Gently.'

She could feel part of her leg swinging crazily but with her arms wrapped around his neck, she couldn't reach down to hold it. She lost consciousness.

Fenner wondered how the Germans did it. They were a hundred yards away and yet somehow they were firing hand-grenades at the dry irrigation ditch where he and his men crouched. The grenades landed short but the bangs unnerved him and he decided to do something about it.

Since taking Primosole Bridge a week earlier, the British had advanced only two miles north, halted by another and deeper irrigation canal, the dry Fosso Bottaceto which crossed the road leading to Catania and which the Germans seized as a natural defensive position. Fenner's platoon had been sent away to rest – a blissful time of clean clothes, sleep, and swims in the sea – but after three days they were sent back into the line.

As the grenades kept coming, Fenner guessed that the Germans had an ingenious device, a sort of small grenade-launcher which you could fire with a large pistol. The British hand-grenades were unusable because they had to be lobbed by hand, but Fenner called for a little two-inch mortar.

The mortar was passed carefully from man to man, every soldier careful not to show his head above ground. The ditch was so low that it only reached to just above your knees and each man had dug a hole to crouch in. If you wanted to urinate you used an empty bully beef tin and chucked it behind you. If you needed to do other business, you waited for the night and did it under cover of darkness.

Fenner set the mortar up and started firing. He had sent a few mortars over with no great success when Captain Glass, his company commander, approached, bent double to stay under cover.

'The Germans have left, you're to take a patrol into the Fosso,' Glass told him.

'But they haven't left, they're still there,' Fenner protested.

'Battalion HQ says they've withdrawn,' Glass replied flatly.

Battalion HQ has got it wrong, Fenner thought, and I should know, the bloody grenades are there to prove it. But there was no point in arguing. He was sure that Glass believed him – the whole platoon had seen the grenades – but Glass had no choice. Fenner decided to take only two volunteers with him. There was no point in risking more lives than that.

He briefed them as best he could: 'What we'll do is we'll take a Thompson gun each, the rest of the platoon will lie in the ditch and shoot at the Fosso, and we will run like Hell towards it.' He didn't have anything else to add as he had no idea what would happen after that.

'Right,' said Glass, 'I'll get the rest of the company to put down fire while you go.' Glass then got up and ran down the ditch towards the platoon which was to Fenner's right.

Fenner heard a bang and then a shout: 'Stretcher-bearers!'

Fenner crawled along the ditch and discovered that Glass had been shot through the thigh. He was in considerable pain and medical staff were giving him morphine and tea. This time, Fenner forced himself to look. Another officer got in touch with battalion HQ, reported Glass's injury and was told that Fenner no longer needed to go on patrol.

No one seemed to know what to do with Glass. He had proved it was impossible to stand up. As his companions, crouching, debated the issue, Glass lay quietly, waiting.

'We'll put up a white flag and carry him back on a stretcher,' one soldier suggested. Several others volunteered to help carry the stretcher.

'No, you don't want to do that, you'll just get more casualties,' Fenner said.

Over the past week, the Germans had repeatedly shot British stretcher-bearers wearing white armbands with the Red Cross sign on them. One was shot from a hundred yards away and died almost immediately. Another, also carrying a wounded man, had his fingertips shot away. Yet another was shot every time he tried to raise himself off the ground to inject morphine into a wounded man.

If the Germans saw British soldiers get up, they shot them – that was what the Germans were paid for. In any case, no one had a white flag to put up. Fenner and a fellow-officer decided to leave Glass where he was until darkness fell. Glass did not complain and Fenner admired his bravery. Fenner realised that Glass was the third commander of Charlie Company to be shot in Sicily in twelve days. The acting-commander Peter Walton had been killed on a beach on the day of the invasion and then Dominic Parker had been wounded at Solarino. Quite a 'chop rate', as the officers called it.

Fenner began thinking that he himself might not keep going for ever. He had already been a little shaken on hearing that a few days ago a corporal, a man with a good record, had shot himself dead shortly before he was due to go back into the line. No one saw it happen and the top brass described it as accidental death. But it occurred to Fenner that it could well have been the act of a brave man who decided to choose the time of his death, rather than continually endure random exposure to it in battle. He pushed such thoughts to the back of his mind. The job was the thing.

More than three hours after he had been shot, Glass was at last carried back for proper medical care.

That morning, after sleeping for only a couple of hours, Mussolini had kept to his daily routine. He read through the daily reports on the enemy's progress through Sicily and on telephone tappings. He received an appeal for clemency from two Dalmatian partisans who had been condemned to death and sent a telegram overturning the sentence. An official from the Interior Ministry briefed him on the latest news and the Japanese ambassador came to ask about his meeting with Hitler.

At lunchtime, he visited two working-class neighbourhoods which had been bombed on the day of that meeting and was gratified when some of the locals applauded him, even though their homes had been hit. Mussolini's spirits were however lowered by what he later described as an 'oppressive sultriness' which sank down on Rome from a motionless sky. To the Militia Commander Galbiati, who accompanied him, Mussolini muttered about the 'lily-livered creatures' and 'riff-raff' of the Grand Council. The party, or the police, would deal with them, he said.

At a late lunch at Villa Torlonia, Mussolini told his wife that he had requested an audience with the King for that afternoon.

'Please, don't go,' Rachele said. She reminded him of hostile remarks the King had made in private three months before and which a lady-in-waiting who was one of her many informants had passed on to her. A guard at the royal residence had also reported that the King feared Mussolini's popularity would make him too powerful. Three times that day, the protocol office at the royal household had called to insist that Mussolini wear civilian clothes, rather than a military uniform for his audience with the King – further fuelling Rachele's suspicions.

As he sipped his soup Mussolini, who followed a mainly liquid diet consisting of up to four litres of milk a day and fruit which he hoped would cure him of his stomach pains, brushed her concerns aside: 'I am a gentleman; we have a treaty with Germany which we cannot betray. The King has signed it too and we will have to discuss the matter together. If necessary, I will stay in command in order to honour our commitments . . . Either that or I hand over command to him, on condition he gives me the powers to arrest the traitors.'

The couple finished their meal in silence.

She joined him in his bedroom while he was changing for the royal audience, and he smiled at her. 'What shall I wear? The white linen suit, a light blue one, or is something heavier better?' he asked.

'Why something heavier in this heat?' Rachele asked.

'Because in the cooler, you know, it gets chilly,' he said. He was so confident that the King needed him that he could joke about her fear that he might be arrested.

Before leaving, dressed in blue serge, Mussolini gathered the papers he planned to show the King. They included the constitution of the Grand Council and other documents which, he would argue, showed it had only an advisory role. The vote was only an opinion, he would insist. As Mussolini left, Rachele stood on the threshold of the villa watching until his car swung out through the gates.

CHAPTER THIRTY-ONE
25 JULY: 1500–2400 HOURS

Rita awoke to find herself lying face upwards on a stretcher on the floor, her whole body save for her head covered in a sheet. Her vision was blurred but she could make out the doctors and nurses milling around and realised she was in the Red Cross hospital near her home. Next to her, also on stretchers and covered with sheets, were her parents and her brother Pippo. She couldn't see them properly but she immediately recognised their voices.

'You will all be all right, but I know I won't. I can feel I'm dying,' she heard Pippo say.

'Hush, Pippo, we will all be all right. Try to rest,' his mother said.

'You, yes, but not me,' Pippo insisted. Orderlies came and took him away.

Then Rita heard her father saying: 'When I think I wanted to kill that doctor when he put a couple of stitches in Rita's chin, after she fell over in the street! I thought he had disfigured my daughter and gave him a punch I was so furious. But that was nothing. Now look at her. Who am I supposed to kill now? Who did this to her?'

Rita felt somebody's hands trying to put something like a mask over her mouth; it smelt strange and she tried to fight them off until her head and her arms were pinned down. A nurse told her to count out loud and again she lost consciousness.

For the past two decades, Mussolini had met King Victor Emmanuel III twice a week at the monarch's official residence, the huge Quirinal Palace which used to be the summer home of popes. The King, a weak figure – 'more Hamlet-like than

Hamlet', as Ciano described him once – had clashed repeatedly with the Duce but, despite their differences, the two men respected each other. Although the King had at first opposed the decision to enter the war at Germany's side, he had since come to support it and this helped to earn him Mussolini's trust.

Punctually at 1700, the Duce's car passed through the gates of Villa Savoia, the King's private home in northern Rome. Armed Carabinieri milled about the grounds, but Mussolini thought nothing of it. As his car approached the villa, he saw the diminutive, moustachioed King, dressed in the uniform of First Marshal of the Empire, awaiting him on the steps of the mansion.

As soon as the two men greeted each other, the King's manner struck Mussolini as odd. The habitually calm monarch was in a highly nervous state. His face was distraught and his speech was halting and indistinct.

'My dear Duce, it can't go on any longer,' the King began, as he led the way to the drawing room. 'Italy is in pieces. Army morale has reached rock bottom and the soldiers don't want to fight any longer. The Alpine regiments have a song saying that they are through fighting Mussolini's war.' The King proceeded to launch into several verses of the song, which he recited in Piedmontese dialect.

The musical interlude over, the King got back to business, biting his nails as he spoke: 'The result of the votes cast by the Grand Council is devastating. Surely you have no illusions as to how Italians feel about you at this moment. You are the most hated man in Italy; you have not a single friend left, except for me. You need not worry about your personal security. I shall see to that.'

With that, Mussolini's 'friend' announced that the dictator would be replaced by Marshal Pietro Badoglio, who would form a cabinet of career officials 'in order to rule the country and go on with the war'. Two years earlier, Mussolini had forced Badoglio, then Chief of Staff, to retire in disgrace over the Greek campaign. And now Badoglio was to take his place.

At the news, Mussolini suddenly slumped in his chair. 'So it is all over then?' he murmured, adding humbly: 'And what will become of me? And of my family?'

'I am sorry, I am sorry, but there was no other solution,' the King replied.

Devastated, Mussolini could only say: 'It's my ruin, my complete ruin.'

Less than twenty minutes after Mussolini had walked into the villa, the King got up to escort him to the door. He shook both Mussolini's hands warmly but avoided the Duce's gaze. Mussolini was struck by how pale the King looked. The monarch appeared to be even shorter than usual; it was as if he had shrunk.

Mussolini walked down the porch steps. A captain of the Carabinieri came up to him and stood to attention. Mussolini halted.

'Duce, in the name of His Majesty the King we invite you to come with us, so that we can protect you from possible violent attacks by the crowds,' the captain said.

Nervously loosening his grasp on a small notebook he had been clenching, Mussolini said in a tired, almost pleading voice: 'But there's no need for that.'

'Duce, I have an order to carry out,' the captain insisted.

'Well then, follow me.' Mussolini started to make for his car.

But the captain blocked his path and pointed to a large ambulance nearby. 'No, Duce. You must get in that,' he said.

Mussolini walked to the ambulance, but hesitated before getting in. Bewildered, he turned towards the villa and saw that the King was watching him from the entrance. The captain took his left elbow and helped him climb inside, where he found more Carabinieri waiting for him, together with two men in plainclothes carrying machine-guns. Mussolini assumed all this was part of the 'personal security' which the King had mentioned. He thought the precautions were exaggerated but it didn't occur to him to doubt the monarch's words.

Mussolini was made to lie in a stretcher and the door of the ambulance was locked. As it pulled away from the villa, he saw the King step back inside the mansion. Out on the road, the ambulance picked up speed and Mussolini clutched the sides of his stretcher to steady himself.

'It's over, it's over! Fascism is dead!' The shouting came from further down the road about an hour before midnight. Almost immediately a soldier told Messina the radio had reported that Mussolini had resigned from power and that Marshal Badoglio was replacing him.

Soldiers all around Messina exploded with joy. 'The war is over!' 'Fascism is dead!' 'We're going home!' they shouted.

In actual fact, Badoglio himself had announced in the same broadcast that 'the war continues', but no one paid any attention. Some soldiers started gathering dead wood from the side of the road to make a bonfire to celebrate the occasion. An officer ordered them to stop as they risked attracting enemy fire but they went ahead and lit one anyway.

Messina didn't know what to think. He believed the news one moment and disbelieved it the next. It seemed impossible that Mussolini and a system so deeply entrenched in Italian society as Fascism was could collapse after two decades with the abruptness of a ripe pear dropping from a tree. Nor could he believe that the ordeal he had been through – covering more than a hundred miles in fifteen days, having to hide all the time from Spitfire and Lightning patrols, and feeding mostly on prickly pears and fruit he stole from orchards – that all that could end so suddenly.

With no opportunity to wash or shave, he smelt foul and looked like a tramp. The cuts he had suffered from barbed wire on his first day of combat had become infected, a mess now of foul-smelling pus and scabs. But Messina ignored them. He was more concerned about the lice which covered his body, especially his hair, under his arms and in his pubic area. They had black crosses on them and looked like tiny German tanks. Some had settled among the scabs over his wounds, feeding on the blood.

He snatched a few hours sleep wherever he could, day or night. On one recent night he had found himself trapped in the middle of an artillery exchange between German and Allied batteries, the drone of the shells sounding like massive hornets. He finally decided the news of Mussolini's arrest wasn't true when artillery shells, attracted by the bonfire as the officer predicted, started landing nearby. In this corner of Sicily, which was all that he cared about, the war was definitely still on.

How Hahn hated the Italians. They were traitors, they always had been, he thought when he heard of Mussolini's fate. Even in the First World War, they had started out proclaiming their neutrality, only to then join the fight against Germany and Austria. And now here they were practically giving up on the Second World War, ditching Mussolini as soon as things got tough.

Where were all the Italian divisions which were supposed to defend Sicily? Now more than ever, Hahn thought, the Germans would be alone in fighting the enemy. Had the Italians no shame?

'Good, got the bastard,' Repard thought when his destroyer's radio broadcast the BBC announcement of Mussolini's fall from power. But what mattered to him most was the fact that neither the Italians nor the Germans had surrendered. As far as he was concerned, nothing had changed: threats to HMS *Tartar* could surface at any moment in his patch – the circle of water and land, with a diameter of a hundred miles, where he had to remain always alert for enemy aircraft and ships.

As the enemy pulled back northwards along Sicily's east coast, Repard tried to disrupt their retreat as much as possible, firing at any sign of movement along the coastal road. Although the enemy was clearly concentrating its forces in the north-east corner of the island, probably in preparation for an evacuation to the mainland, *Tartar* stayed well to the south of that area.

The straits between Sicily and the mainland were so narrow at that point that the destroyer would have been vulnerable to attack not only from the coastal guns, but also from submarines. It was a fact of life – you didn't stick your nose in sticky areas.

When the anaesthetic wore off and Rita regained consciousness that night, she found herself no longer in a stretcher but in a hospital bed, one in a long row in a vast room with very high ceilings. Although her parents and two of her sisters were lying close to her, Rita felt afraid at the sight of dozens of patients in the ward. They all looked badly injured in some way or another, with wounds on heads, arms and legs. Many wore bandages, some of them blood-stained, and the ward echoed with moans of pain.

Rita straightened up a bit in the bed and had the confused impression that she couldn't move either of her legs. She reached down with her left hand under the sheet and instead of touching her left leg, she felt bandages wrapped around a stump below her knee.

Her first thought on discovering the emptiness below her knee was of a pair of clogs which a shoemaker next door had given her and which she hadn't worn yet.

'What about the new shoes? How am I going to put them on? I don't need two shoes now!' Rita exclaimed, tears coming fast.

'Don't worry, Rita. We will buy you another pair later, I will buy you one,' her mother replied from the next bed.

Rita couldn't understand what had happened to her leg. She could still feel both her legs, and even her toes, and yet part of her left leg wasn't there any more. Her brain automatically associated bandages with pain but the stump didn't hurt.

Two doctors stopped in front of Rita and her family. They stared at them in silence for a moment and then one said something to the other but in a voice barely above a whisper that was too faint for Rita to hear.

As soon as they had turned away, she heard her mother speak

to her father. 'Did you hear what that doctor said? Pippo is dead,' her mother said.

'You misunderstood,' her father replied.

'No, I heard what the doctor said. He said: "An entire family. Seven injured and one dead." Pippo was right, we've survived, but he hasn't. Where is he?' her mother said.

Rita was too dazed to grasp the meaning of her mother's words.

After leaving the King's villa, the ambulance took Mussolini to the Roman barracks where the school for Carabinieri cadets was housed. In the courtyard, his slogan was painted in big letters on a wall: '*Credere, Obbedire, Combattere*!' (Believe, Obey, Fight!)

Mussolini was shown to the school commander's office. A camp bed had been placed there and he stretched out on it, exhausted. He was so pale that a doctor was called. His blood pressure was very low but he refused all treatment.

'My physical health interests me no longer,' Mussolini told the doctor. All he asked his hosts was that they show him where he could shave as he hadn't yet done so that day. 'With this ugly beard, I don't feel myself,' he said.

Several officers called on him. The only news they gave him was that the King and Marshal Badoglio had issued proclamations. The war would go on and Rome was quiet, the officers told him. They also informed him that the barracks had been chosen for his own security.

But that evening when Mussolini saw three Carabinieri stationed outside his door, he suddenly asked himself for the first time: was he under protective custody, or was he under arrest?

Across Italy, people celebrated his fall. They ventured out into the night, sometimes dressed in their nightclothes, flooding the streets and piazzas. They spat at his photographs, pulled down his statues, busts and imperial eagles, and threw Fascist badges into the gutter. Waving the Italian flag, they leant out of cars and trucks speeding up and down the streets. Long columns of soldiers marched through towns, singing patriotic songs.

In a street in Rome, a young woman held her baby wrapped in swaddling clothes high up above her head, shouting: 'I want him to breathe this air!' Crowds gathered under Mussolini's balcony at Palazzo Venezia, which he liked to refer to as his 'stage', electric torches now the only source of light in the vast square, and shouted 'Long live the King!' Young men rushed into the offices of the pro-Fascist newspaper *Il Messaggero* near the Trevi Fountain and smashed typewriters, telephones and desks. Slogans which would have been punished with prison only a few hours earlier appeared on walls in the city: 'Down with the Duce' and 'Long Live the Pope'. More prosaically, someone wrote on a wall in Milan: 'Bread, meat and freedom.' For many, the fall of Mussolini meant the end of the war.

In the Villa Torlonia, Mussolini's wife Rachele, with no news of his whereabouts, listened with resentment to the shouts of jubilation that penetrated their home.

PART 4

THE HORSE-RACE

26 July–8 September

CHAPTER THIRTY-TWO

26-27 JULY

About an hour after midnight, Mussolini was roused from his sleep and handed a green envelope from the Ministry of War. He recognised the writing on the envelope as that of Badoglio, his successor as head of the government. The letter inside read:

YOUR EXCELLENCY, CAVALIERE BENITO MUSSOLINI

The undersigned Head of the Government wishes to inform Your Excellency that all the measures carried out in connection with you have been inspired by your own interest, since we have information from several sources of a plot against your life. With all due regret for these circumstances he wishes you to know that he is ready to give orders that you be safely and honourably escorted to whatever locality you may choose.

The Head of the Government:

MARSHAL BADOGLIO

Mussolini immediately dictated a warm reply to Badoglio, thanking him 'for the consideration which he has seen fit to bestow upon me'. He added that he would like to be transferred to the Rocca delle Caminate, an old castle in his native Romagna region which he owned.

Wishing Badoglio success, Mussolini expressed his pleasure at the decision to continue the war at Germany's side 'as the interests and honour of our country require'. He described himself as 'still' the King's loyal servant and ended with the words: 'Long live Italy!'

The pain from the amputation tore Rita from sleep long before dawn. It was so overwhelming that she began to panic, weeping and shouting at the same time. Two Red Cross nurses came to comfort her. They pointed to a boy called Fausto, two years younger than her, who lay nearby in a bed next to his sister and parents. Their home had been hit by a naval shell three days earlier.

'Rita, don't shout. Look at Fausto. He lost his right leg from the thigh down. Look at how he is just lying quietly like a good boy,' one of the nurses said.

'I don't care! My leg hurts!' Rita said.

Later, her mother persuaded her to try and make friends with Fausto. 'Why aren't you crying? Doesn't your leg hurt?' Rita asked. But the boy just turned his back to her.

When the pain abated, Rita's mother explained to her as gently as she could that the blast and shrapnel from a naval shell landing on the house opposite theirs had swept in through the open door. It had thrown Rita from the first room, through the doorway and into the back room.

A piece of shrapnel had most probably sliced through the bone of her leg, leaving her foot attached to her leg by a thin strip of flesh. Although the wound was only a little above her ankle, the surgeon had amputated her leg just below the knee for fear of gangrene. Another injury had paralysed her right foot.

Rita's mother explained that it was a common practice for surgeons to amputate much higher up than where the wound was. Her grandmother had also lost a leg. She had been injured in the right calf, but the surgeon had amputated her at the thigh.

Rita's mother had suffered a deep wound in her side, and no one knew whether the baby could be saved or not. Her father had been injured in the right shoulder, her sister Nina in the forehead, and Tina in the neck.

The nurses had nothing to give Rita to alleviate the pain. There weren't enough bandages to go round, and the dressing on Rita's stump was leaking blood and pus. As the blood dried, it made the bandages as hard to the touch as a plaster cast. It smelt as disgusting as a dead rotting animal. The nurses had no food for the patients either. Rita longed for the piece of flat bread made with chestnut flour which she had stored away in a drawer moments before the blast.

Later, Rita heard the whistling of shells approaching and explosions sounded near the hospital. No one came to move the patients during the raids, so they just lay quietly in their beds.

Hitler entered the small building he used as his teahouse at the heart of the Wolf's Lair, his headquarters in East Prussia, and greeted the six men awaiting him that evening. The Führer had summoned them to Security Zone One, as his area was called, only a few hours earlier without any explanation.

To his entourage, Hitler had remarked that the man behind the plot to topple Mussolini was 'lucky that he pulled that trick in Italy and not on me. I would have handed him over to Himmler immediately.' Everything must be done 'to get hold of this mob, I mean those bastards who dared arrest the Duce'.

In the teahouse, Hitler asked his visitors – five Wehrmacht officers and one SS officer – to give him a brief outline of their careers to date. Listening to Captain Otto Skorzeny, commander of an SS commando unit, Hitler stared silently at him, taking in the six-foot-four frame and the long duelling scar which stretched from the left ear to the chin.

The thirty-five-year-old Skorzeny, a former engineer, did not mention the trouble his temper, which was his worst enemy, had got him into. On one occasion, he had stolen tyres from a military depot at gunpoint because he needed them for his trucks. On another, he had shot down a picture of the Dutch Prince Bernhard in a café in the Netherlands after the owner refused to remove it. A fanatical Nazi, Skorzeny believed there was no such thing as an officer's code of honour; it was only a cloak for cowardice.

'What is your attitude towards Italy and the Italian people?' Hitler asked him.

'I am an Austrian and our attitude towards Italy is prejudiced by events in the previous world war,' Skorzeny replied.

Hitler smiled faintly, and after dismissing all the other officers, began to brief Skorzeny. The Führer talked about Italy and its future: the King would betray Germany and desert the Axis, he was sure of that, because the monarch had shown himself ungrateful to Mussolini, the saviour of Italy, the man who gave it an empire. 'But I will keep faith with my friend Mussolini and will never permit him to be handed over to the Allies,' Hitler said.

Skorzeny wondered what all this had to do with him.

Hitler continued: 'The Duce is, in my view, the last Roman. He is the last visible symbol of the proud old Rome that once ruled the world. His life, his rise to power, and his actions are comparable only to those of an old Roman ruler.

'The Duce is more to me than a confederate, more than the representative and founder of Italian Fascism. He has come close to me as a human being as few men before. He is my great friend. And I never leave my friends in the lurch.

'You, Skorzeny, will free my friend Mussolini and prevent the terrible fate which our enemies have conceived for him.'

The mission must be kept particularly secret, Hitler said, and only five people in all should know about it. Both the German Embassy in Rome and Field Marshal Kesselring, Commander-in-Chief South, must be kept in the dark.

Hitler touched Skorzeny's arm and stared into his eyes. 'Bring me my friend Mussolini. I know you will do your best and that you will succeed.'

Skorzeny believed him completely.

The trek through the mountains to Nicosia was so slow that Johnson felt the very earth of Sicily was against him. The terrain played into the enemy's hands. As they retreated, the Germans left snipers behind who hid among the rocks and fired at the advancing Americans. The Americans were forced to halt until the snipers pulled back – or until they managed to find the snipers, which was not very often.

The Germans blew up bridges and stretches of road, sending rocks and twisted metal tumbling down the mountainside.

Johnson waited hours in the sun for engineers to build a rough passage using heavy timber and planks. The new bridges looked as if they hung from the sky. But you could hardly get anything heavier than a jeep over, so the troops used dozens of mules which they requisitioned from peasants. The mule pack-trains carrying food and supplies looked as if they were serving an army in biblical times.

The men were always short of water, so they never missed a chance to fill their canteens. When they spotted a small pipe cemented into a rocky cliffside, with its little trickle of spring-water, they rushed up to the pipe, waited impatiently for the canteens to fill and then raced back to rejoin their unit, covered in yet more sweat and dust. Everyone ignored the rule that halazone tablets must be dissolved into unpurified water before drinking it.

Once, during that long hard trek, an enemy artillery barrage sent the men scurrying for cover. The cloppety-clop sound made by the mules had probably betrayed the troops. Johnson watched as the mule he had been walking next to seconds earlier stood in the middle of the road, too terrified to move. The red-hot shrapnel – pieces so long they were as deadly as scimitars – cut into the mule's stomach but it still stood there, braying wildly.

The sight of the mule standing in its own intestines, the flies already buzzing over the mess, made Johnson raise his gun and shoot it dead. He thought it was a Hell of a thing to have to do that to an animal. A man knew to jump into a ditch, but a mule didn't, it just went on standing there. But then again it was only a mule. Johnson thought that perhaps he was getting too upset about the animal. Shouldn't he care more about what happened to the men? It was a Hell of a thing.

When Rita, her oldest sister Anna, and her grandmother were transferred to a hospital in Sant'Alfio, north of Catania, two days after they had been injured, Rita was carried to a bed that had been prepared for her. But she refused to use it, preferring to share her grandmother's bed.

The Allied advance, with raids and artillery barrages striking at random throughout Catania, had prompted the evacuation of the most serious cases in ambulances which picked their way slowly through the streets, the drivers fearful of hitting mines. Rita had never heard about mines before and couldn't understand how something buried in the road could explode just because you happened to drive over it.

The move separated Rita from most of her family and no one seemed to know what had happened to them. On her first day at the new hospital, which was in fact a hastily converted school, a doctor took the bandage off Rita's stump and, without anaesthetic, used a pair of tweezers to pick out pieces of shrapnel which he found still embedded in her flesh.

Afterwards, Rita returned to the bed she shared with her grandmother. The two amputees held each other for hours. 'Be good, Rita, it'll pass,' her grandmother said to her, over and over again, as the pain continued to torment the young girl.

For two days Mussolini, sleeping on a camp-bed, had been confined to the commander's office in the Roman barracks. He was given no news of events in the capital or elsewhere. When he asked about his family, he was told that they were all well. At any time, the Carabinieri kept telling him, orders would arrive for his transfer to his country home, the Rocca delle Caminate in central Italy, as he had requested. It was an ideal location as far as his 'personal security' was concerned, they said.

At about 2000 on the evening of the second day, 27 July, during which Mussolini had refused all offers of food, an officer entered his room, and announced: 'Orders to leave have come through!'

An escort accompanied him down to the courtyard. As Mussolini climbed into a car, Brigadier-General Polito of the Military Police marched up and introduced himself: he was to be responsible for Mussolini on the journey.

Certain that their destination was his country home, a long drive north, Mussolini asked no questions. But some time after the car had left the barracks, he saw through gaps in the side curtains, which had been pulled down, that it was heading not north but south.

'Where are we going?' Mussolini asked.

'South,' replied Polito, who was chain-smoking.

'Not to Rocca delle Caminate?'

'That order was countermanded.'

As the journey continued, Mussolini discovered that Polito, a former police inspector, had been named head of the Military Police only two days earlier. He talked volubly to Mussolini about his exploits as a servant of the Fascist regime, including the capture of Sardinian bandits and other outlaws. But he refused to reveal where the party was headed.

CHAPTER THIRTY-THREE
28-29 JULY

For the past month, Montgomery had pestered British and American military chiefs to have his prize possession, a Flying Fortress, fitted with new engines and returned to him immediately.

He had won the aircraft in the spring, in a bet on the Eighth Army's progress in Libya. Bedell Smith, Eisenhower's Chief of Staff, had rashly promised to give him anything he liked if the Eighth Army managed to conquer Mareth and reach Sfax within six weeks. Without hesitation, Montgomery asked for a Flying Fortress together with an American crew which the Americans would pay for – the package to be his private possession until the war's end. Montgomery had part of the plane fitted up as a small comfortable study with two armchairs and a table to use as a desk. 'It is a great thing to have your own aeroplane, to start *when* you like and go *where* you like,' he enthused to a friend, Tom Reynolds.

Shortly after the plane was returned in mid-July complete with new engines, Montgomery sent a cable to Patton in Palermo suggesting they meet on 28 July for what would be their second meeting in just four days and ending: 'Would arrive airfield 1200 hours in my FORTRESS. Query, is this convenient to you.'

For John Henderson, Montgomery's aide-de-camp, the message was like saying: 'Can I come to lunch in my Rolls-Royce?' Despite his ascetic exterior, Montgomery did have a swashbuckling side – rather like Patton's own more bombastic posturing.

Patton did not take kindly to Montgomery's talk of the Flying Fortress and did not bother to answer Montgomery who asked, in another message, whether the runway was long enough for it.

The result was that when the aircraft touched down in Palermo at about midday as planned, Henderson found himself staring in horror through the Perspex canopy of the bubble under the Flying Fortress's nose, where he usually sat, as it charged towards some hangars at the end of the airfield. The strip wasn't long enough for such a huge aircraft, he realised with mounting panic.

Just as Henderson was thinking his end had come, the pilot put all the brakes on one side, revved one engine and swung the aircraft to the right so that it collapsed on the ground. The coveted Flying Fortress was a write-off. Moments later, Montgomery emerged, his face showing no hint of concern – nor frustration – whatsoever.

Shortly before lunchtime, Rosevich heard the sound of motor-cycles and scout cars reaching Palermo's Royal Palace, and raced down the dirty grand staircase, through the Renaissance arcades of the courtyard, to the front gate. Rosevich liked to salute generals – in north Africa, he'd even run across the street to greet a French general because he liked the palm-outwards salute of the French – and the one visiting today was one whose name he had heard many times.

Rosevich stopped just inside the gate and drew himself up ramrod straight to stand to attention, just in time to salute Montgomery as the Eighth Army commander strode through. Montgomery, small and thin, swayed slightly from side to side as he walked. He had a big smile on his face and looked straight at Rosevich as he acknowledged the salute and walked on. The intense sharpness of Montgomery's icy blue gaze impressed him.

Patton gave Montgomery a ceremonial welcome, lining up an infantry company with a band and treating him to a formal lunch. Neither man betrayed any hint of hostility – they were all smiles as they greeted each other. Patton, as suspicious as ever, couldn't understand why Montgomery made a point of stressing the significance of the American drive along the northern coast towards Messina.

That afternoon, Patton summoned Rosevich to take dictation for a letter to General Troy Middleton, commander of the 45th Division, in which he showed his true feelings for his British rival. 'This is a horse-race, in which the prestige of the US Army is at stake,' Patton dictated. 'Please use your best efforts to facilitate the success of our race.' Patton also admitted that he had put on a show for Montgomery in an attempt to show him up for, as he put it, 'doing nothing for me' when they had met four days previously.

Patton was proving a temperamental competitor for the British – General Alexander had compared him to 'a horse that you had to keep a rein on – a dashing steed that always wanted watching'.

On the road to the town of Troina, Johnson heard a shot, looked up and saw Marsha, one of his men, standing perfectly still some five feet from an empty German machine-gun nest. Marsha was staring down at the ground.

'What's the matter?' Johnson asked.

'I'm in a bunch of castrators!' Marsha cried. 'I can see one right next to my foot.'

A castrator was a metal tube, about six inches long, which the Germans stuck into the ground. Inside the tube was a .45 calibre bullet, and at the bottom of the tube was a firing pin with a spring. If you stepped on a castrator the bullet would shoot up through your foot, through your leg and through the rest of your body. On the way it made a lady of you. The Germans put castrators all over the place, on mountain goat paths and anywhere you were practically forced to pass, but especially next to their machine-gun nests so that enemy running up to kill them would step on the devices.

'Well don't move!' Johnson shouted.

'OK, I won't,' Marsha said.

Taking their time, Johnson and the rest of the men sat down under a tree to drink from their canteens. No one was in a hurry to get Marsha out. He had walked straight into a patch of freshly moved earth and everyone knew not to do that kind of thing. They wanted to teach him a lesson. Every so often one of the men would call out: 'You still standing there?' And Marsha would reply in a low voice: 'Yeah!'

After a half-hour, Johnson and a couple of volunteers fixed bayonets and inch by inch they found a clear way out for him.

The Red Cross nurse walked up to Rita's bed on the morning of 29 July, carrying a small wicker basket coloured pink.

'Happy birthday,' the nurse said as she handed it to Rita.

Inside were three green prunes and a boiled potato. To Rita it was a very special present – the daily meal at the hospital consisted of two prunes, or a potato. Rita smiled at the nurse, the first time she had smiled since the shell from the warship had struck her street.

The only good wishes which Mussolini, stranded near a penal settlement on the island of Ponza, received on his sixtieth birthday came from Hermann Goering, the head of the Luftwaffe.

The previous day Mussolini had sailed to the island aboard a corvette, still wearing his blue serge suit which was baggy, unpressed and shabby. According to Admiral Maugeri, who escorted him: 'It looked as if he had been sleeping in it for several days and he probably had.' Mussolini himself had the air of 'a wry, sad and even pathetic clown'. To Maugeri, Mussolini confided: 'I am politically dead.'

During the journey, gestures of support from the ship's sailors touched Mussolini. Emerging from his cabin onto the deck, he had found a message scrawled on the side of the ship in charcoal: 'Courage, Duce, we are with you.' One sailor approached and offered Mussolini his savings which the prisoner accepted as he had no money at all. Another sailor gave him some underwear. Only the captain's intervention – he ordered Mussolini back into his cabin – put a stop to the procession of gift-bearers.

Mussolini was taken to a low, damp house on the edge of a

beach on which fishing boats had been pulled up out of the water. A guard brought him Goering's telegram. Goering and his wife sent their heartiest good wishes. 'Circumstances,' Goering wrote euphemistically, 'prevent my coming to Rome to bring you a bust of Frederick the Great as a birthday present, but this only strengthens the loyalty and brotherly friendship which I wish to express to you on this occasion.'

Normally Mussolini vetoed any mention in the press of his birthday, let alone his age. A few days earlier when Mussolini was still in power, Goebbels had insisted that the German press announce it with great fanfare, ignoring hints from Rome that this was not to the Duce's liking. Despite all this, and the fact that Mussolini had privately described Goering as an 'ex-inmate of a lunatic asylum' after seeing him play with his toy electric railway, today the telegram delighted him. It was his only contact with the outside world.

To Mussolini, the house where he was held was a sad and desolate spot. His room was bare and whitewashed, he had no mattress and slept on the bed-springs, with his greatcoat as a pillow. He was forced to eat all his meals alone, newspapers were banned, and on the two occasions when he was taken for a swim, it was in a deserted and well-guarded spot.

His guards allowed him to write a short note to his wife: 'Dear Rachele, the bearer will tell you what I need. You know what my health allows me to eat, but don't send me much: only a few clothes because I lack them, and some books. I cannot tell you where I am, but I assure you that I am well. Don't worry, and give the children my love. Benito.'

To fight the monotony of the sluggish summer days, he read a book on the life of Christ, and discovered what he described as 'astonishing analogies' between Christ's betrayal and his own. He drew a little comfort from the fact that several illustrious personalities had been banished to Ponza over the centuries, including the mother of the ancient Roman Emperor Nero, and a sixth-century pope.

Mussolini had himself continued the age-old tradition of sending political opponents to Ponza. Languishing on the island when he arrived were two of his most courageous critics – Pietro Nenni, a Socialist leader, and Tito Zaniboni, a parliamentarian on a thirty-year sentence for plotting to shoot the Duce with a sniper's rifle.

It was on the island of Ponza that Mussolini began to realise the full extent of the plot which had stripped him of his power. The future, he believed, would bring Italy's surrender and his own delivery into enemy hands, unless he was poisoned first. To his sister Edvige, he wrote that he saw himself as 'a heap of skin and bones in process of organic decomposition'.

CHAPTER THIRTY-FOUR
30 JULY–1 AUGUST

Messina's heart leapt as the strip of paper on which he had written his name was placed in the peaked cap, together with the names of seven fellow-officers. Army HQ had decreed that a company of Italian soldiers should stay in the nearby hilltop town of Troina alongside the 15th Panzer Grenadier Division. The Panzers had made the American 1st Infantry Division pay dearly for each mile it advanced until then.

Troina was a key bastion on the German Etna Line, which ran inland from the north coast all the way to Catania. The fall of Troina would leave a considerable number of Axis troops in danger of being encircled and Messina learnt that the officer leading the Italian company must fight to the death – which was the way things usually went when the Germans were involved.

None of the officers volunteered, so they agreed to have a name pulled out of a cap. Messina wondered whether, if his name was called, he would have the courage to fight to the death. He felt torn between the desire to keep struggling for his own survival and the fatalism that had engulfed him the last few days.

The deeper he retreated into Sicily, the more he felt that his fate was beyond his control. It was apparently beyond his commanders' control as well: there was never any talk of a plan of action and he doubted there was one. Several times, at only a moment's notice, the men were ordered to pull back to a town or hillside, where they would spend hours setting up defensive positions, only to be ordered just as suddenly to abandon the spot and move on.

The retreat was so slow that Messina felt sure the enemy could have easily caught up with them, if it had wanted to. His contingent had no artillery, and no tanks. But the Allies failed to engage the Italians and they certainly weren't looking for a fight. Troina was to be an exception because there the Italians would be fighting alongside the Germans.

The name pulled out of the cap wasn't Messina's. He silently thanked God.

The following night, 31 July, Johnson and his men marched as quietly as they could along the winding road which threaded its way through the mountains towards Troina. Orders were to sneak up on the enemy at night and attack at daybreak. Preparing for the march, Johnson had been through his unit's equipment to make sure they left behind anything that would rattle or make too much noise.

To him, Troina was just another damn town he had to take. He knew the battle ahead would be tough, because an officer had told him that Troina was Sicily's highest town and strongly defended, and that they would be attacking in battalion strength of about a thousand men. You didn't deploy an entire battalion if you didn't expect trouble.

An explosion ripped through the still night air. So much for the silent march, Johnson thought. He guessed that it came from a little further ahead, and when he drew level with a body lying on the side of the road, he found out what had happened.

A lieutenant had triggered a mine called a Bouncing Betty, which had jumped into the air right in front of him and exploded, but not before the lieutenant had lunged forward to embrace it and fall on top of it. The mine made spaghetti out of the lieutenant. Thanks to him, no one else was hurt.

Johnson had seen a Bouncing Betty before. They were wide as a grapefruit and eight inches long. The Germans buried them, put a trigger on the ground and ran a wire twenty or thirty yards. You'd come along, hit that wire with your foot, and that would set off a black powder charge in the bottom of the mine. The top part would shoot up and explode, sending blades, nails, anything nice the Germans could find, slicing through the air and killing just about anybody within thirty yards.

Johnson hoped that if the soldier next to him stepped on one, the soldier would react as heroically as the lieutenant. He didn't let himself think that he might step on one.

Far to the east, for two weeks now the battle for the Catania plain had been locked in stalemate. The British and the Germans dug in facing each other across a stretch of no-man's-land, unable to move.

On the plain, a new enemy faced the British troops. First hundreds and then thousands of men came down with malaria, and distribution of mepacrine tablets was abruptly increased to one a day per man as commanders realised the seriousness of the problem. In Sicily, malaria was to claim more victims than the fighting did.

After his unit was taken out of the front line to rest, Fenner was ordered to serve as a junior member of a court-martial. Reciting the oath as he stood in a farmhouse near Primosole Bridge, he had to raise his voice as a British mortar battery went into action nearby: 'I swear that I will not on any account disclose or discover the views or opinion of any member of this court-martial unless subsequently asked to do so by due process of law.'

Two soldiers whom Fenner didn't know were on trial. The first had been ordered to drive his carrier to the bridge, at a time when it was being heavily shelled by the Germans. The man had refused to do it three times and was arrested. Charged with refusing to obey an order, he had no real defence although one of his officers tried to stick up for him. The court sentenced him to five years in jail.

The second soldier was up for desertion. He had disappeared before a night attack only to turn up the next morning once the objective had been taken. This man had no real defence either and was sentenced to three years in jail.

Fenner thought the two soldiers got a fair hearing. This was the way the Army had to do things. The government sent the country to war and told the Army to fight and the Army had to fight and maintain discipline. Soldiers didn't like being on the front line but they did their duty, just like their fathers had done more than twenty years earlier.

But he felt sorry for the convicted soldiers. They certainly weren't cowards; they had been in battle before. If only they could have gritted their teeth and hung on a little bit longer, the court-martial would never have happened. On the other hand, they might also have been killed.

Court-martials were not always necessary, he thought. On one of his rounds, Fenner had come across a sentry standing by his Bren light machine-gun. He was leaning against the butt of the gun, fast asleep. Fenner could have charged him with sleeping on sentry duty, which would have meant a court-martial. But he simply prodded the man to wake him up. The idea of putting him under arrest, incarcerating him somewhere, and setting up a court struck Fenner as a total waste of time and effort for a chap who had simply suffered one small lapse.

The attack on Troina began at dawn on 1 August. After marching through part of the night, Johnson and his unit raced up a hill west of the town. His mission was to find somewhere to set up an observation post from which he could direct artillery fire on the enemy. His spirits lifted when he saw an advance by the 39th Infantry Regiment close in on the town.

They soon fell again when the Germans counter-attacked and many soldiers were mown down on the bare hillside which offered little or no protection. The Americans began to run out of ammunition – soldiers scrambled towards the bodies of the dead to grab anything that would help them fight on. Abruptly, out on the right flank of the American line, a single soldier started running back down the hill, away from the Germans. No order was given but soon, the whole line crumbled and all the Americans were running as the Germans shelled them. As

General Allen put it laconically soon afterwards: 'Enemy strength had been underestimated and the 39th was stopped cold.'

Johnson had never seen fear spread so quickly among so many men, but he understood. Fear was contagious. In north Africa he'd once had to knock a man unconscious during a fire-fight. The guy's nervous system had cracked and there was no way Johnson could reason with him. So, praying he wouldn't do the guy permanent injury, Johnson had struck him down with the butt of his rifle.

You couldn't predict how a man would react to combat. Johnson always tried to work things out in advance, to pick out the people he thought would turn out cool under fire. At El Quettar, Johnson had been sure that a tough, macho recruit from Alabama who apparently loved to fight and was as mean as a snake would never let him down. He'll be worth a lot of money, Johnson thought, he's so damn bad that combat won't affect him.

But then, as his unit lay around discussing, as they often did, what they could do to get out of the fighting and how to get out of the war, the recruit got up and said: 'Well, I'll show you what I can do.' Then he took his rifle, put his right hand around the trigger, put his left hand at the end of the barrel, and fired. It blew the holy Hell out of his hand.

Another time, Johnson saw a man stand up in a jeep, put his foot on the windshield and shoot it with his rifle. You got ten years in jail for that kind of thing. A long damned time but some people said that at least you were alive.

The buzzer on Rosevich's desk in Palermo's Royal Palace rang once. He threw aside the *Stars & Stripes* newspaper, jumped up from his chair and hurried towards Patton's office, clutching notebook and pencil.

He would never have dreamt of keeping such an important figure waiting. But on the way, he paused to straighten his tie in a mirror and checked that the rest of his uniform, which included leggings and woollen shirt despite the desert-like heat, was above reproach. Patton thought a sloppy Army made for a lousy Army and had issued a flurry of 'spit and polish' orders about uniforms. He even went about fining soldiers himself for any breaches of his directives. His own staff were the last people he would tolerate violating his orders.

In his office, a vast and sumptuous room with frescos of angels on the ceiling – the most beautiful painting Rosevich had ever seen – Patton sat in a throne-like chair behind an ornate desk, one leg casually crossed over the other. The only noise came from a fan whirring in a corner. Rosevich saluted, settled down and prepared to take dictation.

Patton explained that he wanted to write a model letter for GIs to send their mothers and distribute it to the men. The letter, or so Patton intended, would help to inspire them. But the more Rosevich listened, the more dismayed he became as the General dictated a fictional account of an attack, peppered with four-letter words.

'We stormed up the hill, and we shot them in the arse. Mother, war is real fun,' Patton dictated. Rosevich stopped himself from shaking his head. This is so corny, was all he could think, the boys are just going to laugh at it. Rosevich could live with Patton's liking war – that was what a general was supposed to do – but the letter was so childish that Rosevich felt greatly relieved when Patton's idea came to nothing.

Later that day, a message received by Patton immediately caught Rosevich's attention. The word 'SECRET', in big capital letters, was stamped above and below the message. Rosevich knew he shouldn't, but he often read the messages sent to Patton, even if they were marked 'SECRET', or 'CONFIDENTIAL'. The risk of being caught out wasn't very great, given that it was his job to file them away. And he wanted to know what was going on.

This message was from Eisenhower. It described a concerted drive by the Seventh and Eighth Armies over the next few days which would have 'a profound influence on the future strategy of the whole war'. Eisenhower ordered Patton 'to attack day and night without cessation'.

The message ended on a personal note: 'The Seventh Army has already made a name for itself that will live in American history. Within the next few days it will add immeasurably to the lustre of its fame. I personally assure you that if we speedily finish off the Germans in Sicily, you need have no fear of being left there in the backwater of the war.'

At the end of the message, Rosevich recognised Patton's handwriting. The General had scrawled 'Whoopee!', and underlined it three times.

Johnson had such a perfect view from his observation post that he felt as if he was in a private box at the opera. He'd never been to the opera, but he imagined it must be something like this – through his binoculars, he could see the silhouettes of the Germans in their dug-outs outside Troina.

He had found a shepherd's hut on top of a bare hill which was the closest to Troina, and he and his men had dug a trench which started inside the hut, burrowed under a wall, and ended on the very brow of the hill, facing the town. The men hid all the fresh dirt inside the hut, so that the enemy couldn't see what they had done. There was so much of the stuff inside the hut there was hardly room to squeeze past and get into the ditch.

Halfway through the morning, Johnson started putting artillery onto the German positions on the slopes opposite. The first thing the Germans shelled in reply was the shepherd's hut. As Johnson crouched down in the trench, 88mm shells whacked one side. The hut stayed standing. It was just too full of dirt to collapse.

Johnson spotted a lone German soldier scrambling out of a machine-gun position. The soldier started running up the slope towards the town.

'Let's get him,' someone said.

Johnson picked up the telephone which hooked him straight to the Fire Direction Centre. 'Fire mission. Enemy infantry,' he said, before reading out the letter and the number which identified a square on his map. Each square was 250 yards wide.

He'd never called in artillery to hit a lone soldier before. But the chaos on the first day of the landing, the exhausting march through the mountains, and the failure of the first attack on Troina had left him angry and desperate. It was as though the fleeing soldier had provoked him into a personal fight. Any time someone tried to kill Johnson, he always felt it was a personal problem, something he could resolve only one way.

The first shell from a 155mm howitzer exploded some way behind the soldier. He ran faster. As he got to the top of the hill, another shell exploded. By the time the smoke and dirt cleared, the soldier had disappeared.

'Did we hit him?' Johnson asked.

No one could tell. Perhaps the German had got over the brow of the hill in time.

CHAPTER THIRTY-FIVE
2-5 AUGUST

The courage which the Germans, backed by Italian infantry, showed in defending Troina impressed Johnson. He heard that under cover of night, they infiltrated the American lines down below, got behind the troops, and shot at them with wooden bullets which wouldn't carry far enough to harm their own men. It made no difference to the Americans: wooden bullets killed just as efficiently as metal ones.

The battle for Troina was proving so intense that all artillery units were ordered to provide near constant support for the infantry. From his vantage-point, Johnson kept up a twenty-four-hour watch for the smallest sign of activity, whether it was a few men crawling towards a building during the day, or the glow of a cigarette at night. Day and night, Johnson watched like a vulture and shelled any sign of life.

There was no shade on the hilltop. The sun rose every morning into a spotless sky, and by eleven o'clock in the morning the temperature had reached around 95°F in the shade, of which there was little. The stone walls of the shepherd's hut grew too hot to touch and reflected the sun's glare down onto the men. But however hot it got, no one was allowed to leave the hilltop until nightfall. Some people pleaded with Johnson, saying they had run out of water. Johnson still wouldn't let them go. 'Tough, next time bring a full canteen,' he'd say. 'If the Krauts realise where we are we'll all be dead.'

Two hours before dawn on 3 August, General Allen launched a new assault, this time with four regiments backed by fifteen artillery battalions. But from their vantage-point the Germans shelled any troops within range and the Americans made only slight progress.

The Germans fought on. Occasionally they'd target the shepherd's hut, and after each volley the smoke would clear and the shepherd's hut would still be there. But after a few days it was just a pile of rocks and dirt.

Exhilarated, Hahn saw the British fall as his machine-gunner swept to and fro across the hillside near Paterno on a southern slope of Mount Etna. There were too many casualties for him to keep count.

Stationed with his platoon of seven soldiers on a northern approach to Paterno, Hahn had spent the past couple of days waiting for this. His job, alongside four of the Tigers positioned at the town's approaches, was to gain as much time as possible for the German troops retreating behind him. He had rarely felt so vulnerable, leading just one platoon to protect four tanks.

But his fears evaporated in the early afternoon of 4 August as he saw his machine-gunner cut down the British after they came up the hillside from the River Simeto. There were about sixty of them, some 500 yards away. In no more than fifteen minutes, the platoon stopped the British advance. Hahn wondered whether the fact that it had all been so easy meant it didn't qualify as a real battle.

A few hours later, he spotted through his binoculars an Italian artillery battery, drawn by horses, going up a road on the other side of the river. The Italians must be about to surrender, Hahn thought angrily, because the road led to the British positions.

'Look at the Italians, they're running away!' he shouted to the commander of the Tiger closest to him.

Seconds later, the tank's 88mm cannon roared several times. When the dust kicked up by the explosive shells cleared, Hahn couldn't tell whether the Italians had been killed or wounded. There was no sign of them or of the horses any more. He hoped the Tiger had sorted them out. The Italians were bastards. Traitors.

Late that afternoon, Johnson watched A-36 fighter-bombers approach Troina. He saw one of them peel away and begin its run over the town. The first, 500-pound bomb tumbled down. Several waves of fighter-bombers followed and the dust clouds grew so vast they hid the top of Mount Etna from view.

It was obvious that much of the town had been reduced to rubble. He heard later that a bomb crashed through the roof of the main church where dozens of women and children had sought refuge. The bomb landed in the nave and failed to explode.

'August the third, 1943,' Patton began as Rosevich scribbled. Every time Patton dictated a diary entry, he specified the year – it was one of his idiosyncrasies. That evening, Patton had summoned Rosevich to his tent at his advance headquarters north-west of Troina because he had to dictate his diary for the previous two days.

Patton described a visit to an evacuation hospital where he had talked to 350 newly wounded men, most of them from the 1st Division. One poor fellow had lost his right arm, another had lost a leg. But all were brave and cheerful, Patton reported. Rosevich admired Patton for making regular visits to the wounded. Two days earlier, Patton had come across a man who was dying and had an oxygen mask on, so he knelt down and pinned the Purple Heart on him.

But Rosevich's feelings changed abruptly as Patton continued, in the same slow pace: 'In the hospital, I also met the only arrant coward I have ever seen in this Army. This man was sitting, trying to look as if he had been wounded. I asked what was the matter, and he said he just couldn't take it. I gave him the devil and kicked him out of the hospital. Companies should deal with such men and if they shirk their duty they should be tried for cowardice and shot. I will issue an order on this subject tomorrow.'

Rosevich made an effort not to betray his unease. When taking dictation from Patton, he would smile at any jokes the General made, but otherwise he was careful to look serious at all times.

Afterwards, sitting at his typewriter, he re-read his notes. His brain kept asking questions: Is this right, is it fair? Did things really go the way Patton described or was he glossing over something he didn't want anyone to read in his diary? The question that worried Rosevich most after this hospital visit was: What on earth had driven Patton to do this? Perhaps the pressure of the race for Messina was beginning to tell.

Then Rosevich remembered Patton's references to malingerers, his efforts to motivate troops with visits and speeches before the invasion of Sicily. Patton must believe, Rosevich thought, that if malingering spread, if morale broke down, he might as well forget the war and go home. All his West Point training, all his experience, would have meant nothing.

Patton, as so often in the past, had simply put on a performance, Rosevich thought. Patton had deliberately treated the patient so harshly, knowing that word of the episode would spread among the troops. He was applying the motto he so often liked to quote to his staff: 'Never take counsel of your fears.'

Rosevich could understand why Patton had acted in such a way, but he couldn't justify it. He didn't approve of American generals going around browbeating little GIs. He was sure that most people wouldn't approve either – if word of this got out to the *New York Times*, things would look bad for Patton.

That evening Rosevich played blackjack with his friends as usual. Patton was always generous in giving Rosevich free time, but in the middle of the Sicilian hills there wasn't much to do in the evenings. The bets were always very small, given that they were all on twenty-one dollars a month.

One of Rosevich's friends asked: 'Did you see the General today? Did you talk anything private?'

Rosevich didn't look up from his cards, and just shook his head.

Enormous explosions in the airfield south of Catania and on the slopes of Mount Etna, which continued day and night, told the British entrenched near Primosole Bridge that the Germans were getting rid of their bomb and fuel dumps as they retreated. Fenner's platoon struck out along the straight road towards the city.

A few hundred yards into the advance, Fenner saw the bodies of two British anti-tank gunners lying by the side of the road. He learnt that the bodies had lain there for more than two weeks. They were sergeants whose carrier had dashed through the forward companies in error. Had they missed the sign 'ENEMY BEYOND THIS POINT' which was usually placed at the front line? One had managed to crawl from the burning carrier to a tree; his skin was as black as coal but his hair was bleached white by the sun. Fenner puzzled as to why the Germans didn't bury the enemy dead. The British did whenever they could. Perhaps the Germans were too idle, or perhaps it was a deliberate ploy to demoralise forward troops.

Closer to Catania, the Germans harassed Fenner's men with 88mm cannon and Nebelwerfers, or Moaning Minnies, but the platoon suffered few casualties. His nerves on edge, Fenner led his men through the streets of Catania early on the morning of 5 August. As he inched his way through the devastated city, Fenner dreaded an ambush. The Germans were very good at this, they would ambush you every step of the way if they could. He kept his eyes peeled, constantly scanning street corners and smashed buildings ahead. A sniper, a mine or a booby-trap might be lying in wait for him. A quick burst of machine-gun fire would be enough to send bullets ricocheting off the stone houses and down the street towards him. The Germans even booby-trapped the dead, hiding an explosive charge behind the head with a bit of wire going through the face, so that it would blow up when anyone moved the corpse.

On one street the bombs had spared, they came across some civilians busy breaking into shops and helping themselves to whatever they could lay their hands on. Tense as they were, Fenner and his men laughed at the sight – the way the locals, young and old, scrambled to retrieve dismal pickings struck them as funny. The locals didn't pay much attention to Fenner's platoon. They were too busy smashing windows and looting.

Rosevich reported to Patton's tent in the morning to show him the transcript of the diary entry he had taken down the previous day. Rosevich knew his place and made no comment on the entry in which Patton described how he had kicked an 'arrant coward' out of hospital. Patton checked it through, and added one phrase with his pen: 'One sometimes slaps a baby to bring it to.'

Patton handed the paper back. 'This is fine,' he said.

Then he dictated a memorandum:

HEADQUARTERS SEVENTH ARMY
APO # 758
US ARMY

5 August 1943

MEMORANDUM:

TO: Corps, Division and Separate Brigade Commanders

It has come to my attention that a very small number of soldiers are going to the hospital on the pretext that they are nervously incapable of combat. Such men are cowards, and bring discredit on the Army and disgrace to their comrades who they heartlessly leave to endure the danger of a battle while they themselves use the hospital as a means of escaping.

You will take measures to see that such cases are not sent to the hospital, but are dealt with in their units.

Those who are not willing to fight will be tried by Court-Martial for cowardice in the face of the enemy.

GEORGE S. PATTON, JR,
Lieutenant General, U.S. Army,
Commanding

Rosevich took it all down, stood up to salute Patton and left. As he walked to his desk, he thought how terrible the order was. He knew soldiers found guilty of cowardice could be shot. Of course men should not be malingerers in battle, but there was no predicting how a man would react under fire. What if an entire unit refused to fight? Would Patton have all of them shot?

Rosevich remembered the first time he had been in combat. It was when the Allies were invading north Africa and the ship he was on was approaching the coast. He had felt 500 per cent fear, his body trembling, as enemy planes dropped bombs into the water alongside his ship. Quite a few of the soldiers on board had shouted: 'I gotta get outa here!' They must have been trembling with fear too, but that didn't make them malingerers. It was only human. Rosevich thanked his stars that he was not on the front line.

CHAPTER THIRTY-SIX

6–10 AUGUST

At noon on 6 August Troina fell to a fifth American assault, and soldiers began picking their way through the rubble of the deserted town. Close to 400 fighter-bombers had pounded it for the past three weeks. An officer gave Johnson a dozen German prisoners to take care of. He found a spot on the hillside behind a rock wall, well away from the fighting so that the Germans would not be in danger. He left some of his men to stand guard over them.

Johnson went back to check on them later that day. The prisoners were lying on the ground. Someone had slit their throats.

Johnson questioned his men but no one would tell him anything. He couldn't prove it, but he was sure that he knew who the killer was. That man was different from the rest of them and he was capable of doing that kind of thing. But someone else must have helped him.

Johnson took the man aside. 'Anything like that happen again,' Johnson said, 'you're going to get your arse hung. Because I'll turn your goddamn arse in and make sure it hangs.'

'Go ahead and do it,' the man replied. But Johnson left it at that.

Later, Johnson started wondering what had happened to the German soldier the artillery had shelled five days earlier at his request. He climbed up to the spot on the brow of the hill where the fleeing German had vanished just as the second shell exploded. Johnson wanted to know if they had actually hit him.

He found nothing on the ground, but when he looked up he saw something in a tree. He looked more closely, and saw that it was a piece of a man's breast, the left one. It was slightly larger than his hand and looked just like a piece of meat. Johnson didn't find anything else. He thought how unlucky the soldier had been and imagined his parents receiving a letter saying he was missing in action.

Johnson got back to his men. 'We hit the son of a bitch,' he told them.

'Good,' someone said.

The killing of the Italian prisoners wasn't the first such atrocity committed by Americans in Sicily.

In mid-July, after ferocious fighting for control of an airfield at Biscari, a captain and a sergeant of the American 45th Infantry Division had shot dead seventy-three Italian prisoners in two separate incidents after first lining them up. At their court-martial, the two culprits argued that they had been following orders from Patton, who had told the Division before the landings to watch out for treachery from German or Italian troops who were apparently surrendering. The Americans should 'kill the s.o.b.'s' unless they were certain of their real intention to surrender. Troops should also kill captured snipers who had shot at wounded men and medics.

The court rejected this line of defence and ruled that Patton was in no way to blame. The captain was found 'not guilty' while the sergeant was sentenced to life in jail – he was released a year later. Patton himself wrote to his wife that what he angrily called 'the friends of freedom' were trying 'to cook up another incident about some unnecessary killings – if killings in war are ever unnecessary'.

Hahn dived under the Tiger tank as the artillery shells started hitting the vineyards on either side of the road. The vines grew behind low walls of lava rocks, which Hahn had been warned could turn into hard jagged shards as deathly shrapnel.

The previous day, together with the other men in his platoon, he had hitched a lift on the last Tiger to pull out of the town of

Belpasso near Mount Etna, hanging on as best they could to the turret as the tank ran the gauntlet of heavy British artillery fire and rushed on through roads lined with lava from the volcano's eruptions. Since then he had been ordered to guard an approach road to Nicolosi on Etna's slopes which, dark grey with volcanic ash and twisted rocks of lava, looked like a lunar landscape.

Hahn had barely crawled under the mass of steel when he felt something bizarre on the back of his upper right thigh. He reached back and felt something warm and slippery. When he looked at his hand, he saw there was blood on it.

'Damn,' he said to himself.

He was mildly surprised that he felt no pain and was reassured that he could still move his leg. He kept touching the area gently and noticed that the flow of blood had stopped. It was only a minor injury. He would see to it later. The main thing now was to keep a look-out for any British troops who might try to sneak up on him through the vineyards, and either shoot him or take him prisoner.

He had learnt a few days earlier that soon all German units were to abandon Sicily in an orderly retreat. There was to be no chaos, and no panic. After the collapse of the defences called the Etna Line, they were to gradually retreat behind the volcano, along four more defence lines until they reached the port of Messina from where the evacuation to the mainland would take place.

Hahn was delighted with the news. The Allied artillery, tanks and Air Force made him feel the underdog in Sicily – a feeling he had never had before – and, robbed of his Tiger, he felt that he was not doing as much as he could for the Reich.

The destroyer carrying Mussolini reached the island of La Maddalena, off the Sardinian coast, in the early afternoon of 7 August and the former dictator was allowed to explore the small house which was to be his new prison. Mussolini was pleased to find, lined up on a shelf in the sitting-room, a belated birthday gift from Hitler: a twenty-four-volume edition of the complete works of Nietzsche.

It was a particularly thoughtful gift. Mussolini revered Nietzsche, who was the inspiration behind several of the expressions he liked to use, such as 'live dangerously' and 'the will to power'. Nietzsche's theory of the superman was tailor-made for Mussolini with its emphasis on the ego which defied both God and the masses – Mussolini said the latter were 'stupid, dirty, do not work hard enough and are content with their little cinema shows'.

The beautifully bound volumes were accompanied by an auto-graphed dedication from the Führer himself and a letter from Field Marshal Kesselring who wrote: 'The Führer will be happy if this masterpiece of German literature gives you any pleasure and if you will consider it as a mark of his personal devotion.'

With few other means of whiling time away, Mussolini plunged himself into the first of the volumes. His new home was set on a hillside and surrounded by a dense forest of pine trees, just outside a village. He was more isolated than in his previous prison with more than a hundred Carabinieri and policemen to guard him.

His prison regime, Mussolini complained to Rachele in a letter, was one of total seclusion. 'I know nothing, and first of all I don't know what I have become,' he wrote. His guards granted a request for a mass to be held on the anniversary of the death of his son Bruno, an Air Force pilot who had been killed in a plane crash two years earlier at the age of twenty-three, but he wasn't allowed to attend. He left the villa only once, to go for a walk in the woods under armed escort.

Since Rachele was the only person he was allowed to write to, Mussolini entrusted her with a justification of his rule over Italy: 'My conscience is clear. I have worked for twenty-one years, without rest, with absolute selflessness, with perfect loyalty. You, better than anyone, know how I have acted in the best interest of the people.'

*　　*　　*

At the mobile headquarters which he had set up on a mountain-side near Mount Etna, Montgomery worried about the German retreat. RAF reconnaissance, which was monitoring the Messina Straits, reported heavy enemy traffic from Sicily to the Italian mainland. He was certain that the enemy, as he put it in his diary that day, was 'starting to get his stuff away'. He had tried but failed to find out how the Navy and the Air Force planned to stop the enemy escaping. 'I fear the truth of the matter is that there is NO plan.'

Before the Sicilian invasion, Montgomery had won his battle to rewrite the plans for the landings. But this time he had no authority to impose his ideas on the Navy and the Air Force, however much he hoped to prevent a repetition on the mainland of the very heavy fighting he had witnessed in Sicily which, he wrote to Mountbatten, was 'fiercer than any I have had since I commanded Eighth Army'. The Bosche, as he called the enemy, was a very good soldier indeed – 'he is far too good to be left "in being" as a menace to the world, and *must* be stamped on.'

Montgomery worked off some of his exasperation by caring for a collection of birds which he had accumulated in Sicily. In the caravan which served as his office, a pair of canaries and a hen shared a cage. The most recent addition to the menagerie was a peacock, which a major had sent him by jeep, together with a letter of thanks for a dinner with Montgomery. Montgomery was delighted with the peacock and allowed it to strut about both in his caravan and in the mess.

Henderson, Montgomery's aide-de-camp, and the mess staff didn't much like the peacock as they had to catch it every time the headquarters moved. At the first opportunity, they launched it off an escarpment and watched it flap down the rock-face before disappearing from sight. When Montgomery asked about his pet, he was simply told the bird was nowhere to be found.

* * *

Repard was at action stations as *Tartar* sailed some four miles off Mount Etna when shells arriving apparently out of the blue smacked into the water near the destroyer and gave him yet another wet shirt. *Tartar*'s mission was to keep up with the Army advance along the coast road and target any enemy presence from Catania northwards.

There was no other ship, nor any aircraft, in sight so the gun firing the shells must be on land. A couple more shells followed – six-inch ones, he estimated – but they failed to get closer. He had barely located the heavy gun on a clifftop north of Catania and a few hundred yards from the sea, when the damn thing seemed to slide backwards and disappeared from view. Repard figured it must be mounted on a railway of some sort which pulled it back into a tunnel.

With no air protection whatsoever in the narrow straits between Sicily and the Italian mainland, *Tartar* had to hold fire until night-fall before she could try to silence the gun. But although she stole up close to the coast and waited, like a cat waiting for a mouse to emerge from its hole, the gun failed to reappear.

On the road east, a peasant Messina and his men had found shook his head. 'I have nothing,' he said.

Messina gestured towards his thin, unshaven and dirty soldiers. Their uniforms were little more than rags, and what was left of Messina's own shoes was tied together with string.

'My men have no rations left, just some bread would be enough,' Messina insisted.

'I have nothing,' the peasant repeated.

Messina wasn't surprised by the peasant's hostility: none of the civilians he had come across during the retreat had shown any sympathy for them. The soldiers pressed forward: Messina could feel their anger and their desperation.

'Let's get him, sir,' one soldier shouted.

Messina calmed his men down. He knew the peasant was lying. All the peasants had stacks of flour and potatoes hidden away, he was sure of it, but there was no point in Italians killing their own kind.

After the fall of Troina, Patton pulled Johnson's Division out of the battle for Sicily and ordered the 3rd Infantry Division to move to Santo Stefano di Camastra on the northern coast, from where it would set out on the winding hundred-mile stretch to Messina.

Johnson was too numb to feel much emotion. Thank God this one's over, was all he thought. Now we move on to the next place. He'd been marching and fighting for twenty-seven days and at least fourteen nights. He hadn't had even one shower during all that time. He felt like shit, warmed over twice. After a good clean-up, he spent hours reading everything he could get his hands on. Boxes of paperbacks, a dozen at a time, and some comics started arriving. Johnson let the others fight over the comics and read as many of the paperbacks as he could.

Johnson no longer believed, as he had when he sailed on the eve of D-Day, that war was beautiful, clean and justifiable. He'd learnt on Sicily's mountain roads that war was dusty, dirty, miserable and deadly. He no longer expected anything good to come out of war and had long given up on his hopes that the Germans would quit and go home. The war would go on for ever, it didn't matter how many men got killed. Nobody cared.

Doctors and Red Cross nurses bustled into the ward where Rita and the other patients lay unable to move as bombs exploded with increasing frequency very near the hospital.

'The English are coming!' one of the doctors announced. 'It's too dangerous for you to stay here so we will take you down to the basement where you will be hidden. And when the English get here, don't welcome them, don't applaud them because it's their fault if you're in this state.'

As soon as the medical staff had gone, the patients talked excitedly among themselves. Anything was better than staying where they were, they agreed. A few days earlier, Rita had narrowly escaped being struck by a piece of shrapnel. It hit the wall just where she had been sitting up in bed, a few moments after her grandmother had pulled her down to lie flat. They still had no news of the rest of the family.

Although the basement felt safer, the patients found themselves enduring another ordeal. They were virtually abandoned in a dark corridor-like room, so narrow that two mattresses wouldn't fit on the floor across its width without overlapping. Two patients died of gangrene. Their neighbours covered their faces with sheets, but no one had the strength to carry the bodies outside, and it was hours before orderlies came for them. Lying uncomfortably on their mattress, Rita clung to her grandmother. 'I'm here, I'm here,' the old woman reassured her.

On the morning of 10 August, the door at the end of the basement opened abruptly and light flooded in from the courtyard. Two young British soldiers stood in the doorway, staring in. Rita felt herself lifted up in her grandmother's arms.

'Look!' she heard her grandmother cry out. 'Look at what you have done!'

One of the soldiers rushed forward, the patients making way for him to approach.

'Not us, not us. War,' the soldier said when he got close.

He bent down and stroked Rita's face and hair. Then he took her into his arms. She felt his tears on her face as he hugged her tight and kissed her on the cheek. The soldier brought her out into the light and gave her chocolate and sweets. Rita, starved of proper food for so long, devoured everything he gave her. She felt no animosity towards him, only joy.

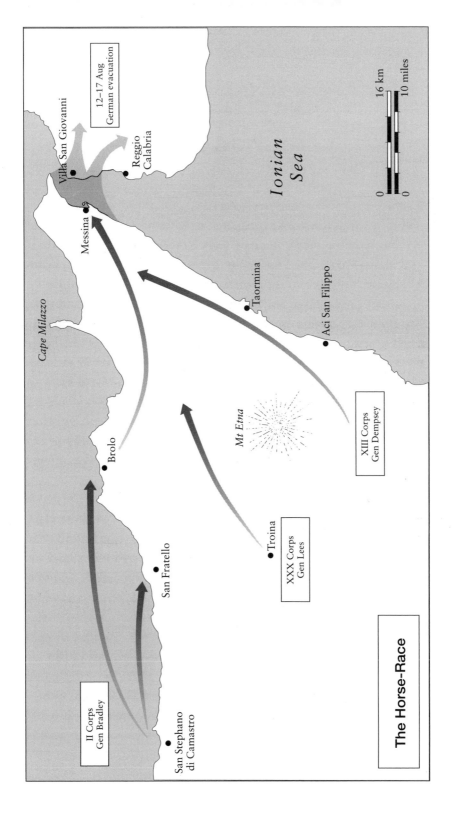

The Horse-Race

12–17 Aug
German evacuation

Villa San Giovanni

Reggio
Calabria

*Ionian
Sea*

Messina

Taormina

Aci San Filippo

Cape Milazzo

Brolo

Mt Etna

San Fratello

Troina

XXX Corps
Gen Lees

XIII Corps
Gen Dempsey

San Stephano
di Camastro

II Corps
Gen Bradley

16 km

10 miles

0

0

CHAPTER THIRTY-SEVEN

11–17 AUGUST

Trudging up a road near the town of Altarella north of Catania, on the morning of 11 August, Fenner heard an explosion ahead and saw a small pack fly up into the air and drop down again. He hurried on to find out what had happened.

Fenner knew the roads were heavily mined. Sicilian authorities had told the British troops as much. Five days earlier, officials from the nearby town of Aci San Filippo had handed a note written in ungrammatical English to a fellow-officer:

> Englishmen
> We dwell at Aci S. Filippo and we have come
> here for telling you that the German soldiers
> have gone away from our country where still
> are mines at the road, for this reason we
> caution you to be attentive and to remove
> the mentioned above mines.
> All people are happy in receiving you and
> they pray you to respect them.
> Hurra Englishmen!
> England for ever!

North of Catania the road was hellish – narrow and flanked by high stone walls and rivers of solid lava with grapevines growing everywhere giving plenty of cover – and the Germans could be anywhere. Within a few miles of Mount Etna, which seemed to brood over the surrounding landscape, the men's feet would sink into four inches of black dust and there was no way you could stop it rising and covering your clothes. All the men could do was make sure they wore their long trousers and tied their puttees tightly around the tops of their boots.

When Fenner got to the scene of the explosion, he discovered that one of the best chaps in the company – cheerful and brave Sergeant Albert Dunn, always a great survivor – lay dead in the dust, his short body blown in half. Barely twenty, Dunn was from County Durham and had served in the company for the past four years. He had won the Military Medal at El Alamein when, armed only with a submachine-gun, he stood his ground and took on a German self-propelled gun, accounting for most of its crew.

Dunn's round face had gone up on posters all over Britain when he was chosen for 'Salute the Soldier Week'. The typical British Tommy, he was pictured carrying a rifle over one shoulder and a pickaxe over the other, his steel helmet on the back of his head.

Fenner was told that he had been trying to defuse a mine which turned out to be booby-trapped. Dunn was an infantryman and shouldn't have attempted such a thing but the gesture was typical of him – he was a courageous chap and he probably thought he was doing everyone a favour by helping to clear the middle of the road so that vehicles and men could get through. The device he tried to clear was a Teller mine; its top fuse would be activated as soon as a vehicle passed over it. But if someone cleaned the earth around it and lifted it, a second fuse anchored into the ground under the mine would make it go off immediately.

Fenner had done a short course on mines and booby-traps, and he wouldn't have dreamt of tackling a mine by himself. Dunn's death moved him more than any other he had witnessed in months. But he didn't stop to see him buried. There was no time.

Under cover of darkness on 12 August and for the third night in a row, the destroyer *Tartar* crept up to the coast north of

Catania with Repard poised to blast away at what he and his men called the railway gun as soon as it showed itself again. The destroyer moved in closer than it had before, attracted by what looked like the headlights of an Army convoy moving along the coast road.

Suddenly, the lights went out and the railway gun emerged from its tunnel.

A shout in Repard's headphones shattered the stillness. 'E-boats on the starboard bow!' someone cried from the bridge. Then he heard the Captain calling for full speed and hard-aport. Repard felt his seat vibrate as *Tartar* began to accelerate before swinging out to sea.

'We've been caught with our pants down. We're in for the high jump,' Repard thought. The headlights must have been a lure. E-boats, armed with both guns and torpedoes, were faster than *Tartar*. There would most likely be no advance warning of the torpedoes: the underwater Asdic (sonar) device which had detected the sound of the E-boats' engines couldn't distinguish between their roar and that of torpedoes equipped with propellers.

As the destroyer belted away from Sicily, Repard ordered a few shots over the stern at the heavy gun. The explosions caused by his shells appeared to be more or less in the right place, and he hoped that his shells had at least blocked the entrance to the tunnel. He would have loved to go ashore and see for himself the results of the shelling around the gun's emplacement. He knew there were ancient Roman ruins in Catania, and thought briefly that *Tartar* must have added to them.

The destroyer steamed on and he struggled to pick out the outlines of the E-boats against the dark mass of the coast, his eyes straining in the night. His binoculars failed to pick up anything in the darkness, and for a long while the radar couldn't distinguish between the cliffside and the E-boats, with the result that he had no idea where to fire. The E-boats must have been lying in wait under its shadow, ready to spring their ambush. No lights gave away their position.

Repard pictured the torpedoes running through the water towards him. When the radar finally picked up echoes from two E-boats, two miles to the west, Repard immediately swung his guns onto the bearings but the zigzag course set by the Captain made the destroyer heel heavily, and placed the mast in the guns' line of fire. In any case, Repard still couldn't see the E-boats and there was no point in blazing off into the night. Eventually it didn't matter any more. The radar revealed that the E-boats had called off the chase.

The last thing Messina saw on Sicilian soil, at lunchtime on 16 August, was a jumbled mass of dead Italian soldiers lying crushed under the collapsed metal slabs of a warehouse. The bitter-sweet smell was so nauseating and asphyxiating in the hot sun that Messina and some 800 other soldiers hurried on to the quayside as fast as they could. Opposite, across two miles of water, he could see the Italian mainland where he hoped he would at last be able to get his strength back and fight the invaders again once his unit had been re-equipped.

Awaiting the men was the last ferry boat still running. A crew-member handed a bright red lifejacket to Messina. He put it on – he knew how to swim, but he wouldn't have the strength to do so for long. He found a spot on deck, where the men huddled so close together there was no room to stretch his legs.

As the ferry prepared to sail, the Captain announced that if an Allied plane flew close to the ship, the soldiers on board should remain immobile. 'If anyone shoots at the plane, we will become a military objective and we can be attacked,' the Captain said.

The ferry set out across the strait and Messina began to pray silently. It had steamed only half a mile out of the harbour when six Spitfires approached and began diving down, one after the other, only pulling out some sixty feet above the sea.

The men were all wearing the red lifejackets. To the Spitfire pilots, Messina thought, they must look like the centre of a giant bull's-eye. He quietly recited the prayers his parents had taught him: 'My Lord, save me. Holy Mary, help me. Let the souls of my dead relatives pray to the Lord for me.' More prosaically, he repeated over and over again: 'Holy Mary, let me get to the other side. Holy Mary, let me get to the other side.'

He tried to hide his trembling from the men squatting close to him. Their own eyes were full of fear, their faces haggard and their backs bent by the humiliation of defeat. This was truly the Ghost Division.

One soldier nearby said he'd heard that Americans attacked the ferries at sea, whereas the British had the decency to wait until the ships were no longer in open water and had reached the other side. Messina prayed that the man was right.

The ferry had barely reached the dock in the harbour of Villa San Giovanni on the mainland when the Spitfires began diving again, this time raking the ferry with cannon shells and machine-gun bullets. Messina fled the ship as did all the other men. He ripped the lifejacket off as he ran and reached a railway line close to the quayside where he burrowed into a drain barely big enough for him. From his hideout, he saw two Blenheim Bristols bomb the ship, making it lean towards the quayside like a wounded colossus.

The destruction of the ferry meant that Messina's unit was the last one out of Sicily. Crouching in his drain, he mumbled a prayer of thanks to the Virgin. He also prayed that he would never have to fight again; he knew all too well what the Allies could inflict on an infantryman with no artillery, tanks, Air Force or Navy to protect him.

Shortly after dawn on the following day, 17 August, Hahn posed for a photograph as he stood on the boat taking the last Tiger out of Sicily. He was so overjoyed at leaving Sicily and proud of his own record there that he gave little thought to the fact that his army had suffered defeat. In any case, Sicily was so far away from Germany that losing the island didn't represent a threat to his homeland.

Soon after the picture was taken and the boat had set out for the mainland, enemy bombers attacked the docks it had sailed from. To the tank-crew, it looked as if a blanket of bombs was being thrown over the docks which were still only a few hundred yards away from their boat.

Anti-aircraft guns on the Sicilian coast fired back, succeeding in hitting a few of the planes. Hahn and his companions were both delighted and terrorised by such success as they feared that one of the stricken aircraft could crash on top of them. Bombs fell closer and closer to the boat, the columns of water so thick they hid the port of Messina from view and the shock waves rocking the boat to and fro.

Hahn reached the Italian mainland unharmed. Of the crews attached to the seventeen tanks in his company, only some thirty men had come through Sicily without being either killed, wounded or taken prisoner.

By 0830, the Axis forces' own Dunkirk was complete. It was the climax to a determined and masterly defensive battle which had been fought along successive defence lines, with the Germans virtually dictating the pace of the Allied advance. The lines became shorter as the Germans backed into the north-east corner of Sicily, allowing more and more men to be evacuated.

Although Hitler's habit was to always keep his troops in the dark about the possibility of a withdrawal, commanders in Sicily had defiantly launched the evacuation as early as 11 August, and made sure that German troops knew about it. Far from demoralising soldiers, as Hitler feared, the knowledge that they would not be left to die or to be taken prisoner in Sicily actually boosted their morale.

The evacuation procedure was orderly and disciplined, with units directed to assembly points and then assigned a precise time and place for embarking, so that ferry boats, barges and assault craft, many of them designed for the invasion of Britain, spent as little time as possible in port. German soldiers were permitted to embark only if they were still in possession of their personal weapons. An order distributed in the Hermann Goering Division warned: 'These weapons are *tickets* for the ferry. Without these, soldiers will be ruthlessly prevented from crossing.'

Some 53,000 German troops, including 15,000 wounded, escaped to the mainland. Fifty-one tanks and some 10,000 vehicles were also carried across. Baron von Liebenstein, the Naval officer who oversaw the evacuation, could quite justifiably boast: 'We have not given up a single German soldier, weapon or vehicle into enemy hands.' The Italians were just as successful with their evacuation, using three steamers, a train ferry and motor rafts. This odd fleet transported to safety 62,000 men, as well as vehicles, artillery pieces and even twelve mules.

Still haunted by the Gallipoli disaster, the Allied Navy steered clear of the narrows in the Straits of Messina, fearing the shore batteries. According to the German Admiral von Ruge, the sight of his fleet's patrols anywhere near the straits caused Royal Navy ships to turn tail.

Similarly, the Air Force failed to make much of an impression, despite their efforts to increase the pressure in the last three days. Wary of the anti-aircraft guns, the Air Force was reluctant to risk an approach and in the first ten days of August the Germans reported losing only four craft, including a Siebel Ferry, a contraption based on two engineer pontoons. The air attacks killed only one German. Von Ruge noticed that Allied aircraft activity suffered from predictability. 'The Anglo-Saxon habit of lunch hour also helped considerably,' he said.

Major-General Rodt, commander of the 15th Panzer Grenadier Division, also noted in an after-action report that the Allied Air Force was set in its ways. The most likely raid-free times were what the German troops called 'the enemy's tea-breaks', from 1600 to 1800 daily. The early misty hours of the morning were also quiet and the Germans found that they got troops across the straits much more efficiently during the daytime than at night when the air attacks were heavier.

It took Patton seventeen days to cover the last hundred miles to Messina and win the race against Montgomery. The 'Truscott trot' was not enough to get the Americans and their supplies along the narrow coast road, which proved impassable for tanks and heavy vehicles. Officers fanned out into the surrounding countryside to requisition some 400 mules and a hundred horses – often at gunpoint as it amounted to robbing Sicilian peasants of their livelihood.

Frustrated by the German resistance which doggedly fought for every mountain village and threatened to make him lose the race for Messina, Patton ordered three separate amphibious landings along the coast. But only the first of these, at San Fratello, was completely successful. The second, at Brolo, saw the Americans suffer 167 casualties. The last, at Cape Milazzo, turned out to be both pointless and farcical as the seaborne troops were greeted by Americans who had already reached it. Late on the night of 16 August, the first Americans finally entered Messina.

On the following morning Rosevich drove through the city to rejoin Patton. The General, who was still feeling shaky after suffering from sandfly fever which had confined him to bed with a high fever for two days, was so elated by his success that he took his dagger to some photographs of Mussolini and ripped them to shreds.

But when Rosevich saw the devastation in Messina, he did not feel like celebrating. So much of the city was flattened you couldn't tell where the streets began or ended. He had never seen such devastation. The fact that there didn't appear to be anyone – alive or dead – in the city, apart from a couple of soldiers in a passing jeep, deepened his gloom. 'How are they ever going to build this city up again?' he wondered.

Rosevich thought of the men, soldiers and civilians who had been injured or killed over the past few weeks. He had never seen a wounded man or a dead body close up. But some days earlier Patton had described in his diary seeing one man who had had the top of his head blown off. The hospital staff, he said, were just waiting for him to die. The man was such a horrid bloody mess that Patton felt the sight of him risked making him, as he put it, 'develop personal feelings about sending men to battle. That would be fatal for a General.'

Patton had to all appearances overcome any such misgivings when he dictated his diary entry about the conquest of Messina later that day. What mattered to him now were British dirty tricks: 'In the town of Messina we met three British tanks and a few men who had arrived at 10:00 o'clock under the command of a general. It is very evident that Montgomery sent these men for the purpose of stealing the show. They had landed from one LCT (Landing Craft, Tanks) about fifteen miles south and had come directly up the road. I think the general was quite sore that we had got there first, but since we had been in for eighteen hours when he arrived, the race was clearly to us.'

God, Patton said, had been most generous to him, and if he had to fight the Sicily campaign again, he would make no change in anything he had done. But he added: 'So far in this war I have been a chip floating on the river of destiny. I think I had best keep on floating – I will surely be used some more though at the worst, things look gloomy.'

He made no mention, Rosevich noticed, of the fact that enemy artillery firing from the mainland had struck the car following Patton as his motorcade entered Messina. The city was still under attack and all the men in the car were injured. Nor did Patton mention that more enemy artillery interrupted the victory parade and claimed more victims.

Just like after the fall of Palermo, tributes poured in to hail the General who, thirty-eight days after the initial landings, had ended the battle for Sicily. 'All of us are thrilled,' President Roosevelt wrote. The message from Montgomery was full of praise: 'The Eighth sends its warmest congratulations to you and your splendid Army for the way you captured Messina and so ended the campaign in Sicily.'

But some time later, at a conference in Catania which both Patton and Montgomery attended, the British Lieutenant-General showed his reluctance to share the spotlight with his American ally. One of the subjects under discussion was fraternisation which in effect meant whether soldiers could talk to Sicilian women.

Patton came quickly to the point. 'Fornication ain't fraternisation, that is if you keep your hat on and the weight on your elbows,' he observed.

The military chiefs around the table roared with laughter, but Montgomery looked peeved. Patton had stolen attention from him.

CHAPTER THIRTY-EIGHT
18 AUGUST–7 SEPTEMBER

In the three weeks since meeting Hitler on the day after Mussolini's fall from power, the SS Captain Skorzeny had spared no effort in his search for the former Duce. Skorzeny had quizzed senior German officers and diplomats in Rome and eavesdropped in cafés and restaurants, but to no avail. Then Hitler himself intervened. The Führer told the Rome government that Field Marshal Kesselring had a birthday gift – the complete works of Nietzsche – he wished to give to Mussolini in person. But Rome refused to allow a meeting.

Skorzeny challenged anyone who claimed to know something about Mussolini's whereabouts, pretending to doubt their word in an attempt to provoke them into saying more. The trail suddenly warmed. From a fruit-seller on the coast near the island of Ponza and an Italian Navy officer, he learnt that Mussolini had been held there for a while. But he had since vanished.

A few days later, Skorzeny overheard another Navy officer say that Mussolini was in Sardinia. He rushed over to the island and, after a couple of false leads, learnt from a prostitute that Mussolini was not on Sardinia itself but on the nearby island La Maddalena. Skorzeny sent a member of his team, wearing the uniform of an Italian sailor, to investigate and succeeded in pinpointing the villa where Mussolini was held.

On 18 August, Skorzeny took off from a Sardinian airfield in a He-111 plane for a reconnaissance flight. He planned to take photographs of the villa and the nearby coastline with his Leica camera. The plane was about to reach La Maddalena when the pilot received a warning that enemy aircraft were in the area. Skorzeny ordered the pilot to stay on course all the same and managed to take a few photographs from the forward gun turret. He was still taking pictures when the plane suddenly gave a violent jerk and plunged into a sharp dive.

The He-111, one of its engines destroyed by an enemy plane, crashed into the sea, the impact shattering the nose window. With the help of a crew-member, Skorzeny managed to swim free of the cabin, taking with him both his camera and a life raft. An Italian ship picked them up after an hour, and its captain asked no questions.

Undaunted, Skorzeny began to plan a seaborne raid on the villa with powerful launches and minesweepers. He obtained Hitler's approval for the plan but before he could put it into effect, Mussolini disappeared yet again. Skorzeny resumed his quest.

The lengthy letter from Eisenhower to Patton was a shocking eye-opener for Rosevich. The contents of the letter which he was told to file cast a very bad light on the General. Dated 17 August, it included reports medical staff had sent to Eisenhower about Patton's treatment of the two men he had called cowards.

Rosevich knew about the first man's case but the reports were much more detailed than the General's diary entries. Patton, the reports said, had asked the GI what was the matter and the man replied: 'I guess I can't take it.' Patton then flared up, slapped him across the face with his gloves, grabbed him by the scruff of his neck and kicked him out of the hospital tent.

The second case was news to Rosevich. A week later on 10 August, at another aid station, the General slapped another man he called a 'goddamned coward' and 'a yellow son of a bitch'. Patton then struck the man again with such force that his helmet liner was knocked off into the next tent. Patton even reached for his pistol, shouting: 'I ought to shoot you myself, you goddamned whimpering coward.'

The need for toughness on the battlefield, Eisenhower wrote, 'does not excuse brutality, abuse of the sick, nor exhibition of uncontrollable temper in front of subordinates'. Eisenhower demanded that Patton apologise to those concerned.

Although Rosevich disapproved of the General's conduct, he felt sorry for him. The letter had come at a difficult time for his superior. Over the past few days, Patton's jubilation at winning the race for Messina had quickly evaporated and he was often morose, almost depressed. Twice Rosevich had seen him reading books on ancient military history, through a pince-nez which he had only ever seen in schoolbook portraits of presidents. Patton was so fascinated by the battles of Hannibal, Caesar and Napoleon that he believed, according to his aide Codman, he had fought in them himself.

Rosevich didn't believe in reincarnation and figured that the reason the General was plunging himself into the past was because he was worried about his own prospects. In his letters, Patton had revealed that he and the Seventh Army would miss the coming invasion of the Italian mainland, but he had no idea whether or not he would he part of the amphibious invasion of northern France due in the spring.

Late on the afternoon of 20 August, Patton summoned Rosevich to take dictation for his diary. The General was anxious to set the record straight about the two incidents. 'My motive was correct because one cannot permit skulking to exist,' Patton dictated. 'It is just like any communicable disease. I admit freely that my method was wrong and I shall make what amends I can. I regret the incident as I hate to make Ike mad when it is my earnest study to please him . . . I feel very low.'

Rosevich noted that Patton had stopped short of a full apology.

Soon after the fall of Messina, word reached Johnson that some twenty American soldiers were going to be hanged for raping local women. The executions were to take place in a piazza in the town of Palma di Montechiaro on the southern coast, where his Division was now encamped.

Most of the condemned men were front-line troops. He had

heard the story several times – a soldier charges into a house, it's empty save for a woman too afraid to say anything, so the soldier thinks: 'I'll take care of this one and no one will know the difference.' And if the woman turns him in, the soldier hangs.

Johnson could have gone to watch but he had no desire to do so – he'd seen enough deaths. It was a terrible waste of men and crazy that, although the fighting had stopped, the killing continued.

Rosevich was sitting at his desk on the morning of 21 August when he saw Codman, Patton's aide, lead a GI apparently in his mid-twenties into the General's office. Rosevich had seen many visitors call on Patton since the end of the campaign. Everyone wanted to salute the Conqueror of Sicily. Patton had charmed a party of journalists, reconstructing the campaign for them, and quoting one of his favourite mottoes, Danton's exhortation to the defenders of Verdun in 1792: '*Il nous faut de l'audace, encore de l'audace, toujours de l'audace.*' (We need audacity, more audacity, always audacity.)

The meeting with the GI lasted less than a half-hour, and afterwards Codman ushered the man out without introducing him to anyone. Later, Codman told Rosevich that the GI was one of the two soldiers whom Patton had branded a shirker. Codman didn't go into any details. 'The General was told to apologise and he did,' was all he said. Rosevich could imagine what having to apologise to a private meant for a man like Patton, and was impressed.

That evening, Bob Hope came for dinner. Codman told Rosevich that, after Patton gave a speech, Hope described the General as 'a pretty good comedian, and a great entertainer'. Rosevich saw irony in the compliment. He had seen Patton so down in previous days that he was sure the General's jovial manner was a front. It was an act – like the one he had performed to motivate the troops before the Sicily campaign began.

Rosevich was sure he had guessed right when, a little later, he saw Patton's diary entry about the Hope dinner: 'Bob Hope and his troupe called on me at the office later and we had them to dinner and they sang and carried on until after midnight. I put myself out to be amusing and human as I think it may help, particularly if this business about the shirkers comes up.'

A few days later, with the curfew lifted at last, Rosevich was free to amuse himself as he saw fit. On one of his walks through the narrow flagstoned streets of Palermo's Saracen city-centre, he saw a lovely-looking girl and went up to talk to her. He spoke very poor Italian and she understood only a couple of English words, but somehow he managed to ask her out dancing, and she accepted. He could hardly believe his luck.

Every Friday evening, the military organised dances in a church basement. Rosevich arranged for an Army truck to fetch the girl and then pick him up on the way to the dance. He knew nothing about her, apart from the fact that she was very pretty and that her father had an orange farm. But he could feel himself falling for her.

When the Army truck arrived, Rosevich rushed out to greet her. He pulled open the door of the truck and his face fell. Inside, smiling at him, was not only the girl but also, it seemed to him, her whole family – and Sicilian families were never small. Rosevich managed to smile back, squeezed in between two women he guessed were the girl's mother and grandmother, and off they all went.

On 22 August, the following message was distributed to the men of the Seventh Army:

Soldiers of the Seventh Army: Born at sea, baptised in blood, and crowned in victory, in the course of 38 days of incessant battle and unceasing labour, you have added a glorious chapter to the history of the war.

Pitted against the best the Germans and Italians could offer, you have been unfailingly successful. The rapidity of your dash, which culminated in the capture of Palermo, was equalled by the dogged tenacity with which you stormed Troina and captured Messina.

Every man in the Army deserves equal credit. The enduring valour of the Infantry, and the impetuous ferocity of the tanks were matched by the tireless clamour of the destroying guns . . .

But your victory has a significance above and beyond its physical aspect – you have destroyed the prestige of the enemy.

Your fame shall never die.

GEORGE S. PATTON, JR
Lieutenant-General, U.S. Army
Commanding

Mussolini's three-week stay on the island of La Maddalena ended abruptly. The sight of a German plane flying low over the area prompted Mussolini to hope that Hitler might soon engineer his release and apparently unnerved the Italian government. On 27 August, he was transferred to a small house some 3,000 feet up on the Gran Sasso mountain in the Apennines in central Italy.

Soon after his arrival, and still kept ignorant of his fate, Mussolini asked one of his guards, a police inspector, why he was being held there.

'You are considered an ordinary prisoner,' the inspector replied.

'And what is your job, then?' Mussolini insisted.

'The same as before. To see to it that you don't try to get away and, above all, that no one tries either to free you or to do you harm.'

The small house serving as Mussolini's prison was opposite the start of a funicular railway leading up to a wide plateau at 6,000 feet. Mussolini noted with satisfaction that both the funicular and a lodge on the plateau were built during his rule. Perhaps he realised the irony of the plateau's name: the Campo Imperatore (Emperor Field).

Gradually Mussolini's guards eased the regime at what he called 'the highest prison in the world'. Although the number of

Carabinieri watching over him was increased, he was allowed to read the newspapers, listen to the radio and play cards with his guards in the evenings. The change made Mussolini suspicious: wasn't it like the last cigarette granted to a prisoner before his execution?

'I don't know what will become of me,' he wrote in a letter to Rachele. He asked her to take care in bringing up their two youngest children, the teenagers Romano and Anna Maria – it was the closest he came to expressing the belief that his death might be near.

Fenner and the three Durham battalions stood to attention outside the picturesque town of Taormina on 30 August as Montgomery drove up in his jeep. The car stopped and Montgomery, his face, arms and knees burnt almost black by the Sicilian sun, stood up on the rear seat.

'Break ranks, come nearer, sit down and smoke if you want to,' Montgomery began.

The men, who formed a square in a dried-up river bed, relaxed. They were in a boisterous mood after the fall of Sicily. On the march to Taormina, knowing they were out of reach of the Germans, they had belted out the old songs – 'Tipperary', 'Pack up your troubles' – with several lewd versions.

Montgomery congratulated them, saying they had fought long and hard under his command in both Africa and Sicily. Now they needed a rest and he would see they got it. In the meantime, he was going to take the rest of the Eighth Army over to the Italian mainland.

'I have got some chaps over there, they tell me the form is good. And never forget! Wherever I go, I shall send for my 50th Division,' Montgomery said, to loud groans from the men.

Montgomery raised his hand and the men were quiet again. 'You never know, I may go home,' he said, prompting mocking cries of 'Ha, ha', cheers and only a few boos.

Fenner was impressed: here was Montgomery taunting the

longest-serving infantry division in the Eighth Army, and getting away with it.

Some days later, Fenner was walking down a road north of Catania when a familiar figure came into view. It was Morris, the soldier who had deserted just before the battle for Primosole Bridge. Wearing slacks, a shirt and a cap with the Durhams' badge on it, Morris looked quite well turned out. But he had no equipment with him.

Morris walked up to Fenner and the two talked briefly. Morris told Fenner he had hidden in a cave before the battle and after it a Sicilian woman had taken him in. Fenner ordered him to report back to the battalion.

Soon afterwards, a letter from Morris arrived. He had reported back, now would Fenner put in a good word for him before his court-martial? Fenner felt sympathy for Morris. Of course there were better men in the battalion; they had seen as much action as him and they had stuck around. But there was goodness in Morris and he had simply suffered a bit of a lapse.

Besides, Fenner was the only commissioned officer Morris could ask and who else would speak up for him? The others were either wounded or dead. Fenner testified that Morris was a good chap and a good soldier, that he had been with the battalion ever since the Durhams had arrived in north Africa and had seen plenty of action. Despite Fenner's intervention, Morris was sentenced to five years in jail.

Repard had never had it so easy at night. After the conquest of Messina, HMS *Tartar* had sailed through the strait between Sicily and the Italian mainland with impunity and its mission now was to target any enemy presence on the coast of Calabria, ahead of a new Allied invasion.

Although it was late at night, Repard had no difficulty in pinpointing his target from five miles offshore. A red glow moving steadily along the coast told him all he needed to know about the progress of a steam train. The glow was a superb aiming point and it took only one broadside to produce a great flash and a shower of sparks as the train exploded.

Repard thought of the people on the train and how horrifying it must have been to be hit out of the darkness by an entire broadside. But he had never seen for himself the effect of his shells on land targets. He quickly dismissed the thought and congratulated his men on their accuracy.

CHAPTER THIRTY-NINE
8 SEPTEMBER

After crossing from Sicily to the mainland, Messina had marched through the mountains of Calabria, using shepherds as guides, and then travelled by train to the Livorno Division's headquarters in Cuneo in northern Italy. With a white powder disinfectant, doctors treated the cuts on his body left by the barbed wire he had forced his way through on his first day in battle.

Granted leave as he awaited new orders – he fully expected the Division to be reconstituted and sent to counter the Allied advance up the peninsula – Messina finally reached his Naples home on 8 September. His mother and two sisters hugged and kissed him, then ran a very hot bath, all three picking at the lice on his body.

Cleaner and smarter than he had ever been in the past three months, Messina called that evening on his family doctor, a close friend. As they sat talking, a voice suddenly interrupted the music coming from the doctor's radio.

The two men listened as the hoarse, monotonous voice of Marshal Badoglio, the new head of government, announced: 'The Italian government, having recognised the impossibility of continuing the unequal struggle against the overwhelming enemy power and against more grievous disasters afflicting the nation, has requested an armistice from General Eisenhower, commander-in-chief of the Anglo-American Allied forces.'

The news brought tears to Messina's eyes. He cried not only because of frustration and anger at what he had been through, but also because of the shame he felt at his country's humiliation. He was afraid of what might happen now. He was afraid of the Germans' reaction. He hoped they would pull out and leave the Italians in peace, but instead they might well consider Italy had become enemy territory and stay to fight.

From his Swiss hospital bed, where he learnt of Italy's surrender, Hahn cursed the ally he had fought to defend. He had come down with malaria shortly after leaving Sicily, his temperature 42 degrees, and had been sent to a Swiss hospital for treatment.

As soon as possible, he promised himself, he would get out and fight again for Germany. Germany had lost the battle for Sicily, but it would win the war. German newspapers and the radio kept talking about Hitler's secret weapons. Hahn had no idea what these might be, but sooner or later he would find out.

Johnson had been out for a picnic with a driver – his C-rations tasted better away from camp. On their way back in the evening, they drove the jeep into a village piazza where people were crowding around a couple of bonfires.

Many of the locals came rushing up to them, and Johnson thought they were going to pull his head off. But all they wanted was to kiss him on the cheeks and pat him on the back. They chanted, '*Finito. Tutto finito!*' again and again. He learnt the Italians had surrendered.

The Sicilians pressed some wine into Johnson's hands, and he drank. The wine was so dark you could stick your finger in it and it would turn purple. He watched as the people danced around the bonfires, holding bottles of wine in their hands, and cheering. The war might be '*finito*' for them, he thought, but he was sure that his war was far from over.

At the prison hospital in Lucca, Snell's first thought when he heard of the surrender was that now he would have no need for his escape kit. The Italian guards disappeared, and the word spread through the wards that the prisoners would be allowed to leave the following day.

Snell, like his fellow-patients, was jubilant and wanted to set out immediately. But the senior British officer at the prison had received an order from Allied High Command that they should stay where they were. The top brass had decided it would be foolhardy to allow vast numbers of Allied prisoners to roam the country as they sought to rejoin the front line.

Snell was so frustrated he found it hard to concentrate when the British Army chaplain, a prisoner like the rest of them, held a service of thanksgiving in the ward. In any case the ceremony didn't mean much to Snell, because he wasn't religious. For him the news of the surrender meant freedom, and freedom to go back to fighting the war.

But during the night he was awoken by bursts of machine-gun fire. German soldiers had arrived and from now on they would guard the hospital. He felt double-crossed and kicked himself for not leaving earlier. So much for giving thanks, he thought – thanks for bloody what?

Shortly after *Tartar*'s ship-radio announced the surrender, Repard pulled out his diary and scribbled only: '!!!!!'. He allowed himself to relax for a moment. 'The assault continues,' he wrote. 'We expect air attack and possibly German E-boats. But we are confident that it won't be very difficult.'

By the end of the Sicily campaign, 'Lucky *Tartar*', as the destroyer came to be called, had travelled 200,000 wartime miles and suffered not a single casualty. A week earlier she had witnessed the landings of Allied troops coming from Sicily on the Italian mainland.

He wondered how much longer her luck would hold, now that she was bound for another Allied landing at Salerno, 150 miles to the north and near the Bay of Naples. Here, again, the Navy would chance hundreds of ships and landing craft well within the range of Italian home-based bombers – and, what's more, with only scanty air cover. But surely, now that the Italians had dropped out of the war, the landings would be a pushover?

*   *   *

Fenner celebrated with drinks of both local wine and VAT69 which someone had managed to obtain. The officers called in a driver from Glasgow, who doubled up as the company barber and also had a good voice. The driver-barber sang Scottish songs, and some of the officers joined in. Everyone got pretty tight – deservedly so.

Fenner made no plans for the immediate future, let alone for after the war. Life for now meant guarding an Italian POW camp, training to keep fit and relaxing by swimming nude in the sea – no one had any bathing trunks. He was sure the war leaders and the generals thought the surrender was a terrific thing, but for him it meant only that a little bit had fallen off the Axis. The rest was very strong and had to be dealt with. He would still have to carry on fighting the Germans.

A few days later, he went back along the route he had taken from Catania to find the grave of Albert Dunn, the sergeant who had been blown up while clearing a booby-trapped mine. He found it in a corner of a field which was being used by a squadron of light aircraft designed for air observation. The pilots had a hell of a job; they had to fly above the front line directing artillery fire while trying to avoid fire from German as well as British shells.

Fenner stood silently in front of the grave for a minute or so. For the first time in Sicily, he had all the time he needed to stop and think near the remains of a fellow-soldier he had known. To go through so much, and then to die like that, he thought, just the day before the Sicilian campaign had ended for his battalion. He pictured the broad smile so often stamped on Dunn's round face.

Fenner was thankful to be alive and unharmed. Of the three platoon commanders in Charlie Company, he was the only one who had not been wounded in Sicily. When Fenner walked away, a couple of pilots from the squadron asked him about the grave and he told them what had happened. He was glad that they wanted to hear Dunn's story.

* * *

8 September

The news of the surrender meant nothing to Rita when word of it was passed on from neighbour to neighbour down her street as church bells rang out all over the city of Catania.

Her return home had been delayed by her discovery, as she touched the calf of her right leg, of something hard and sharp buried under her skin. Again without anaesthetic, a surgeon removed a piece of shrapnel two inches long and one inch wide, the cause of the paralysis in her right foot.

When her father had fetched her from hospital, he brought her news that her brother Pippo had died an hour and a half after the explosion, his stomach lacerated by shrapnel. The family had no idea where his body was. Her father lifted her into a horse-drawn cart for the trip to the house in the city-centre, which they had abandoned that April. Catania's main street, the Via Etnea, was lined by piles of rubble and almost deserted, in depressing contrast to the times when, before the war, she had ridden down it in a carriage hired by her father, coloured feathers dancing on the horse's head.

Her delight in seeing her house again evaporated when she realised that she could not walk into her old home unaided, and she felt sad again when the sight of everyone gathered together except for Pippo brought his absence home to them all. For three days she pestered her parents, asking them how on earth she was going to get around the house now. She had practically never sat still as a child and she had no intention of doing so now. Then a carpenter who lived nearby made her a wooden crutch which he painted white and Rita, laughing uproariously, was free to race everywhere – she preferred to run rather than walk, because she thought her injury would be less visible that way. Out in the street she even played with a skipping rope.

But more than anything else Rita enjoyed looking after her baby sister, Carmela, to whom Rita's mother, despite her serious injury, had given birth three days after the shelling. Rita played with Carmela, made sure she was fed at the right times and kept her clean and warm. Carmela became the focus of Rita's days.

309

EPILOGUE

Patton called the battle for Sicily 'the shortest Blitzkrieg in history', but his words fail to convey the blunders which plagued the campaign – the acrimonious confusion over its planning, the cost in lives of the initial haphazard airborne landings, Montgomery's rush headlong into a trap short of Mount Etna, Patton's own vainglorious advance on Palermo, and the failure of the Allies to stop the Axis evacuation.

In the more realistic assessment of a War Office action-report, the Sicilian campaign was described as a 'strategic and tactical failure', and a chaotic and deplorable example of 'everything that planning should not be'. Cooperation between the British and the Americans was found wanting, with one of the worst aspects Patton's obsession with winning a race against Montgomery.

Acting virtually alone for the whole campaign, save for the first few days, some 60,000 German troops succeeded in exploiting Sicily's rugged terrain to stall an Allied force more than seven times as big. Montgomery's Eighth Army saw 11,843 men killed in action, wounded or missing, while Patton's Seventh Army reported 8,781 men dead, wounded, or taken prisoner. German losses were close to 29,000, while Italian losses were about 144,000, including 2,000 killed and 137,000 captured.

What was the point of it all? The conquest of Sicily certainly helped to achieve some of the Allies' original aims. It did provide a stepping-stone to the Italian mainland, helped to control shipping routes in the Mediterranean, and – much faster than the Allies had expected – ousted Mussolini from power.

But the Sicilian campaign failed to prompt Hitler to thin the ranks of his armies in France, and any illusions that it would prove the start of a road to Berlin were soon shattered. Unlike the demoralised British Expeditionary Force evacuated from Dunkirk, the Germans who escaped from Sicily did so with most of their equipment and their morale high enough for them to soon pin down the Allies at Salerno, Monte Cassino and Anzio.

Of all the Allied commanders involved in the Sicilian campaign, only Eisenhower admitted he had made a mistake. He acknowledged that his forces should have begun the offensive with landings on both sides of the Strait of Messina, in order to cut off all Sicily and obtain the surrender of all Axis troops on the island. After the war, Germany's Field Marshal Kesselring, the former Commander-in-Chief South, wrote that he had expected the Allies to land in Calabria as well as in Sicily. In that case, he added: 'Sicily would have become a mousetrap for all German and Italian forces fighting down there.'

No such trap was ever set and German troops fought so well after Sicily that the offensive on the Italian mainland did not end until May 1945. Of all the Allied campaigns of the war, it claimed the heaviest losses. The road to Berlin did not start on the beaches of Sicily but on those of Normandy a year later. As the Americans had feared at the Casablanca summit of January 1943, when they challenged the British to justify invading Sicily, victory on the island was more of an end in itself than a means to an end.

For the Sicilians, the Allied victory had an ominous underside. The secret pact which had seen American military intelligence work with the Mafia in the run-up to the invasion turned into an unexpected blessing for the gangsters. In the towns the Allies liberated, the jailed men of the Mafia described themselves as anti-Fascists and claimed the status of political prisoners. The Allied military government which administered Sicily freed many of them, and as many as 90 per cent of the 352 new mayors whom it named were either Mafiosi or politicians of the Separatist movement, which was closely tied to the Mafia.

As Lord Rennell, the head of the Allied Military Government, ruefully reported in August: 'I fear that in their enthusiasm to remove the Fascist *podestà* (mayors) and the municipal officials of rural towns, my officers, in some cases out of ignorance of local society, have chosen a number of Mafia bosses or have authorised such persons to propose docile substitutes ready to obey them.' The Mafia soon reasserted its supremacy over the island.

Benito Mussolini's disappearance following the invasion of Sicily was short-lived. The SS Captain Skorzeny tracked the former dictator down to the hotel on the Gran Sasso mountain where he was being held, torturing two Carabinieri officers in the process.

On 12 September, Skorzeny swooped down with commandos aboard assault gliders and landed in a boulder-strewn meadow by the hotel. Skorzeny charged the hotel and the police guards offered no resistance. In tears, Mussolini embraced him, saying: 'I knew my friend Adolf Hitler would not abandon me.' Mussolini boarded a waiting two-seater Storch aircraft behind the pilot. Then Skorzeny insisted on squeezing his big frame into the plane too. The aircraft, making a perilous take-off over the edge of a 3,000-foot drop because of the excess weight, managed to fly Mussolini away without mishap.

Later, installed by Hitler as the head of a new puppet government based at Salò on the edge of Lake Garda in northern Italy, Mussolini plotted his vendetta against the Fascist leaders who had dared to oust him from power. In January 1944, five of them were shot by firing-squad – among them his son-in-law, Count Ciano, who turned to face his executioners just before they opened fire. Mussolini's wife Rachele had insisted that Ciano should be shot.

More than a year later, in April 1945, partisans seized Mussolini and his mistress Clara Petacci near Lake Como in northern Italy as they tried to flee to Austria. Both were shot dead and their bodies strung up, heads down, in a piazza in Milan, enabling the crowd to vent its hatred on the corpse of the Duce by spitting at it, striking it with their hands and beating it with sticks.

* * *

Epilogue

Contrary to David Repard's expectations, the landings at Salerno, south of Naples, proved no pushover. The Italians were no longer playing ball but the Germans were still full of fight. A bombardment liaison officer, who had lived on HMS *Tartar* for two weeks before the landings and trained with Repard, was parachuted in to help guide the shelling of the coast. Repard was saddened to hear that the officer, after reporting German troops advancing towards him, radioed back to the destroyer: 'I think they are on to me.' Shortly afterwards, Repard worked out from the charts that the officer was bringing down *Tartar*'s fire on his own position in order to kill enemy soldiers. Then contact with him was lost.

At the end of 1943, Repard was awarded the Distinguished Service Cross (DSC) for his service on *Tartar*. Three weeks after he left *Tartar*, the officer who took over from him was killed in his seat. Repard went on to fight in the Atlantic aboard HMS *Byron*, and took the surrender of the first German U-boat to abandon the war in Scotland in May 1945. The U-boat's red and black ensign, complete with swastika, hangs on a wall in his cottage north of London.

Repard says the war made him grow up fast – he turned from a boy just out of school who believed battle would be the most exciting rugby match he had ever played in, into an officer responsible for men old enough to be his father. He says he has 'drawn a line mentally' around the sinking of the hospital ship SS *Talamba*, and that he cannot afford to keep thinking about it as it belongs to the past. 'Looking back, I see the war as a period that was simply ghastly in terms of what we were doing. But it had to be done, and I'm proud to have been a part of it,' he says.

Repard's marriage to Peggy Bowyer was written up by the newspapers, as she is the daughter of Daphne Mitford, and related to Lady Churchill. They had met at a *thé dansant*, and their first outing was a trip to the local cinema, aboard Repard's scarlet MG sports car. They have three children.

Repard's diary of the Sicilian campaign ends with a quotation from Jan Smuts, the South African leader, speaking at the Guildhall in London in 1943: 'If the courage my contemporaries once gave to war can be used by their successors on behalf of peace, the martyrdom of man may lead at last to their redemption. Let the greatest war in history become the prelude to the great peace.'

More than two weeks after the Italian surrender, Tony Snell finally managed to escape from his German guards. On the night of 26 September, he jumped from a train near the town of Mantova with Lieutenant Peter Lewis of the Durham Light Infantry who had been wounded in the shoulder and captured at Sicily's Primosole Bridge. The two men met up in the darkness by whistling 'Lili Marlene'. Dressed in their uniforms, they headed south hoping to meet up with Montgomery's Eighth Army. Farmers gave them civilian clothes, and for four days they sheltered in farmhouses at night.

For two months they hid in safe-houses in Modena watched over by Mario Lugli, an Italian partisan who headed a network for escaped Allied troops. Lugli asked Snell to inspect a high plateau with a view to turning it into a secret aerodrome for evacuating prisoners, and for landing arms and ammunition for the partisans. With another young partisan, Snell took a bus and then walked to the spot where he realised the place could only be used for arms drops. He drew maps of the area which he hid in a child's skiing cap that he could throw away if necessary.

With the help of an attractive young woman, Anna Martinelli, who stole the necessary stamps and seals from the city hall, returning them after use, Snell and Lewis took a train to Milan and on the morning of 4 December, they reached Switzerland after a four-and-a-half-hour walk across the snow-draped Alps. They knocked on the door of a farmhouse, and Snell told the woman who opened it, in French: 'We are British escapers from Italy.' 'Oh really,' she replied. 'You are the first two we've had today.'

Snell was flown home in October 1944 and became one of the first pilots to fly Meteor jets operationally after he joined the new

504 Squadron. His escape and the help he gave the partisans during it earned him the Distinguished Service Order (DSO).

After the war he joined an amateur dramatics society, but then decided he had to try and do it properly. He acted in several films for television and the cinema, before starting a career as a cabaret entertainer in the late 1960s with his late wife Jackie. They toured more or less reputable haunts in America, his main act one in which he played the part of a pianist in a whorehouse honky-tonk during the Gold Rush. The act culminated with Jackie, posing as a waitress, shooting him with a blank pistol and Snell collapsing on the piano keyboard.

In the early 1970s, he moved to the British Virgin Islands when an acquaintance offered him a job managing a small fleet for tourists. He has since opened a restaurant – called The Last Resort, after an advertisement at a dockside petrol pump which proclaimed 'Last Gas For 3,000 Miles' – and he still performs the odd one-man show.

He cannot raise his right army fully because in Switzerland doctors broke his right arm once more but set it wrongly. Some of the fingers of his left hand are still numb, but that doesn't stop him playing the piano. He rarely talks about his war although he does answer questions from visitors. Of his survival, he says only: 'I was lucky of course, incredibly lucky. Definitely. And I have no idea why.'

Joseph Rosevich served Patton until June 1945, following him across France and into Germany. In the last weeks, Rosevich remembers a relaxed Patton, confident now about the war's outcome, dictating a letter to Eisenhower and then calling him back three times into his office to add some jokes. Both men laughed as they reworked the letter. When the two separated, Patton wrote Rosevich a letter commending him 'for the superior performance of duty'.

It was the cheerful moments that Rosevich remembered when, on 9 December 1945, he heard of the collision between Patton's

Cadillac, flying the General's four-star pennant, and a truck outside the German town of Mannheim. The crash left Patton paralysed from the neck down and he died in his sleep twelve days later. As Patton himself said, it was 'a helluva way to die'.

Rosevich got himself embroiled in a dispute with Patton's family after he gave copies of parts of the General's diary, which he had kept, to the author Ladislas Farago. Farago was writing a biography of Patton and Rosevich made him promise that nothing embarrassing to Patton or his family would be published. The family protested, and Farago had to fight to obtain permission to use the diary in his 1963 book, *Patton: Ordeal and Triumph*. Today, Rosevich says that he was wrong to keep the copies and then hand them to Farago. 'I'm sorry,' he says simply.

As a New York schoolteacher after the war, Rosevich was inspired by Patton's constant striving after the highest possible standards in virtually everything he did. Rosevich made his pupils memorise Hamlet's most famous speeches – at first they thought it was an impossible assignment, but then they stood up in front of the class and recited them, thoroughly enjoying the experience. 'That was a lesson Patton taught me, *L'audace, toujours l'audace*,' (audacity, always audacity) Rosevich says.

David Fenner's brigade sailed home to England in October aboard a Dutch ship rumoured to be the only 'wet ship' in the convoy – but the only alcohol on board was Dutch gin which took some getting used to. Stationed in Cambridge, he learnt at the officers' mess in January that Montgomery had decided that his unit would be part of the assault troops on D-Day in Normandy that summer. When the news was announced, a fellow-officer turned to Fenner and told him: 'David, you can't go on for ever.'

A month after hearing the bad news, Fenner was having a drink at a hotel bar with some friends when he spotted two young women. One of them was an attractive blue-eyed blonde. Fenner went up to her and offered to buy her a drink. Her name was Audrey and, unknown to him, she had pointed out Fenner to her friend beforehand, saying: 'That one's mine.' The two saw each other regularly until Fenner left Cambridge.

He landed at Gold Beach on 6 June and less than a week later his unit was charged by an SS Panzer Division whose soldiers included members of the Hitler Youth – good fighters but also murderous as they killed prisoners. During the fighting, a piece of shrapnel lodged itself in Fenner's foot and he was invalided out. 'The wound saved my life. If I'd gone on much longer in Normandy, I would have been killed,' he says. Less than a year later, he married Audrey. They have two children and live in a house by a stream on the Dorset coast.

Fenner suffered from nightmares for a few years after the war – he dreamt that he was under attack and that he couldn't do anything about it. He stayed with the Army, working as an instructor at the Durhams' officer cadet school, and after tours of duty in Germany and Canada, he headed the Nuclear, Biological and Chemical Defence School in Wiltshire. 'The Army needed an infantryman who could translate all the scientific gobbledegook about ghastly things, like nerve gas, into simple language that a soldier could understand. The Army is quite sensible, in a way,' he says.

Serving with the Durham Light Infantry is one of the things he is proudest of having done.

Werner Hahn caught malaria in Sicily, and when he was back in the line near Faenza in northern Italy a small piece of shrapnel lodged in his skull above his right ear. Medics performed surgery on him by candlelight. In February 1945, he was again in hospital with a new bout of malaria when he heard news on the radio of massive bombing raids on Dresden, the city where his parents lived. Four weeks later, he received a letter telling him that his mother had been killed by a bomb.

Hahn went on believing that Hitler's secret weapons would ensure victory until the last month of the war. His unit surrendered to the Americans in the Italian Alps in May 1945. When he returned to Dresden which was in the Russian occupation zone, he discovered that all the universities were full and he had to abandon his dream of studying to become a doctor. Instead he made a career in the new German Army, rising to the rank of commander of a tank battalion before retiring.

A widower with two children, he lives in a small Bavarian village and is still angry at having, as he puts it, lost five years of his life. 'Millions of people sacrificed for nothing, just because a madman ordered it,' he says. 'If only we had known the truth about what we were fighting for . . .'

For more than a month following Italy's surrender, Livio Messina hid in Naples as the Germans launched raids across the city to round up young Italian men for deportation to Germany. When the Allies entered the city in October 1943, Messina welcomed his former enemy as liberators. He volunteered to work for them as an interpreter, his wages helping to pay for the upkeep of his family through the terrible winter that followed when many in Naples starved to death and young women offered themselves to Allied troops for a loaf of bread.

Messina says his war ended only in early 1948, when he finally obtained a secure job as a secretary in the state railways, which allowed him to meet the needs of his family. He later qualified as a lawyer and moved to Rome where he married and had a daughter.

The Sicilian campaign was Messina's only experience of combat. He says it taught him 'to love life, because I realised how easily I could lose it'.

For about a year, Rita Francardo and her family lived with the illusion that her brother hadn't died in the shelling of their home and would return one day. Whenever Rita's mother heard a boy calling for his mother in the street, she would turn round hoping to see Pippo.

Epilogue

Pippo never came back. In the summer of 1946, the local authority decided to exhume bodies from a mass grave in the cemetery and give them a proper burial. Rita's mother spent hours there hoping to find Pippo's corpse. She would pick up a skull and stare at it, saying: 'Who are you? Is it you, Pippo?' A friend of the family recognised the body of their dead son by the clothes he was wearing, but Pippo had been naked on the operating table and his remains were never found.

One day shortly after the end of the war, when Rita's father had started working again as a taxi-driver, he announced that the whole family would go to the cinema that evening. The cinema had been one of Rita's favourite pastimes before the war. 'I can't come, I can't walk,' Rita said. Her father replied: 'You are coming to the cinema because if you don't go, no one goes.' When everyone was ready to go out, her father picked her up and hoisted her onto his shoulders. Delighted, Rita shouted: 'Look, I'm still me, I'm still Rita and I'm going to the cinema!'

At the age of eleven, Rita started carrying out odd tasks in the offices of an association dedicated to civilian war victims. She has spent the rest of her life working for the association, helping victims to come to terms with their injuries, and to obtain compensation from the state.

She considers herself a 'normal' person and says there are only two things she cannot do. One is to go for a swim in the sea – she hates the sea, and feels that the sea hates her in return. Nor can she bring herself to pass through the neighbourhood in which the shell struck. But other than that, she feels there is nothing she could not accomplish if she put her mind to it. Her greatest joy in life is her daughter, Letitia.

Rita feels no hatred. 'Did the people who fired the shell want to hit me? No. Whoever fired the shell, it wasn't their fault. I blame war, not them,' she says. She hopes that telling her story will serve a purpose. 'I don't want people to say: "Poor thing, look at what she went through." I want people to realise what war really is. And if you live through war, you will want the peace to last for ever.'

Alfred Johnson left Sicily on his birthday, 21 October 1943 – 'twenty years old and an old man', as he puts it today. He says he was a happy-go-lucky boy before the war, and that Sicily dashed his illusions. 'I had hoped that war would be big and beautiful and clean and justifiable, but it's not. It's dirty and low-down and deadly. I never again felt the romance of war, and all I wanted to do from Sicily until the end was to kill Germans,' he says.

Johnson missed the hell of Omaha Beach in Normandy on D-Day because he was in hospital in England with pneumonia. When he recovered, he took the 1st Division patch off his shoulder and played dumb in an attempt to avoid being sent back to it. But he was found out and rejoined the Division in Normandy, fought in the Battle of the Bulge on the border between Belgium and Germany, and took part in the liberation of Nordhausen concentration camp where the SS left sick prisoners to starve to death. The Americans found more than 3,000 corpses and forced several hundred German civilians to help them evacuate the bodies. Johnson found himself confronted by an old German who refused to do the work, until he put his gun in the man's mouth.

Johnson's Division spent 432 days in the line, more than any other combat division in Europe. He jokes that you could follow him all the way from Africa to Czechoslovakia by his foxholes. He got a Bronze Star for Valour in north Africa, but he's damned if he can remember what he got it for – it could also be that he would rather simply forget because 'medals are for killing people'.

When he got home, to be welcomed by fireboats squirting huge jets of water and tooting their horns in front of the Statue of Liberty, he discovered that his parents had separated and both had moved away. He didn't have their address, only a New Orleans post office box number, 7203, for his brother. Sitting in a telephone booth, he waited for an hour and a half until a kind operator finally managed to locate his brother.

Johnson joined the Air Force after the war, and became responsible for recruitment in much of Florida before retiring. The war still dogs him. Years after he retired, he was in a church when lightning struck the steeple. The next moment he found that he had dived behind a pew and that people were laughing at him and asking what the hell was wrong with him. The noise had sounded just like a 155mm shell. 'The war catches up with you and there are times when you just can't handle it,' he says.

He lives with his wife Nora near the Alabama state capital, Montgomery. As he delights in saying, they have three children, four grandchildren, and two great-grandchildren. 'It's only recently that I've become happy-go-lucky again – because I'm having a second childhood, I suppose,' Johnson says.

For Johnson's eighty-first birthday, his son Vic wrote a poem about his father's recollections of Sicily, which ends with a tribute:

> Past the Straits of Gibraltar
> And Algiers by the sea,
> A world of wonder lay waiting
> For a young lad such as he.
>
> By the time it all was over,
> So many people were lost.
> The sweet taste of victory
> Offset by the lives it cost.
>
> They gave up their tomorrows
> For us to have a better life today.
> Their sacrifice and sorrows
> A debt we cannot repay.

ACKNOWLEDGEMENTS

In Sicily, Francesco Aiello, mayor of Vittoria; Longo and Castronuovo, Associazione nazionale vittime civili di guerra, Catania; Giuseppe Pisasale of the Associazione nazionale combattenti e reduci, Catania; Sister Giuseppina Caruso; Professor Santi Correnti; Ezio Costanzo; Anna, Carmela and Letizia Francardo, and Antonio; Monsignor Santo D'Arrigo; Domenico De Meo; Aldo Ingrassia; Daniele Loporto; Tullio Marcon; Professor Rosario Mangiameli; Enzo Minissale at *La Sicilia*; Lorenzo Maugeri; Nicoletta Moncada; Anselmo Nonuccio at *Il Giornale di Sicilia*; Teresa Reitano; Sergio Sciacca; Franco Siciliano.

In Rome, the staff of the Archivio, Ufficio Storico, Ministero della Difesa; Giuseppe Arcaroli of the Associazione nazionale vittime civili di guerra; Sophie Arie; the staff of the Biblioteca della Fondazione Ugo Spirito; Lutz Klinkhammer at the Istituto Storico Tedesco; Enrico Boscardi at the Centro studi e richerche storiche sulla guerra di liberazione; Crispian Balmer; Giampaolo Cadalanu; Charlotte Eagar; Ronald Grosso, Director, Mediterranean Region, American Battle Monuments Commission; Tom Huggan, Defence Section, British Embassy; Enzo Orlanducci of the Associazione nazionale reduci di prigionia; Alessandra and Romano Mussolini; Mario Savini Nicci of the Croce Rossa Italiana; Harry Shindler, Italy Star Association; Stefano Stucci, press officer, British Embassy; Micaela Taroni.

Elsewhere in Italy, Joseph Bevilacqua, Superintendent, Sicily/Rome American Military Cemetery, Nettuno; Raffaele Cristani of the veterans' association of the Livorno Division; Sergio Distefano; Mimmo Franzinelli; Cesare Minnala; Gianni Oliva; Arrigo Petacco; Federico Peyrani; Luigi Sartori; Marghera; Loretta Veri at the Fondazione Archivio Diaristico Nazionale, Pieve Santo Stefano.

In the UK, David Addison; Julie Baker of the Air Historical Branch (RAF), Ministry of Defence, Stanmore; Raymond Baxter; David Blake at the Royal Army Chaplains' Department Association, Andover; the British Legion; Alan Brown of the Airborne Forces Museum, Aldershot; Alastair Campbell at RHQ the Argyll and Sutherland

Acknowledgements

Highlanders; Ian Cooke; Randall Cross and Ian English of the Durham
Light Infantry Association, Durham; Brian Cull; John Dickie; Keith
Durbridge of the George Cross Island Association, Southampton;
Peter Elliott at the RAF Museum, Hendon; Peter Harclerode of the
Parachute Regimental Association, Colchester; James Holland; Vic
Johnson, for permission to quote from his poem 'The Campaign in
Sicily'; Andrew Kewley of the 46th (Liverpool Welsh) Royal Tank
Regimental Association; John Longman at RHQ Royal Tank Regiment,
Wareham; Angus Mansfield; Tony Martin at the Queen's Own Buffs
Regimental Association, Canterbury; Barbara Mortimer of the UK
Centre for the History of Nursing, Edinburgh; Stephen Prince at the
Naval Historical Branch, Royal Navy, Portsmouth; Lady Ann Riches
of the Middlesex Hospital Nurses' League; Mary Parrott; Sebastian
Ritchie at the Air Historical Branch, RAF; Bill Ryan; Tom Smyth at
RHQ the Black Watch, Perth; Eric Taylor; John Timbers at the Royal
Artillery Charitable Fund, London; Alec Waldron; H. Waring at the
Queen's Own Royal West Kent Regiment Museum, Maidstone;
Andrew Wise at *RAF News*.

At the Imperial War Museum, John Stotford Pickering of the Sound
Archives, Roderick Suddaby and Simon Robbins of the Department of
Documents, Jane Rosen of the Department of Printed Books, Chris
Dowling of the press office.

In America, Alfred Alvarez at the Airborne & Special Operations
Museum Foundation, Fayetteville; the American Legion; the *Army
Times*; Martin Blumenson; Sam Carter; Richard Ciccolella; Hugh
Cole; Carlo D'Este; Austin Fernald; George Gentry at the 18th Infantry
Regiment Association; Eric Gillespie and Andrew Woods at the
Colonel Robert R. McCormick Research Center, 1st Division Museum,
Cantigny; Nigel Hamilton; the 82nd Airborne Museum, Fort Bragg;
Susan Linpeomann at the United States Military Academy, West Point;
Walter Meeks at the 3rd Infantry Division Museum; Sean Olgon at
the Special Collections Division, Mugar Library, Boston University;
Herbert Pankratz at the Eisenhower Library; Joanne Patton; Betty
Rucker at the 82nd Airborne Division, Fort Bragg; John Shirley of the
Society of the Third Infantry Division; Brian Sobel; Barry Statia, the
National D-Day Museum, New Orleans; Edward H. Thomas; Veterans
of Foreign Wars.

In Germany, Wolfgang Bach; Horst Frickinger and Franz Götte of the
veterans' association of the 29th Infantry Division; Helmut Hagendorfer;
Hilmar Lotz and Wilfried Seide of the veterans' association of the

Hermann Goering Division; Fritz Eckert of the veterans' association of the 1st Fallschirmjäger Division; Franz Kurowski; Eugen Scherer.

In Malta, Ray Polidano of the Malta Aviation Museum.

Debbie Baldwin and Irwin Arieff; Audrey and David Fenner; Giovanna Punzo and Antonio Cristofari; Eileen and Peter Taylor.

PHOTOGRAPHIC ACKNOWLEDGEMENTS

Corbis: 4, 11, 15, 26; © Cornell Cappa Photos by Robert Capa © 2001/Magnum Photos: 21, 23; Imperial War Museum: 1, 5, 7, 9, 13, 14, 17, 19, 22, 25, 27, 28; The National Archives: 2, 3; courtesy the author: 6, 8, 10, 12, 16, 18, 20, 24,

SOURCES AND BIBLIOGRAPHY

UNPUBLISHED SOURCES

The Imperial War Museum, London, Department of Documents
The papers of:
R. Aitchison, First Lieutenant, MTB84, Royal Navy
G. Ball, Flight Lieutenant, 43 Squadron
Charles Barker, Brigadier, 1st Battalion, Gordon Highlanders
Art Bastone, Corps of Military Police
Richard Bingley, Second Lieutenant, 1st Battalion, the Parachute
   Regiment
Albert Bromley, Corporal, 4th Armoured Brigade, 7th Armoured Division
G. R. Brown, 2nd Battalion, the South Staffordshire Regiment
John Carpenter, Spitfire pilot, 92 Squadron
B. R. Christy, 368 Battery, 92nd Field Regiment Royal Artillery
C. R. Eke, 754th Army Field Company
George Feggetter, Surgeon, RAMC
David Fenner, Lieutenant, 6th Battalion, Durham Light Infantry
P. Hay, Lieutenant, HMS *Tartar*
Wilfrid Hill, chaplain, 1st King's Own Yorkshire Light Infantry
Arthur Hines, 41 Royal Marine Commando
John Johnstone, 2nd Battalion, Parachute Regiment
Ernest Kerans, 9th Battalion, Durham Light Infantry
P. Lovett, Private, 46th Royal Tank Regiment
Ian Mackay, medical officer, 64th Medium Regiment, Royal Artillery
Reg Marshall, Captain, Airlanding Anti-Tank Battery, Royal Artillery, 1st
   Airborne Division
Bernard Montgomery, Lieutenant-General, Eighth Army
K. G. Oakley, Able Seaman, F1 Beach Commando
Gerald Page, orderly, 14 Field Ambulance
David Repard, Sub-Lieutenant, HMS *Tartar*
John Scollen, Captain, 4th (Durham) Survey Regiment, Royal Artillery
J. Tomlinson, Captain, 214th Field Company, 38th (Irish) Brigade

The Lord Tweedsmuir, Colonel, Hastings and Prince Edward Regiment

I. Weston Smith, liaison officer, Tac HQ, General Leese's 30 Corps

Douglas Wimberley, Lieutenant-Colonel, 1st Battalion, the Queen's Own Cameron Highlanders

J. Windeatt, HQ liaison officer, 36 Infantry Brigade

Imperial War Museum, London, Sound Archives:

Edward Ardizzone, British official war artist

James Bellows, Private, 1st Battalion, Royal Hampshire Regiment

Richard Bingley, NCO, 1st Battalion, Parachute Regiment

Frederick Brookes, NCO, 101 Artillery Beach Landing Group

George Brown, NCO, 2nd South Staffordshire Regiment

Anthony Colgan, driver, 9th Battalion, Durham Light Infantry

Les Colquhoun, photo reconnaissance pilot, 682 Squadron

Harold Coxen, officer, 1st Parachute Regiment

John Cummings, 3 Commando

Albert Dance, NCO, Glider Pilot Regiment

James Donaldson, Private, 2nd Battalion, the Devonshire Regiment

Sidney East, Private, 2 Squadron Glider Pilot Regiment

David Elliott, stretcher-bearer, 7th Medium Regiment, Royal Artillery

Ronald Elliott, Signaller, 9th Battalion, Durham Light Infantry

Patrick Fitz, seaman, HMS *Abercrombie*

Robert Foulds, NCO, 7th Medium Regiment, Royal Artillery

Kenneth Giles, NCO, 7th Medium Regiment, Royal Artillery

Nicholas Hammond, officer, Special Operations Executive

Jack Hancock, sapper, Army/Air Photographic Interpretation Unit

Sydney Hardman, NCO, 46th Battalion, Royal Tank Regiment

Walter Harris, NCO, 90th Field Regiment, Royal Artillery

Martin Hastings, 2nd Battalion, Devon Regiment

Frederick Holmes, Private, 1st Battalion, Hampshire Regiment

Bertram Holt, NCO, Glider Pilot Regiment

Sydney Hook, seaman, LST 403

Neville Howell, NCO, 73rd Anti-Tank Regiment, Royal Artillery

Marjorie Hunt, nursing officer, Queen Alexandra's Royal Army Nursing Corps

Alfred Ingram, sapper, 295 Field Company, Royal Engineers

William Jalland, Durham Light Infantry

Norman Jewell, officer commanding HMS *Seraph*

George Kite, Private, 2nd Battalion, South Staffordshire Regiment

Peter Lewis, officer, 8th Battalion, Durham Light Infantry

Sources and Bibliography

Edwin Lunch, seaman, HMS *Beaufort* and HMS *Delphinium*
John McGregor, officer, 5th Battalion, the Black Watch
Clifford Milway, officer, 103 Field Company, Royal Engineers
Gordon Mitchell, officer, 1st Battalion, Parachute Regiment
John Morgan-Griffiths, NCO, 1st Battalion, Parachute Regiment
Sidney Nuttall, Private, 1st Airborne Division
Gerald Osborne, 1st Battalion, the Black Watch
Peter Parrott, Spitfire pilot, 72 Squadrom
Isaac Preddy, NCO, Welch Regiment
David Repard, Sub-Lieutenant, HMS *Tartar*
George Richardson, Corporal, 6th Battalion, Durham Light Infantry
Percival Tyson, NCO, 5th Battalion, East Yorkshire Regiment
Alec Waldron, intelligence officer, Glider Pilot Regiment
John Watts, medical officer, Royal Army Medical Corps
William Watson, officer, 6th Battalion, Durham Light Infantry
Charles Westlake, NCO, 7th Medium Regiment, Royal Artillery
Derek Whitehorn, beach party officer, F1 Commando, Royal Naval
    Commandos
John Wiseman, officer, Special Air Service

Colonel Robert R. McCormick Research Center, 1st Division Museum,
    Cantigny:
*Battle Report – Sicilian Campaign – 7th Field Artillery Battalion – HQ
    – 1st Infantry Division*
*History – HQs and HQsCo., 3rd Battalion, 1st Infantry Division, Aug.
    1942–July 1945*

Dwight D. Eisenhower Library, Abilene, Kansas:
Diary of Stan T. Bahner, Corporal, 171st Field Artillery Battalion

United States Military Academy Library, West Point:
The papers of General George S. Patton, Special Collections Division

University of Catania, Italy:
Reitano, Teresa. *Storia di guerra ai civili nel luglio–agosto 1943 in Sicilia*,
    Tesi di laurea 2001–2, Università degli Studi di Catania, Facoltà di
    scienze politiche

University of Milan, Italy:
Peyrani, Federico. *I carri armati Tiger in Sicilia: La Schwere Panzer*

Abteilung 504 (luglio–agosto 1943), Tesi di laurea 1997–8, Università degli Studi di Milano, Facoltà di lettere e filosofia

Miscellaneous sources:
Snell, Tony. *Answers to questionnaire. Report on Italian helpers and evasions and escapes of F/Lt. A. N. Snell*, 8.4.1946
Allied Air Interdiction for Operation HUSKY (Sicily), May–August 1943, HERO (Historical Evaluation & Research Organisation), 1971

Recollections, interviews:
Alfred Alvarez, forward observer, 7th Field Artillery Battalion, 1st Infantry Division
Paul Ambro, 10th Engineer Battalion, 3rd Infantry Division
Mary Bates, nurse, Queen Alexandra's Imperial Military Nursing Service
Marjorie Bennett, nurse, Queen Alexandra's Imperial Military Nursing Service
Giuseppe Bertaina, 33rd Infantry Regiment, Livorno Division
Alec Blackburn, 158th (Welsh) Field Ambulance, RAMC
Herman Chanowitz, Third Infantry Division
Raffaele Cristani, Lieutenant, 28th Artillery Regiment, Livorno Division
Richard Crum, machine-gun squad, 26th Infantry Regiment, 1st Infantry Division
Jack Dailey, Sergeant-Major, 30th Infantry Regiment, 3rd Infantry Division
Berthold Dölle, Corporal, 504th Heavy Panzer Battalion, Hermann Goering Division
Geoff Durand, 128th (H) Field Regiment, Royal Artillery
Walter Ehlers, 18th Infantry Regiment, 1st Infantry Division
Fred Erben, Sergeant, 16th Infantry Regiment, 1st Infantry Division
William Falcone, radio operator, 1st Signal Company, 1st Infantry Division
Alfonso Felici, Third Infantry Division
Edoardo Fraire, 33rd Infantry Regiment, Livorno Division
Rita Francardo, refugee, Catania
Karl Goldschmidt, Second Lieutenant, 504th Heavy Panzer Battalion, Hermann Goering Division
Gerald Gray, Spitfire pilot, 111 Squadron
Alfred Günther, 504th Heavy Panzer Battalion, Hermann Goering Division
Werner Hahn, Lance-Corporal, 504th Heavy Panzer Battalion, Hermann Goering Division

Sources and Bibliography

Charles Hangsterfer, headquarters company, 16th Infantry Regiment, 1st Infantry Division

Wally Harris, Sergeant, 90th (City of London) Field Regiment, Royal Artillery

Richard Heaven, Major, 456 Light Battery, Royal Artillery

John Henderson, aide-de-camp to General Montgomery

James Hill, gunner, 26th Infantry Regiment, 1st Infantry Division

Alfred Johnson, Sergeant, 16th Regimental Combat Team, 1st Infantry

Louis Johnson, Corporal, 18th Infantry Regiment, 1st Infantry Division

Arnold Lambert, Sergeant, 16th Infantry Regiment, 1st Infantry Division

William Lee, Rifleman, 26th Infantry Regiment, 1st Infantry Division

Livio Messina, Second Lieutenant, 1st Battalion, 33rd Infantry Regiment, Livorno Division

Lewis Moncrief, 5th Field Artillery, 1st Infantry Division

Philip Morehouse, Headquarters, 1st Infantry Division

Romano Mussolini, son of Benito Mussolini

Tom Nott, radio operator, 324 Wing, RAF

Charles Page, 5th Field Artillery Battalion, 1st Infantry Division

Anthony Pascuzzi, 5th Field Artillery Battalion, 1st Infantry Division

Virgil Passaniti, Master-Sergeant, 675th Army Ordinance Company, 31st Fighter Group

R. Pinchin, Sergeant, 8th Battalion, Durham Light Infantry

Ken Plumridge, Spitfire pilot, 111 Squadron

Giovanni Poli, Major, 33rd Infantry Regiment, Livorno Division

Anthony Pridham, 8th Battalion, Durham Light Infantry

E. Raybould, Beaufighter pilot, 600 Squadron, RAAF

David Repard, Sub-Lieutenant, HMS *Tartar*

Harley Reynolds, Sergeant, 16th Infantry Regiment, 1st Infantry Division

George Richardson, Corporal, 6th Battalion, Durham Light Infantry

Ron Rickwood, Private, 7th Battalion, the Green Howards

L. Rivett, navigator, 13 Squadron

Joseph Rosevich, Sergeant, private secretary to Lieutenant-General George S. Patton

William Ross, 46th Battalion (Liverpool Welsh) Royal Tank Regiment, Royal Armoured Corps

Luke Seanlan, gunner, 127th (H) Field Regiment, Royal Artillery

Prentice Smith, forward observer, 32nd Field Artillery Battalion, 1st Infantry Division

Tony Snell, Spitfire pilot, 242 Squadron

Bill Stevenson, 50th Northumbrian Infantry Division
Harry Stokes, 9 (Airborne) Field Company, Royal Engineers
Rocco Telese, Third Infantry Division
Bill Underwood, company commander, 2nd Battalion, the Royal Scots Fusiliers
Bruno Vagnetti, Private, 33rd Infantry Regiment, Livorno Division
K. Weller, Spitfire pilot, 72 Squadron
Gordon Wilmot, 2nd Battalion, the South Staffordshire Glider Unit

PUBLISHED SOURCES

Aga Rossi, Elena. *Una nazione allo sbando: L'armistizio italiano del settembre 1943 e le sue conseguenze*, Il Mulino, 2003
Alexander of Tunis, Field-Marshal Earl. *The Alexander Memoirs, 1940–45*, Cassell, 1962
Associazione Nazionale Vittime di Guerra, ed. *Italia martire: sacrificio di un popolo 1940–1945*,
Associazione Nazionale Vittime di Guerra, 1965
Astor, Gerald. *Terrible Terry Allen*, Presidio Press, 2003
Attanasio. *Sicilia 43–47: Gli anni della rabbia*, Mursia, 1984
Sicilia senza Italia. Luglio Agosto 1943, Mursia, 1976
Ayer, Fred. *Before the Colours Fade*, Cassell, 1965
Bandini, Franco. *Claretta: profilo di Clara Petacci e dei suoi tempi*, Sugar Editore, 1960.
Barnett, Correlli. *Hitler's Generals*, Weidenfeld & Nicolson, 1989
Baudin, Jean, ed. *Vita e morte del soldato italiano nella guerra senza fortuna*, Ferni, 1970
Bedeschi, Giulio, ed. *Fronte italiano: C'ero anch'io. La popolazione in guerra*, Mursia, 1987
Begg, Richard Campbell and Peter Liddle. *For Five Shillings a Day: Personal Histories of WWII*, HarperCollins, 2000
Bianchi, G. F. *Perché e come cadde il fascismo. 25 luglio, crollo di un regime*, Mursia, 1970
Blair, Clay. *Ridgway's Paratroopers: The American Airborne in World War II*, Naval Institute Press, 2002
Blumenson, Martin. *The Patton Papers 1940–45*, Houghton Mifflin, 1974
Sicily: Whose Victory?, Macdonald, 1969
Patton: The Man behind the Legend, 1885–1945, Jonathan Cape, 1986
Bosworth, Richard. *Mussolini*, Arnold, 2002
Bowlby, A. *The Recollections of Rifleman Bowlby*, Leo Cooper, 1969

Sources and Bibliography

Bradley, Omar. *A Soldier's Story*, Random House, 1999
  and Clay Blair. *A General's Life*, Simon & Schuster, 1983
Breuer, William. *Drop Zone, Sicily: Allied Airborne Strike, July 1943*,
  Presidio Press, 1997
Brickhill, Paul. *Escape – or Die: Authentic Stories of the R.A.F. Escaping
  Society*, Pan, 1954
Bryant, Arthur. *The Turn of the Tide*, Doubleday, 1957
Buckley, Christopher. *The Road to Rome*, Hodder & Stoughton, 1945.
Bufalino, Gesualdo and Nunzio Zago, eds, *Cento Sicilie: Testimonianze
  per un ritratto*, La Nuova Italia, 1993
Bullock, Alan. *Hitler: A Study in Tyranny*, Penguin, 1952
Butcher, Harry C. *My Three Years with Eisenhower*, Simon & Schuster,
  1946.
Campbell, Rodney. *The Luciano Project: The secret wartime collabora-
  tion of the mafia and the US Navy*, McGraw-Hill, 1977
Capa, Robert. *Slightly out of Focus*, Modern Library, 2001
Carius, Otto. *Tigers in the Mud: The Combat Career of German Panzer
  Commander Otto Carius*, Stackpole, 2003
Caruso, Alfio. *Arrivano i nostri*, Longanesi, 2004
Chatterton, George. *The Wings of Pegasus*, Macdonald, 1962
Chiesura, Giorgio. *Sicilia 1943*, Sellerio, 1993
Churchill, Winston S. *The Second World War: Victory in Africa*, Cassell,
  1964
Ciano, Edda. *La mia testimonianza*, Rusconi, 1975
Ciano, Galeazzo. *Diario 1937–1943*, Rizzoli, 1980
Clancy, Tom and Carl Stiner. *Shadow Warriors: Inside the Special Forces*,
  Pan, 2003
Codman, Charles R. *Drive*, Little, Brown, 1957
Colarizi, Simona. *L'opinione degli italiani sotto il regime 1929–1943*,
  Laterza, 1991
Corvaja, Santi. *Hitler and Mussolini: The Secret Meetings*, Enigma, 2001
Costanzo, Ezio. *Sicilia 1943: Breve storia dello sbarco alleato*, Le Nove
  Muse, Catania, 2003
  L'estate del '43: I giorni di guerra a Paternò, Le Nove Muse, Catania,
  2001
Cull, Brian with Nicola Malizia and Frederico Galea. *Spitfires over Sicily:
  the Crucial Role of the Malta Spitfires in the Battle of Sicily,
  January–August 1943*, Grub Street, 2000
Darby, William O. and Baumer, William H. *Darby's Rangers: We Led the
  Way*, Presidio, 1980

De Felice, Renzo, *Mussolini l'alleato*, Einaudi, 1990
  Mussolini, Einaudi, 1965–90
De Guingand, Francis. *Operation Victory*, Hodder & Stoughton, 1947
Deakin, F. W. *The Brutal Friendship: Mussolini, Hitler and the Fall of Italian Fascism*, Phoenix Press, 2000
D'Este, Carlo. *Bitter Victory: The Battle for Sicily July–August 1943*, Collins, 1988
  Eisenhower: A Soldier's Life, Weidenfeld & Nicolson, 2003
  A Genius for War: A Life of Gen. George S. Patton, HarperCollins, 1996
Devlin, Gerard, *Paratrooper!*, Robson, 1979
Doenitz, Karl. *Memoirs*, Cassell, 2002
Duggan, Chris. *Fascism and the Mafia*, Yale University Press, 1989
Duncan Smith, W. *Spitfire into Battle*, John Murray, 1981
Dupuy, Col. T. N., ed., *Allied Air Interdiction Operations for Operation Husky, May–August 1943*
Edwards, Roger. *German Airborne Troops 1936–45*, Macdonald, 1974
Eisenhower, Dwight. *Crusade in Europe.* Johns Hopkins University Press, 1997
Ellis, John. *Cassino: the Hollow Victory*, Aurum Press, 2003
Fairbanks, Douglas. *A Hell of a War*, St Martin's Press, 1993
Faldella, Emilio. *Lo sbarco e la difesa della Sicilia*, L'Aniene, 1956
  L'Italia nella seconda guerra mondiale, Cappelli, 1960
Farago, Ladislas. *Patton: Ordeal and Triumph*, Ivan Obolensky, 1963
Farrell, Nicholas. *Mussolini: a new life*, Weidenfeld & Nicolson, 2003
Fracassi, Claudio. *La lunga notte di Mussolini: Palazzo Venezia, luglio 1943*, Mursia, 2002
Garland, Albert and Howard McGaw *United States Army in WWII: Mediterranean Theater of Operations, Sicily and the Surrender of Italy.* Washington, Government Printing Office, 1986
Gavin, James M. *Airborne Warfare*, The Battery Press, 1980
  On to Berlin, Viking Press, 1978
Grandi, Dino. *25 luglio '43*, Il Mulino, 1983
Gunther, John. *D-Day*, Hamish Hamilton, 1944
Hamilton, Nigel. *Master of the Battlefield: Monty's War Years, 1942–1944*, Hamish Hamilton, 1983
Heiber, Helmut and David M. Glantz. *Hitler and His Generals: Military Conferences 1942–1945*, Greenhill Books, 2002
Hirshon, Stanley P., *General Patton: A Soldier's Life*, HarperCollins, 2002
Holland, James. *Fortress Malta: An Island Under Siege 1940–1943*, Orion, 2003

Horden, Bert. *Shark Squadron Pilot*, Independent Books, n.d.

Howard, Michael. *Strategic Deception in the Second World War*, Pimlico, 1992

Infield, Glenn. *Skorzeny: Hitler's Commando*, Military Heritage Press, 1981

Innocenti, Marco. *L'Italia del 1943: Come eravamo nell'anno in cui crollò il fascismo*, Mursia, 1993

Ismay, General the Lord. *The Memoirs*, Heinemann, 1960

Jackson, W. G. F. *The Battle for Italy*, B.T. Batsford, 1967

Jewell, Norman. *Secret Mission Submarine*, London, 1944

Kennedy, Irving. *Black Crosses off my Wingtip*, General Store Publishing House, 1994

Kershaw, Ian. *Hitler 1936–45: Nemesis*, Penguin, 2001

Kesselring, Albert. *Memoirs of Field-Marshal Kesselring*, Novato, Presidio Press 1989

Klinkhammer, L. *L'occupazione tedesca in Italia*, Bollati Boringhieri, 1993

Kuhn, Volkmar. *German Paratroops in World War Two*, Ian Allan, 1978

Kurowski, Franz. *The History of the Fallschirm Panzerkorps Hermann Göring*, J. J. Fedorowicz, 1995

Leonardi, Dante. *Luglio 1943 in Sicilia*, Società Tipografica Modenese, 1947

Lepre, Aurelio, *L'occhio del Duce: Gli italiani e la censura di Guerra 1940–1943*, Mondadori, 1992

Lewin, Ronald, ed. *Freedom's Battle, vol. 3: The War on Land 1939–45*, Pimlico, 1994

Lewis, Peter. *The Price of Freedom*, Pentland, 2001
  and Ian English. *Eighth Battalion, the Durham Light Infantry 1939–45*

Linklater, Eric. *The Campaign in Italy*, HMSO, 1951

Macksey, Kenneth. *Kesselring*, David & Charles, 1978

Mack Smith, Denis. *Mussolini*, Paladin, 1983

Macmillan, Harold. *War Diaries*, Macmillan, 1984.

Majdalany, Fred. *Cassino: Portrait of a Battle*, Cassell, 1999

Mangiameli, R., ed. *Sicily Zone Handbook 1943*, Salvatore Sciascia, 1994

Marcon, Tullio. *Assalto a tre ponti: Da Cassibile al Simeto nel luglio 2003*, Ermanno Albertelli, 2002

Maugeri, Lorenzo. *6 Agosto 1943: I Panzer Tiger a Belpasso*, Memorie, 2003

McBryde, Brenda. *Quiet Heroines: Nurses of the Second World War*, Chatto & Windus, 1985

Mitcham, Samuel W. *The Battle of Sicily*, Random House, 1991

Mitchell, Raymond. *Marine Commando: Sicily and Salerno, 1943*, Robert Hale, 1988

Molony, C. J. C. *History of the Second World War. The Mediterranean and Middle East, vol. 5: The Campaign in Sicily, 1943, and the Campaign in Italy, 3rd September 1943 to 31st March 1944*, HMSO, 1973

Montagu, Ewen. *The Man Who Never Was*, Spellmount, 2003

Montanelli, Indro and M. Cervi. *L'Italia della disfatta*, Rizzoli, 2001

Montgomery, Bernard. *Memoirs*, TAB Books, 1990

    El Alamein to the River Sangro and Normandy to the Baltic, St Martin's Press, 1974

Morris, Eric. *Circles of Hell: the War in Italy 1943–45*, Hutchinson, 1993

Mussolini, Benito. *My Rise and Fall*, Da Capo Press, 1998

Mussolini, Rachele. *La mia vita con Benito*, Mondadori, 1948

    The Real Mussolini (as told to A. Zarca), Saxon House, 1973.

Mussolini, Romano. *Apologia di mio padre*, Edizioni Eme, 1969

    Il Duce mio padre, Rizzoli, 2004

Mussolini, Vittorio. *Vita con mio padre*, Mondadori, 1957

Nanni, Camillo. *La Livorno: divisione fantasma*, International Magazines, n.d.

Navarra, Q. *Memorie del commesso di Mussolini*, Longanesi, 1983

Nello, Paolo. *Dino Grandi*, Il Mulino, 2003

Nicolosi, Salvatore. *La Guerra a Catania*, Tringale, 1983

Oliva, Gianni. *I vinti e i liberati: 8 settembre 1943–25 aprile 1945*, Mondadori, 1994

O'Reilly, Charles. *Forgotten Battles: Italy's War of Liberation, 1943–1945*, Lexington Books, 2001

Otte, Alfred. *The HG Panzer Division*, Schiffer, 1989

Pack, S. W. C. *Operation Husky: The Allied Invasion of Sicily*, David & Charles, 1977

Pantaleone, M. *The Mafia and Politics*, Chatto & Windus, 1966

Patton, George S. *War as I Knew It*, Houghton Mifflin, 1995

Petacco, Arrigo. *La Nostra Guerra 1940–45: L'avventura bellica tra bugie e verità*, Mondadori, 1995

    L'archivio segreto di Mussolini, Mondadori, 1997

Piggott, Juliet. *Queen Alexandra's Royal Army Nursing Corps*, Leo Cooper, 1975

Pond, Hugh. *Sicily*, William Kimber, 1962

Pöppel, Martin. *Heaven and Hell: The war diary of a German paratrooper*, Spellmount, 1988

Sources and Bibliography

Prien, Jochen, *Jagdgeschwader 53: A history of the 'Pik As' Geschwader May 1942–January 1944,* Schiffer Military History, 1998

Ridgway, Matthew B. *Soldier: The Memoirs of Matthew B. Ridgway,* Greenwood Press, 1974

Regan, Geoffrey. *Blue on Blue: A History of Friendly Fire,* Avon, 1995 *Air Force Blunders,* Carlton, 2002

Rissik, David. *The D.L.I. at War: The history of the Durham Light Infantry 1939–45,* Durham, 1952

Rocca, Gianni. *L'Italia invasa 1943–45,* Mondadori, 1998

Ruggero, Ed. *Combat Jump: The Young Men Who Led the Assault into Fortress Europe, July 1943,* HarperCollins, 2003

Santoni, Alberto. *Le operazioni in Sicilia e in Calabria, luglio–settembre 1943,* Stato Maggiore dell'Esercito, 1983

Shirer, William L. *The Rise and Fall of the Third Reich,* Simon Schuster, 1960

Sobel, Brian M. *The Fighting Pattons,* Praeger, 1997

Spinosa, Antonio. *Mussolini: il fascino di un dittatore,* Mondadori, 1989

St George Saunders, Hilary. *The Red Beret,* Michael Joseph, 1950

Steinhoff, Johannes. *Messerschmitts over Sicily,* Nautical & Aviation Publishing Company of America, 1987

Summersby, Kay. *Eisenhower Was my Boss.* Prentice-Hall, 1948

Taylor, Eric. *Front-line Nurse: British Nurses in World War Two,* Robert Hale, 1997

Terraine, John. *The Right of the Line: The Royal Air Force in the European War 1939–1945,* Wordsworth, 1997

R. Townshend Bickers. *The Desert Air War 1939–1945,* Leo Cooper, 1991

US Army. *US Army Campaigns of World War II. Sicily,* Government Printing Office, 1993

Venè, G. F. *Mille lire al mese: la vita quotidiana della famiglia nell'Italia fascista,* Mondadori, 1988.

Von Senger und Etterlin, F. *Neither Fear nor Hope,* Macdonald, 1963

Ward, S. G. P. *Faithful: The Story of the Durham Light Infantry,* Nelson, 1962

Whiting, Charles. *Slaughter Over Sicily,* London, Leo Cooper 1992

Young, Peter, *Storm from the Sea,* Greenhill Books, 2002

ARTICLES

Calvino, Italo. 'Il Duce's Portraits: Living with Mussolini', in *The New Yorker,* 6 January, 2003

Senior, R. 'The Durham Light Infantry at the Primosole Bridge', in *The Army Quarterly*, vol. XLIX, no. 1, October 1944

Smith, Robert. 'The Red Devils in Sicily', in *Stand-to*, vol. 3, no. 3, March 1952

INDEX

Index

Index

Index

Piazza Venezia, Rome 175
Polito, Brigadier-General 254, 255
Ponte Grande bridge, near Syracuse 66
Ponte Olivo airfield 117
Ponza island 259–1, 296
Port Said 3
Poston, Captain John 30
Primosole Bridge 176–8, 179, 184,
  193–4, 230, 234, 264, 274, 303, 314
Prince of Wales' Theatre, Coventry
  Street, London xviii

Quirinal Palace, Rome 239

R-boats 44
Rastenburg, East Prussia 192
Red Army 59, 192
Red Cross 218, 236, 239, 250, 259, 283
Red Devils (of First Airlanding Brigade)
  66
Red Two beach, east of Gala 45, 71–2
Rennel, Lord 311–12
Repard, Sub-Lieutenant David xi, 107
  in charge of firing *Tartar*'s guns 7,
    25
  unorthodox uniform 7, 51
  appearance 7
  background and childhood 8
  joins the Navy 8
  experiences on HMS *Sheffield* 19–20
  death of enemy soldiers on *Tartar*
    20–21
  sent to rest camp 22–3, 24–5, 52
  his girlfriend Jane 25
  part of invasion force 52, 55, 56,
    63–4, 78–80
  diary 55, 313–14
  and enemy searchlights 73–4, 78–80
  and assault of coastal batteries 83
  friendly fire 93
  and bombing of *Tartar* 102–3
  and the hospital ship 107, 110,
    111–14, 117–18, 122–3, 142–3,
    147, 148, 313
  Junker attacks 139–40, 142–3
  and HMS *Eskimo* 147
  writes to his mother 148
  replenishes *Tartar*'s stores 168–9
  tries to disrupt the enemy's retreat
    243
  and the elusive 'railway gun' 282,
    288
  encounter with E-boats 288–89
  blows up a steam train 303–4

and Italian surrender 307
  awarded the DSO 313
  on HMS *Byron* 313
  marriage 313
Reynolds, Tom 256
Richards (an American Indian) 96
Rocca delle Caminate, Romagna 249,
  254, 255
Rodney, HMS 52
Rodt, Major-General 292
Romans 41
Rome
  ancient 211
  raid on (19 July 2003) 201, 202, 203,
    205
  Mussolini on 226
  'oppressive sultriness' 237
Rommel, Field Marshal Erwin 6, 26, 31,
  138
Roosevelt, Franklin D. 11, 216, 295
Roosevelt, Brigadier-General Theodore
  38
Rosevich, Sergeant Joseph xi, 315–16
  in north Africa 257
  listens to Patton's speech 33–5
  Patton's secretary 34, 35–6, 68, 138,
    266–68, 272–3, 315
  background 34, 35
  appearance 34
  sees Patton in tears 69
  and Patton's rivalry with
    Montgomery 164–5
  and Mims 169–70
  and Patton's race towards Palermo
    212
  in the Royal Palace, Palermo 215,
    216, 257
  in north Africa 257, 276
  and Patton's treatment of malinger-
    ers 272, 273, 275–6
  in Messina 293
  and enemy artillery 294
  and the Bob Hope dinner 299–300
  dancing 300
  commended by Patton 315
  dispute over Patton's diary 316
  a New York schoolteacher 316
Royal Air Force (RAF)
  and Sicily invasion plan 12
  Spitfire Fund 53
  friendly fire on 93
  and discipline 103
  reconnaissance 281
Royal Indian Navy 27

345

Index